Catholic Sisters, Narratives of Authority, and the Native American Boarding Schools, 1847–1918

Catholic Sisters, Narratives of Authority, and the Native American Boarding Schools, 1847–1918

Elisabeth C. Davis

LEXINGTON BOOKS
Lanham • Boulder • New York • London

Published by Lexington Books
An imprint of The Rowman & Littlefield Publishing Group, Inc.
4501 Forbes Boulevard, Suite 200, Lanham, Maryland 20706
www.rowman.com

86-90 Paul Street, London EC2A 4NE, United Kingdom

British Library Cataloguing in Publication Information Available

Library of Congress Cataloging-in-Publication Data

Names: Davis, Elisabeth C., 1989– author.
Title: Catholic sisters, narratives of authority, and the Native American
   boarding schools, 1847–1918 / Elisabeth C. Davis.
Description: Lanham : Lexington Books, [2025] I Includes bibliographical
   references and index. I Summary: "This book examines Catholic Native
   American Boarding Schools run by Catholic Sisters between 1847 and 1918.
   Using previously unexplored archival material, Elisabeth C. Davis
   examines how Catholic Sisters established authority over their students
   and the local indigenous community"—Provided by publisher.
Identifiers: LCCN 2024033219 (print) I LCCN 2024033220 (ebook) I
   ISBN 9781666952520 (cloth) I ISBN 9781666952537 (epub)
Subjects: LCSH: Off-reservation boarding schools—United States—History—
   19th century. I Catholic schools—United States—History—19th century. I Nuns as
   teachers—United States—History—19th century. I Authority—Religious aspects—
   Catholic Church. I Indian children—Education—United States—History—
   19th century. I Indians of North America—Cultural assimilation—History—19th
   century. I Indians, Treatment of—United States—History—19th century.
Classification: LCC E97.5 .D37 2025 (print) I LCC E97.5 (ebook) I
   DDC 973.04/9700904—dc23/eng/20240819
LC record available at https://lccn.loc.gov/2024033219
LC ebook record available at https://lccn.loc.gov/2024033220

♾️ ™ The paper used in this publication meets the minimum requirements of American National Standard for Information Sciences—Permanence of Paper for Printed Library Materials, ANSI/NISO Z39.48-1992.

To Sue and Ken, my parents

Contents

List of Illustrations

FIGURES

TABLE

Acknowledgments

In many ways, this book is unique. Unlike many first books, this one does not come from my dissertation, but rather from my trying to recover from a successful dissertation defense. While my dissertation committee did not oversee this book, I must thank Erik Seeman, Susan Cahn, Tamara Thornton, and Catherine O'Donnell for all their feedback on the dissertation, which helped me develop as a historian.

This book is forever indebted to the CUSHWA Center for Catholic Studies at Notre Dame University for the generous funding I received. The Mother Theodore Guerin Research Travel Grant allowed me to travel to various archives throughout the country to do invaluable research. The Summer Research Grant allowed me to do last-minute research at the Notre Dame Library, which helped so much in historicizing the financial workings of the Bureau of Catholic Indian Missions (BCIM).

I cannot thank enough the wonderful archivists and community historians with whom I worked throughout this project: Amy Cooper Cary, Eleanor Craig, Helen Jacobson, Catherine Lucy, and Reba Weatherford. I am also grateful to the interlibrary loan departments at SUNY at Fredonia, Rosemont College, University of Connecticut, and Transylvania University, who hunted down rare books and requested copies of the BCIM microfilms for me ad nauseam. I cannot thank you all enough. Your work is undervalued, but without it, historical analysis would never happen.

Thank you to all those who looked at drafts of various chapters or early drafts of the full manuscript: Gregg Bocketti, Susan Cahn, Richard D. Deverell, Jeffrey O'Leary, and Nancy Shoemaker. Your feedback helped me figure out how I wanted to put these relatively unrelated narratives into conversation with each other. I am also grateful for conversations with James Carroll,

Kathleen Holscher, Darby Ratliff, and Mark Thiel throughout the research process.

While working on various parts of this project, I sat on a committee overseeing an NEH Sharp Grant through the American Catholic Historical Association that worked with the Catholic Truth and Healing Commission. I learned so much listening to committee chair Patrick Hayes as well as fellow committee members Kathleen Holscher, Jack Downey, and Maka Black Elk.

A special thank you to Joseph Mannard, who has been a mentor to me since I sent him a "fan letter" while still a green grad student. Joe has been a willing soundboard and source of support for years. I am so grateful for everything.

My family and friends have always supported me, even though they cannot fully understand my obsession with "nuns" and are forever trying to figure out ways to describe what I do. As I wrote this, I particularly thought of my godsons and nephews, who are young now. I hope someday you'll be able to read this book and understand why "Aunt Lis" is forever moving and chasing stories.

I must thank my ever-patient husband and our darling fur-babies. You all listened to my rambling as I tried to figure out where I was going. You tolerated my frantic middle-of-the-night typing as I finally figured out the analysis. Thank you. I love you.

Preface

The image on the front of this book comes from St. Peter's Mission in Montana. The school was located on a Blackfeet mission and run by the Jesuits between 1884 and 1898, and the Ursuline Sisters between 1884 and 1918. The picture depicts a group of Ursulines sitting with a group of Native students, engaged in a variety of demonstrative activities. Three Sisters sit or stand surrounded by a variety of Indigenous girls. On the left, one Sister holds something on her lap, possibly a map, as girls examine it from above and below. On the right, another Sister holds a child while looking left. In the rear, a final Sister stands looking down. Most of the students are engaged with their teachers, while only three look straight at the camera: two center front and one in the right rear. One more, on the right front, looks at the camera shyly, almost a sidelong glance. The rest of the students are engaged in a variety of activities. None of the Sisters look at the camera. (See figure P.1.)

This image portrays a tranquil moment, with no chaos. Everyone is cool and calm. The girls are completely docile. The photo leaves no doubt in the mind of the reader that the Sisters are in complete control. These women have succeeded in their mission; the girls are fully (or at least presented as being) assimilated. The girls are all wearing Euro-American style clothes, complete with aprons on the older girls. The younger girls are dressed in white, a symbol of religious and physical purity. Surrounding the students are symbols of their education, such as a musical instrument on the left and books in the front. Most importantly, there is a religious statue in the center, presumably of the Blessed Virgin or St. Peter, demonstrating the girls' status as devout, practicing Catholics.

The purpose behind this picture is clear: it is meant to demonstrate how well the female students at the school at St. Peter's Mission had converted to the Catholic faith. There is no evidence of the girls' Native background. We

Figure P.1. Ursuline Nuns with a Group of Female Students at St. Peters Mission in Montana Near Cascade Mountain. *Source: Originally published in Lydia Sterling Flintham, "Leaves from the Annals of the Ursulines," Catholic World Vol. 66 Issue 393, 331.*

could substitute white girls into the image, and it would just be an image of a traditional, Catholic white girls' school. These Native girls were not so-called "noble savages," dressed in their traditional clothes, but were rather examples of good Catholic girlhood. They are examples of a successful assimilation story.

Yet, there is another meaning. The Sisters never look at the camera—they are too busy with their students. As I look at it, I am reminded of an archivist who once told me that Catholic Sisters have always been too busy "doing" to write down their stories. These Sisters are definitely "doing." They are busy with acts of assimilation, teaching their charges the fine arts, such as painting in the rear, or a white education, with what looks like a geography lesson in the front. They have become actors of settler colonialism, assimilating their charges to white values. While never looking at the image, the Ursulines wanted the world to see their achievement. The Ursulines' work among the Blackfeet, the image proclaims, was successful.

The image was originally published in a December 1897 article in the periodical *The Catholic World*. I was amazed at how well it illustrates the overarching theme of this book. Unlike most of the other sources in this book, this one was meant to be viewed publicly, accompanying an article on the work of the Ursulines among the Blackfeet in Montana. The text accompanying the image boldly extolled the work of the Ursulines, proclaiming, "A country's greatest pride should be its women. . . . Thus the world looks to women for all that that is noblest, and it has been rightly said that though man educates the people, yet women educates man."[1] Placing the Ursulines among this idea of noble women, the article women on to describe their work at the St. Peter school. It outlined the students, the daily life at the school, as well as the role of the Ursulines there.

The *Catholic World* article and image are explicitly different from the other sources used in this book in that they were staged for public consumption; most of the sources I discuss were not. However, like the archival sources, the image captured the essence of how Catholic Sisters viewed themselves when working with indigenous children. The Ursulines were demonstrating their authority over their charges and were successful in their mission. They were bringing what they viewed as civilized to native persons, effectively being "women [who] educates man." These intertwined narratives are ones that the communities discussed within this book would strive to promote in a variety of ways.

NOTE

1. Lydia Sterling Flintham, "Leaves from the Annals of the Ursulines," *Catholic World* 66, no. 393 (1897): 319–320.

Abbreviations

COMMON ABBREVIATIONS

BCIM   Bureau of Catholic Indian Missions
CSJs   Sisters of St. Joseph of Carondelet
OSFs   Sisters of the Third Order of St. Francis
SBSs   Sisters of the Blessed Sacrament
SHCJs   Sisters of the Holy Child Jesus
SMs   Sisters of Mercy
SSJs   Sisters of St. Joseph

PRIMARY ARCHIVES AND REPOSITORIES ABBREVIATIONS

AADP   Archives of the Archdiocese of Philadelphia. Philadelphia, Pennsylvania.
CISDRC Dickinson College. Carlisle Indian School Dickinson Digital Resource Center.
        http://carlisleindian.dickinson.edu
CSJCA   Sisters of St. Joseph of Carondelet. Congregation Provincial Archives. St. Louis, Missouri.
LHC   Sisters of Loretto. Loretto Heritage Center and Archives. Nerinx, Kentucky.
MUL   Marquette University Archives, Marquette, Wisconsin
OSFA   Order of the Sisters of St. Francis of Philadelphia Archives. Aston, Pennsylvania

SHCJA   Sisters of the Holy Child Jesus. American Providence Archives. Bryn Mawr, Pennsylvania.
SPA   St. Patrick Roman Catholic Church Archives, Carlisle, PA
SSJPA   Sisters of St. Joseph. Philadelphia Archives. Philadelphia, Pennsylvania.
NDA   University of Notre Dame. Archives and Special Collections. South Bend, Indiana.

Glossary

In many ways, this is a Catholic history, complete with its own lexicon. I am forever grateful to the reviewer who reminded me to be kind to the reader who may not be familiar with this terminology. What follows is a basic dictionary of Catholic terms important to this narrative. Rather than arranging them alphabetically, I am arranging them in order of importance.

Woman religious: A woman religious is a person who devotes her life to the church in some formal way. A woman religious can describe a nun or a Sister.

Nun: A woman who takes formal vows, particularly those of enclosure. Ideally, a nun will not engage with the world. They remain sequestered for their life after taking formal vows, praying and doing spiritual work.

Sister: A woman who takes informal vows. She will live with a religious community but will engage with the world as a teacher, nurse, social worker, and so on. Most of our images of Nuns are actually Sisters, as they engage with the world about them. All the women discussed in this book are Sisters.

Mother superior: The leader of a women's religious community. This leader can be at a local level or of a group.

Congregation: A collection of local convents/houses that are part of the same community, such as the Sisters of St. Joseph. They are joined together by a Constitution, which delineates the power structure, the goals of the community, and the relationship of the local houses to each other. The Papacy must approve of the creation of a Congregation.

Convent: Where Nuns or Sisters live. May also be known as a house.

Motherhouse: Where the head of a congregation is located.[1]

Laity: A person who does not take formal vows or is not a member of the clergy. They are members of a parish but not a member of a religious congregation.[2]
Clergy: A priest who is ordained.[3]
Parish: Typically a single church, its community, with one priest. There can be multiple parishes in a geographical location, such as a city.[4]
Diocese: A collection of parishes. It can be based upon a city or a larger geographical region. In the nineteenth century, most dioceses covered large geographical locations, sometimes up to full states.[5]
Bishop: The head of a diocese. He has authority over all priests, nuns, and Sisters within his jurisdiction.[6]

Various religious communities worked with Indigenous communities. These included two that are mentioned throughout this history in passing.

Jesuits: Formally known as the Society of Jesus. The Jesuits were founded in 1540 in France. Limited only to men, the Jesuits have worked with Native communities since the sixteenth century, as missionaries traveled to French settlements in what is now Canada. In the United States, the Jesuits were the main missionaries among the Native Nations.[7]
Benedictines: Formally known as the Order of St. Benedict. Established in the sixth century, the Benedictines were initially a contemplative order, meaning they lived in monasteries. However, various groups broke away in the nineteenth century in order to become missionaries. Both men and women can be Benedictines. In the United States, both male and female Benedictines have worked with the Native populations.[8]

NOTES

1. "Nuns," *Catholic Encyclopedia,* accessed April 3, 2024, https://www.newadvent.org/cathen/11164a.htm.
2. "Laity," *Catholic Encyclopedia,* accessed April 3, 2024, https://www.newadvent.org/cathen/08748a.htm.
3. "Priest," *Catholic Encyclopedia,* accessed April 3, 2024, https://www.newadvent.org/cathen/12406a.htm.
4. "Parish," *Catholic Encyclopedia,* accessed April 3, 2024, https://www.newadvent.org/cathen/11499b.htm.
5. "Diocese," *Catholic Encyclopedia,* accessed April 3, 2024, https://www.newadvent.org/cathen/05001a.htm.
6. "Bishop," *Catholic Encyclopedia,* accessed April 3, 2024, https://www.newadvent.org/cathen/02581b.htm.
7. "The Society of Jesus," *Catholic Encyclopedia,* accessed April 3, 2024, https://www.newadvent.org/cathen/14081a.htm.
8. "The Benedictine Order," *Catholic Encyclopedia,* accessed April 3, 2024, https://www.newadvent.org/cathen/02443a.htm.

Introduction

"As the surest prospect of advancing the work of civilization among the Indians, we had formed the resolution to send out five or six Religious Lades (alias Nuns)."

In 1847, Jesuit missionaries decided to open several industrial schools for Indigenous children in Kansas and Missouri.[1] While there were male missionaries stationed in the west, there was a shortage of manpower. The Jesuits knew that they needed more help, particularly if they wanted to work with girls. There was but one solution. As J. Van Velde, a Jesuit priest who would become the Bishop of Chicago and later the Bishop of Natchez, Mississippi, wrote,

> As however the surest prospect of advancing the work of civilization among the Indians chiefly depends on the education of the female children, we had formed the resolution to send out five or six Religious Lades (alias Nuns) who by vow and profession devote themselves to the education of girls.[2]

In essence, Van Velde was doing what every Catholic priest had done for time immemorial when they needed help: it was time to send in the nuns.

The Catholic clergy have relied upon women religious to run the various diocesan educational and social work endeavors from the medieval period to today. This role expanded in the early nineteenth century, as Catholic missionaries began to settle and form the institutions that would become the backbone of the American Catholic Church. Responding to increasing European immigration, the need for parochial schools and health care, Catholic priests knew that it was the Sisters who kept the diocese running. As historian Margaret Hogan noted, "From the priests' perspective, the diocese needed women religious—to provide these services but even more importantly to

1

model good Christian behavior and highlight the virtues of religious devotion."[3] It was not only with whites in the various dioceses that Catholic Sisters worked; it was also with Indigenous Americans.

While not the first missionaries to work with Indigenous communities, Catholic women religious have run Native boarding Schools and day schools across the United States since 1847. Prior to 1978, Catholic Sisters ran approximately 74 boarding schools for Indigenous children. The schools were numerous, varying in organization and duration, lasting from only a few years to several decades. The government supported some schools, while others relied on private donations. The Sisters also taught supplementary religious education courses to Catholic students at the federal schools, such as the Carlisle Indian Industrial School. These women attempted to understand their place within this world, creating a narrative of authority over their students, Protestants, and local communities. In doing so, the Sisters were able to craft a narrative of success in the larger scheme of cultural and political imperialism at the turn of the twentieth-century United States.[4]

While there has been increasing awareness of the topic of Catholic boarding schools in the aftermath of the 2021 public revelations about Catholic boarding school atrocities in Canada, the role of women religious in the nineteenth century has not been fully explored.[5] From the earliest female-run Catholic school, the Osage Mission in Kansas, to continuing missions among the Dakota and Lakota today, Catholic Sisters were political, social, and religious actors, participating in the cultural genocide of Indigenous Americans. Their actions and goals reflected larger white societal biases, as they attempted to "Kill the Indian . . . Save the Man," to quote the infamous founder of the Carlisle Indian Industrial School, Richard Henry Pratt.[6] As such, Catholic women religiously deserve to be part of the larger narrative of Indigenous boarding schools. This book is an attempt to rectify this gap in the historiography, focusing on the role of women religious at various Native schools from 1847 to 1918. The timeline corresponds with the opening of the first school by Catholic Sisters in Kansas through the closing of the Carlisle Indian Industrial School. In this book, I examine the case studies of the Sisters of Loretto (Lorettines) in Kansas, the Sisters of the Holy Child Jesus (SHCJs) in Minnesota, the Sisters of St. Francis (OSFs) in Oklahoma, and the Sisters of St. Joseph (CSJs) on the Arizona-California border.

My analysis relies on the idea of authority. The *Cambridge Dictionary* defines authority as "the moral or legal right or ability to control," expanding with the explanation of "a group of people with official responsibility for a particularly area of activity."[7] The *Oxford English Dictionary* defines authority as "power or right to give orders, make decisions, enforce obedience; moral, legal, or political supremacy."[8] In the most simplistic terms, I take authority to mean, who is in charge, who has the ability to shape and control circumstances? In this case study of Catholic Sisters at the Boarding Schools, I do not simply mean who oversees the students, but also who is in charge of presenting their story to the world.

In crafting their narrative, the Sisters largely focused on creating a narrative of success. Going back to the *Cambridge Dictionary,* success is "the achieving of the results wanted or hoped for," with the caveat of "something that achieves positive results."[9] What were the Sisters attempting to achieve? Like their counterparts in the government, as well as educational reformers, Catholic Sisters on the mission schools were determined to assimilate children into white cultural values. But that assimilation rested upon two distinct, but often interrelated, foundations. First, the Sisters had to have control, or authority, over the children. Second, the children, and the larger Indigenous community, had to accept that the Sisters' lessons, ideas, and beliefs were supposedly superior to their own traditions and cultures. Whether the local communities accepted this idea or not, the Sisters had to at least prove to themselves that it had happened.

The archival sources from which my analysis derives were often not meant to be seen by outsiders. There were letters between the Sisters themselves or Sisters and the clergy; they were annals and convent histories written primarily for the eyes of members of the community. The stories the Sisters told were not for others but primarily for themselves. These stories became part of the community's lore, largely demonstrating the Sisters' ability to navigate a world and situation over which they had little control. They were a way of answering the unspoken question of whether these missions were successful and how the Sisters were crafting their legacy.

These sources were more than just the personal legacies of these individual communities. They demonstrated the success of the missions through the Sisters' authority over their Indigenous subjects, the Sisters were also trying to prove the triumph of Catholicism over supposed Indigenous heathenism. An article from Utah's *The Intermountain Catholic* from 1904 described the Catholic mindset of the period:

> It must be a crusade which will reach every state, every diocese, every parish, every Catholic home and heart in the republic. No Catholic should shirk his responsibility. Such a movement, if carried out, and this involves little or no difficulty, will not only save our Indian schools, but strengthen and expand our missionary work among the 200,000 Native Indian buried in paganism.[10]

Driven by this sense of vocation, all Catholic missionaries were to do his or her bit, particularly those on the front lines at the schools.

Catholics saw themselves as succeeding where the Protestant and American governments had failed. Henry Ganss, the parish priest who worked with Catholic students at the Carlisle Indian Industrial School, boasted in 1904 that

Our success in educating, Christianizing and civilizing the Indian was phenom-
enal, marvelous, and I might add miraculous. Our schools were thronged, our
missionary churches crowded. . . . The dawn of a new era appeared on the hori-
zon. Hope and courage filled the heart of the Indian, gratitude and thanksgiving
the heart of the just white man.[11]

While such language was hyperbole, Catholics felt that they had to live up
to the hype.

Catholics viewed their work as an effort of love, rather than of enterprise.
Speaking in 1915, William Ketcham, the head of the Bureau of Catholic
Indian Missions (the BCIM), the organization that oversaw all Catholic educational work with Native persons, suggested that "it is evident that the Indian
can never be of benefit to the church. The money and men she devotes to
them are to her a material loss," but "there are many who yet believe in things
spiritual, in the salvation of the soul, in victories and achievements which the
corporeal senses cannot discern."[12] Ketcham suggested that the salvation of
the soul was more important than any monetary funds. However, that salvation came at the expense of Indigenous autonomy, sovereignty, and tribal
identity, something of which Catholics of the period were not fully aware.

The Sisters working in the missions had a vested interest in promoting the
mission of the Church. The various groups of women religious were the main
group to work with Native children, outside of the male Jesuit and Benedictine
missionaries. Moreover, their position in Catholic society in the nineteenth
century was ever-expanding, as they opened more hospitals, schools, and social
work practices. As Catholic Sisters tried to figure out their place in American
culture, they also worked with the local bishops to negotiate their own levels
of autonomy.[13] Just as it would in the local parishes, failure at the Indigenous
schools could mean the displeasure of the local bishops. The Sisters were thus
determined to prove their worth in the great new work with the Native nations.

HISTORICAL CONVERSATIONS

In writing this monograph, I have incorporated several historiographical
themes, weaving them into a larger historical narrative of American expansion and change in the nineteenth century. In many ways, this book engages
with a larger historiography of imperial politics and education at the turn of
the century America. Both Cristina Stancui's and Elisabeth M. Eittreim's
recent works on education and assimilation note that white assimilationalist
goals ultimately strove to keep Indigenous persons, and others affected by
these policies, such as immigrants and those within American protectorates,
in a state of dependency. By linking the boarding schools to larger trends,

Stancui and Eittreim remind the reader of the larger socio-political contexts of the school, particularly the implicit imperialist agenda within assimilationist educational endeavors.[14] Catholic Sisters were educators in their own right, teaching students not only catechism but also aspects of trade education, such as the domestic arts for girls and technical arts for boys. Through such an education, Catholic Sisters were determined to pass on white values, although with a Catholic twist.

This book is also a Catholic history. Jay Dolan is most noted for arguing for Catholic participation within the larger American body politic. Regarding the Catholic role in the Native American boarding schools, Francis Paul Prucha truly started the conversation that included religion and the Catholic missions. Prucha's classic work focused on the relationship between the government and Catholic Institutions, particularly the BCIM, amid the political upheavals of the late nineteenth century. However, he often emphasized Catholic exceptionalism rather than critically analyzing the power structures inherent within these missions. While largely forgotten by the historiography, Prucha's work served as the metaphorical grandfather to the field of Catholic and Indigenous histories.[15] Indeed, this book is a direct descendant of Prucha's work, exploring the role and importance of the Catholic mission and boarding schools throughout nineteenth-century America.

Most importantly, this is a woman's history. The field of Catholic women's history has often been relegated to the sidelines, with cultural perceptions of Catholic Sisters and Nuns as recluses influencing any analysis. While most of the historiography on nineteenth- and early twentieth-century female reformers and educators has focused on examining the role of Protestant women within this imperial enterprise, this book notes that Catholic Sisters had the same mission.[16] Catholic Sisters worked to enforce gendered settler colonial roles upon the Indigenous nations, such as emphasizing certain types of labor and clothing. Thus, while outside of the role of mother and wife, Catholic Sisters were as much imperial actors as their Protestant counterparts.[17]

In noting the importance of Catholic Sisters' role in expanding the assimilationist goals, this book joins a vibrant conversation on Catholic Sisters at large. Exemplary works by Anne Butler, Carol Coburn, Joseph Mannard, Margaret McGuiness, Martha Smith, and others have argued to restore Catholic women to their proper place in American history, placing them at the center of social and cultural changes and reform movements.[18] Recent work has looked at Catholic Sisters' roles at the Native American boarding schools, notably Anne Butler's history of Catholic Sisters in the American West, Margaret McGuiness' biography of Katharine Drexel, and Kathleen Holscher's history of the *Zellers vs. Huff* case (initially heard in New Mexico in 1948 and upheld by the Supreme court in 1951). These histories joined a larger conversation that links Catholic Sisters with settler society and nascent imperialisms, exemplified by Amanda Bresie's 2014 article on Drexel, aptly titled "Mother Katharine Drexel's Benevolent Empire."[19] This book expands on previous histories' critical approach to the Catholic missions to look beyond Drexel to other groups of women religious. It is the first book of its kind to present various religious communities that worked on the Native missions and at the Catholic boarding schools.

ACTUS DRAMATUS

The case studies within this book chart the first Indigenous school run by Catholic Sisters in the 1840s through the role of Catholic Sisters at the federal schools, ending in 1918 with the closing of the Carlisle Indian Industrial School. Chapter 2 focuses on the Sisters of Loretto, who opened a school for Osage girls in Kansas in 1847, delineating how the Sisters navigated this new situation, being one of the first boarding schools in the nation. Chapter 4 examines the Minnesota school run by the Sisters of the Holy Child Jesus, looking at the joint ideas of Indigenous authenticity and performance. Chapter 6 is a follow-up to chapter 2, being a case study on the Osage school run by the Sisters of St. Francis in Oklahoma, examining competition between the religious school and federal school. Chapter 7 analyzes the Sisters of St. Joseph's school with the Quechan in California, in which the Sisters took on more authoritative roles, undermining Indigenous sovereignty.

Although having different origins, these congregations were dedicated teachers; they had other schools, either with Indigenous communities, immigrant communities, or American-born communities. Most importantly, these groups have not fully been studied to the extent that others have, such as Katharine Drexel's Sisters of the Blessed Sacrament (SBSs) or those who worked with the Lakota and Dakota. In doing so, I hope to introduce the reader to the varied and nuanced experiences of Catholic women religious at the Native American boarding and day schools.

While illustrating different situations, these case studies all deal with the question of authority, particularly how the Sisters demonstrated their control in uncertain situations. Like many historians, I attempt to enter and reconcile all these historical conversations through my case studies, which place Catholic women religious within the major historical events of westward expansion, imperialism, and the boarding school movements. In each case study, I examine the larger historical influences upon the individual schools. Influenced by work on nineteenth-century settler colonialism and imperialism, I take a critical approach to these women, seeing them as imperial actors crafting their own narrative of success within the settler colonialism/internal imperialism of the nineteenth and twentieth centuries.

Interwoven with these case studies are chapters 1, 3, and 5. Chapter 1 looks at assimilation attempts prior to the Civil War. Chapters 3 and 5 then divide the post–Civil War era in two, looking first at the first of federal funding for contract schools and then with the defunding of these same missions. These sections provide important historical changes that occurred in the larger history of Indigenous assimilation processes and boarding schools. These sections are to help demonstrate the change-over-time that occurred throughout the nineteenth century. This book closes with a conclusion, and an abbreviated conversation on the continuation of Catholic Native education after 1918.

I've organized this book with a certain readership in mind; it is a series of self-contained case studies that can be read together or individually. While I hope that specialists in the fields of women's religious and Catholic history will read and use this text, I want to make it accessible to undergraduates. Years of teaching undergraduate courses has taught me that students often struggle with book chapters that flow into each other. I wrote this book as a series of contained case studies so that undergraduates will be able to read only one chapter and have all the pertinent material at their fingertips.

I am aware of the limitations of this monograph. It is a series of just a few case studies, rather than a comprehensive survey of every community that worked with Native students. Moreover, I focus on individual aspects of these mission schools rather than providing a full history of each mission school. To help, I have assembled a table of schools run by Catholic women religious in the appendix. The material is taken from the Catholic Truth and Healing community. It is meant to give a broader timeline of Catholic women's involvement in Native education. It is also meant to show just how involved Catholic Sisters were—the number of communities involved is higher than we might think.

CULTURAL CONCERNS AND TERMINOLOGY

My work largely relies upon white sources; I am examining white ideas of assimilation and imperialism in an age of cultural genocide. The main reason for this perspective is simply the sources. With few exceptions, I have not been able to find Indigenous voices from these schools from the time period. Sadly, most of what exists are white convent annals and letters, located primarily within local convent archives or the BCIM, held at Marquette University.

Some readers may find some of these sources' language to be offensive. I have not censored my quotes, maintaining terms such as "squaw." I realize how hurtful, bigoted, and harmful this term is to Native women, reflecting white perspectives and interpretations of Indigenous gender and culture.[20] However, I want to be as historically accurate as possible, fully representing the white mindset of the nineteenth and early twentieth centuries. To censor or change these terms would take away from the narrative that Catholic Sisters crafted for and of themselves.

NOTE ON SOURCES

Unless otherwise noted, all newspaper sources came from the Chronicling America Database.

NOTES

1. J. Van de Velde, S. J. Letter to W. Medill, July 27, 1847, LHC, Osage Mission, St Ann's, St Francis historical data & memoirs RG-SCH, VII Box II-8, Sisters of Loretto, Loretto Heritage Center and Archives, Nerinx Kentucky (LHC).
2. J. Van de Velde, S. J. Letter to W. Medill, July 27, 1847.
3. Margaret Hogan, "Sister Servants: Catholic Women Religious in Antebellum Kentucky" (PhD Dissertation, University of Wisconsin–Madison, Madison, WI, 2008), 59.
4. Nancy Marie Spears, "New Archive Sheds Light on Indian Boarding Schools Run by the Catholic Church," *The Imprint,* June 8, 2023, https://imprintnews.org/top-stories/new-archive-sheds-light-on-indian-boarding-schools-run-by-the-catholic-church/242011; Dan Stockman, "Inside the Effort to Identify Catholic-Run Boarding Schools for Indigenous Children*," Global Sisters Report,* March 30, 2023, https://www.globalsistersreport.org/news/inside-effort-identify-catholic-run-boarding-schools-indigenous-children; Dan Stockman, "Newly Published List Shows Catholic Sisters Ran 74 US Native American Boarding Schools," *National Catholic Reporter,* May 9, 2023, https://acquia-d7.ncronline.org/news/newly-published-list-shows-catholic-entities-ran-87-us-native-american-boarding-schools.
5. Ian Austen and Dan Bilefsky, "Hundreds More Unmarked Graves Found at Former Residential School in Canada," *New York Times,* June 24, 2021, https://www.nytimes.com/2021/06/24/world/canada/indigenous-children-graves-saskatchewan-canada.html; "Canada: 751 Unmarked Graves Found at Residential School," *BBC News,* June 25, 2021, https://www.bbc.com/news/world-us-canada-57592243; Kevin Clarke, "A Burial Site for Indigenous Children was Found in Canada. Could it Happen in the United States?," *America: The Jesuit Review,* June 14, 2021, https://www.americamagazine.org/faith/2021/06/14/kamloops-burial-sites-indigenous-children-native-american-boarding-schools; "Secretary Haaland Announces Federal Indian Boarding School Initiative," *U.S. Department of the Interior,* June 22, 2021, accessed July 1, 2021, https://www.doi.gov/pressreleases/secretary-haaland-announces-federal-indian-boarding-school-initiative.

6. Richard Pratt, "Kill the Indian, Save the Man," CISDRC.

7. "Authority," *Cambridge Dictionary,* Cambridge University Press & Assessment, accessed October 3, 2023, https://dictionary.cambridge.org/us/dictionary/english/authority.

8. "Authority," *Oxford English Dictionary,* Oxford University Press, accessed October 3, 2023, https://www.oed.com/search/dictionary/?scope=Entries&q=authority&tl=true.

9. "Success," *Cambridge Dictionary,* Cambridge University Press & Assessment, accessed October 3, 2023, https://dictionary.cambridge.org/us/dictionary/english/success.

10. "Burden on Mother Katharine," *The Intermountain Catholic* (Salt Lake, Utah), May 1, 1904.

11. Henry Ganss, "Our Work for the Indian," *The Indian Advocate* (Sacred Heart, OK), May 1, 1904.

12. William Ketcham, reproduced in "Plea for the Catholic Indian Schools," *The Irish Standard* (Minneapolis, MN), February 20, 1915.

13. Elisabeth Davis, "We Know Not God's Designs in Permitting a Separation: Women Religious, the Consolidation Controversies, and the Nineteenth Century American Catholic Church," *Journal of Religious History* 47 (December 2023): 566–585.

14. Cristina Stanciu, "Americanization on Native Terms: The Society of American Indians, Citizenship Debates, and Tropes of "Racial Difference"," *Native American and Indigenous Studies* 6, no. 1 (2019): 111–148; Cristina Stancui, *The Making and Unmakings of Americans: Indians and Immigrants in American Literature and Culture, 1879-1924* (New Haven, CT: Yale University Press, 2023). Also see Robert F. Berkhofer, *Salvation and the Savage: An Analysis of Protestant Missions and American Indian Response, 1787-1862* (Lexington, KY: University of Kentucky Press, 1965); Elisabeth M. Eittreim, *Teaching Empire: Native Americans, Filipinos, and US Imperial Education, 1879-1918* (Lawrence, KS: University of Kansas Press, 2019).

15. Jay P. Dolan, *The Catholic American Experience: A History from Colonial Times to the Present* (New York: Image Books, 1985); Jay P. Dolan, *Catholic Revivalism: The American Experience 1830-1900* (Notre Dame, IN: University of Notre Dame Press 1978); Francis Paul Prucha, *The Churches and the Indian Schools 1888-1912* (Lincoln, NE: University of Nebraska Press, 1979).

Also see Margaret Bunson, *Faith in the Wilderness: The Story of the Catholic Indian Missions* (Huntington, IN: Our Sunday Visitor, 2000), 69–138; Peter J. Rahill, *The Catholic Indian Missions and Grant's Peace Policy, 1870-1884* (Washington, DC: Catholic University of America Press, 1953), 119–168; Leslie Woodcock Tentler, *American Catholics: A History* (New Haven, CT: Yale University Press, 2020).

16. For example, Robert F. Berkhofer, *Salvation and the Savage: An Analysis of Protestant Missions and American Indian Response, 1787-1862* (Lexington, KY: University of Kentucky Press, 1965); Linda Clemmons, "'Our Children Are in Danger of Becoming Little Indians': Protestant Missionary Children and Dakotas, 1835-1862," *Michigan Historical Review* 25, no. 2 (1999): 69–90; Harald Fischer-Tiné et

al., eds., *Spreading Protestant Modernity: Global Perspectives on the Social Work of the YMCA and the YWCA, 1889-1970* (Honolulu, HI: University of Hawai'i Press, 2021); Joseph L. Grabill, *Protestant Diplomacy and the Near East: Missionary Influence on American Policy, 1810-1927* (Minneapolis, MN: University of Minnesota Press, 1971); Martin E. Marty, *Righteous Empire: The Protestant Experience in America* (New York: Harper & Row, 1977); Katherine D. Moran, *The Imperial Church: Catholic Founding Fathers and United States Empire* (Ithaca, NY: Cornell University Press, 2020); Michael Newson, "Pan-Protestantism and Proselytizing: Minority Religions in a Protestant Empire," *Widener Law Review* 15 (2009): 1–91; Barbara Reeves-Ellington et al., *Competing Kingdoms: Women, Mission, Nation, and the American Protestant Empire, 1812-1960* (Durham, NC: Duke University Press, 2010); John Stuart, "Beyond Sovereignty?: Protestant Missions, Empire and Transnationalism, 1890–1950," in *Beyond Sovereignty: Britian, Empire and Nationalism,* ed. Kevin Grant et al. (London: Palgrave Macmillan, 2007), 103–125; John Wolffe, "Protestant–Catholic Divisions in Europe and the United States: An Historical and Comparative Perspective," *Politics, Religion & Ideology* 12, no. 3 (2011): 241–256.

17. For example, Amanda Bresie, "Mother Katharine Drexel's Benevolent Empire: The Bureau of Catholic Indian Missions and the Education of Native Americans, 1885-1935," in *Remapping the History of Catholicism in the United States,* ed. David Endres (Washington, DC: Catholic University of America Press, 2017), 71–94; Anne M. Butler, *Across God's Frontiers: Catholic Sisters in the American West, 1850-1920* (Chapel Hill, NC: University of North Carolina Press, 2012); Mary M. McGlone, *Called Forth by the Dear Neighbor: A History of the Sisters of St. Joseph in the United States* (St. Louis, MO: US Federation of the Sisters of St. Joseph, 2020); Margaret McGuiness, *Katharine Drexel and the Sisters Who Shared Her* Vision (Mahwah, NJ: Paulist Press, 2023).

18. Carol Coburn and Martha Smith, *Spirited Lives: How Nuns Shaped Catholic Culture and American Life, 1836-1920* (Chapel Hill, NC: University of North Carolina Press, 1999); Mary Ewans, *The Role of the Nun in Nineteenth-Century America* (Thiensville, WI: Caritas Communications, 2014); Margaret McGuiness, *Called to Serve: A History of Nuns in America* (New York: New York University Press, 2013); Joseph G. Mannard, ""Our Dear Houses Are Here, There and Every Where": The Convent Revolution in Antebellum America," *American Catholic Studies* 128, no. 2 (2017): 1–27; George C. Stewart, *Marvels of Charity: History of American Sisters and Nuns* (Huntington, IN: Our Sunday Visitor, Inc., 1994).

19. Amanda Bresie, "Mother Katharine Drexel's Benevolent Empire," 1–24; Butler,*Across God's Frontiers*; Kathleen Holscher, *Religious Lessons: Catholic Sisters and the Captured School Crisis in New Mexico* (New York: Oxford University Press, 2012); Karl Markus Kreis, ed. *Lakotas, black robes, and holy women: German reports from the Indian missions in South Dakota, 1886-1900* (Lincoln: University of Nebraska Press, 2007; McGuiness, *Katharine Drexel;* Irene Mahoney, *Lady Blackrobes: Missionaries in the Heart Of Indian Country* (Golden, CO: Fulcrum Publishing: 2006).

20. "Editorial Note: The Use of the Word Squaw," *Native Northeast Portal,* accessed August 27, 2023,http://Nativenortheastportal.com/editorial-note-use-word -squaw; "Is 'Squaw' Really an Offensive Name and to Whom?," *Berkshire the*

Edge, February 1, 2022, https://theberkshireedge.com/is-squaw-really-offensive-and-to-whom/; Valerie Lambert and Michael Lambert, "Teach Our Children Well: On Addressing Negative Stereotypes in Schools," *American Indian Quarterly* 38, no. 4 (2014): 524–540; Renya Ramirez, "Healing, Violence, and Native American Women," *Social Justice* 31, no. 4 (98) (2004): 103–116; Dwanna L. Robertson, "Invisibility in the Color-Blind Era: Examining Legitimized Racism against Indigenous Peoples," *American Indian Quarterly* 39, no. 2 (2015): 113–153; "Setting the Record Straight about Native Languages: Squaw," *Native Languages of the Americas,* accessed August 27, 2023, http://www.Native-languages.org/iaq5.htm.

Chapter 1

A Brief History of Religion, Assimilation, and Education Prior to 1860

In 1896, *The Indian Advocate,* a periodical run by Catholic missionaries in Oklahoma, proudly proclaimed "Catholic missionaries are pioneers in civilizations and the friends of literature where they penetrate among savage people."[1] Throughout its run, *The Indian Advocate* told tales of the missionaries of the colonial era as well as the early decades of the republic, placing them within a larger history of American history and development.[2] Yet, within the American narrative, Catholics were only part of the westward expansion that characterized the expansion of the nation at large in the decades prior to the American Civil War.

In my U.S. 1 survey classes, I start my lecture on the post-Revolutionary period with the broad statement: "The year is 1783; the Revolution has ended . . . now what?" In addition to its dramatic effect on students, the question embodies the debates Americans faced in the decades between the American Revolution and the Civil War. The United States was a nascent nation, more loosely allied than united, trying to balance local and federal loyalties and the divide between slave and so-called free states. This was an era of westward expansion with its accompanying development of a larger, more bureaucratic government, tempered by a continued belief in the importance of small government. It was a fundamentally white, Christian nation marked by increased religious and ethnic diversity.[3]

During the Antebellum era, most Americans made a connection between religion and civilization, defining one based on the other. A public-school education was based around religious values, with readings from the Bible and devotions. The decades between the Revolution and the Civil War were filled with religious revivals. Responding primarily to the rise of the cities and new industrialism, religious reformers hoped to bring their followers peace in a world they thought had gone mad. They saw religion as the panacea to the modern world's ills, providing a direct connection with the divine and a sense of community. The various evangelical denominations argued that it was only their way that led to salvation, claiming other forms of Christianity were a sign of backwardness.[4]

During the antebellum era and after, Christianity implicitly meant Protestantism. While the Constitution promised that the government would "respecting an establishment of religion, or prohibiting the free exercise thereofshall make no law," that ideal was more about the flexibility to practice whichever form of Christianity one chose. However, some local and state ordinances restricted some Christian denominations, such as Catholics (or Papists), whom Protestants viewed with suspicion due to their loyalty to the Pope in Rome and emphasis on celibacy. Catholics actively protested what they viewed as Protestant intolerance, particularly the use of Protestant Bibles in public schools, but largely saw little change.[5] Christianity meant Civilization; Civilization meant Protestantism. As David Emmons wrote in his book on Irish immigration, "true American republicanism was also based on Protestantism; it, too, was privileged, and the 'wages of Protestantism' were also built into the system."[6] Protestant ideals dominated initial responses toward Indigenous assimilation.

The link between Christianity, civilization, and education was both explicit and implicit in the nineteenth century. Most of the Native American boarding schools were established prior to the separation of religion from the public schools, meaning Bible studies, in particular those of the Protestant Bible, was an essential aspect of education for any school child in the United States.[7] Going as far back as the colonial period, missionaries to Indigenous persons saw conversion and adherence to Christian traditions as key to the civilization process, taking them from the supposed level of savages and elevating them.

This religious mindset would change after the Civil War, with the institutionalization and regulation of the schools working with Indigenous persons. While the government allowed the mission schools, typically religious schools that received government funding, it emphasized the need for a secular or Protestant education. Catholic schools, however, often continued to focus on religious conversion, particularly when they received little to no government funding (as we shall see in later chapters).[8]

PROTESTANT MISSIONARY WORK

Protestant missionary work dominated the history of Native Assimilation in the United States. Such work started off slowly, originating in the 1600s. After the founding of the Virginia Company, King James I wrote a letter to the new community, asking that they convert the Indigenous nations and teach them British values. However, the government put little money into this project, asking the clergy to raise money to support such missions.[9] Other early missions were part of this ad hoc approach to cultural assimilation.

In 1631, John Eliot founded the first proto-boarding school in Roxbury, Massachusetts. The school was for prisoners of war and largely provided an industrial education. Eliot suggested that his students later attend "praying towns" in order to learn about Christianity. Between 1651 and 1674, Eliot created 14 praying towns with over one thousand inhabitants. Like missionaries before and after him, Eliot believed Christianity was the first step on the road to white, Christian "civilization." In addition to religious education, the praying towns also provided a basic education, including reading and writing, as well as some elements of a classical education, such as the Greek language. Unlike the boarding schools of the later era, most of the instruction at the praying towns was in the local Indigenous language; indeed, twice as many students could read and write their own tongue versus those who could read in English.[10]

Other Protestant missionaries created schools throughout the seventeenth and eighteenth centuries. With the expansion of English colonies along the eastern coast, missionaries founded the Society for the Propagation of the Gospel in New England in 1649. The society's goal was to support various attempts at conversion, from printing the Bible in Indigenous languages to supporting Harvard's, Dartmouth's, and William and Mary's education programs for Indigenous students. Education outreach expanded quickly. For example, Thomas Mayhew and his son established a mission in Martha's Vineyard in the 1650s. Inspired by the Great Awakening revivals of the mid-eighteenth century, Eleazar Wheelock founded a school; his most famous Indigenous student, Samson Occom, continued this work on various reservations. Unlike later endeavors, these early Protestant missions focused not on full cultural assimilation but rather a middle ground in which Indigenous persons learned about Christianity in their own language. These missions used translated Bibles and had Indigenous teachers. However, these missionaries, particularly Wheelock, suggested that students should be separated from their parents and communities to fully develop European values.[11]

The nineteenth century saw the expansion of Protestant-run schools. The first two were run by Moravians and Presbyterians: the Moravians established one in Georgia in 1805 for the Creeks and the Presbyterians in 1806 for the Cherokee. Protestant missionaries expanded their missions in the succeeding decades, with the Presbyterians dominating the early decades of the century. In total, by 1832, Protestant missionaries ran 46 out of 51 mission schools. Unlike their predecessors, these schools focused on an English-only education emphasizing conformity to white Anglo-European values versus syncretism.[12] Despite their isolation from the larger system,

Catholics had been working as missionaries for as long as, if not longer than, their Protestant counterparts.

CATHOLIC MISSIONARY WORK

Catholic missionary and assimilation work among the Indigenous nations started in the sixteenth century. With their "conquest" of New Spain, primarily Central America and the southern part of the modern United States, the Spanish believed it was part of their mission to convert Indigenous persons and teach them Spanish culture. While the Spanish initially tried to use the encomienda system, the system focused more on coercive labor rather than cultural assimilation. In 1542, Charles VI of Spain sent Franciscan friars to the newly claimed territory in the Americas to establish missions. These missions were supported by the Spanish government, which linked conversion to the acknowledgment of Spanish sovereignty. However, the goal was for these schools to become secular institutions within a decade; this did not come to pass.[13]

The Spanish missions were similar to the boarding schools of the later centuries. Franciscan and Jesuit friars and Spanish soldiers forced Indigenous persons to live there, often using these persons as political hostages. Missionaries initially focused on converting women and children, whom the Spanish hoped would go out and convert entire communities. While there were set times for prayer, mission residents spent most of their time doing manual labor, a theme within the later industrial schools. Indigenous members of the missions lived in gender-segregated dormitories. The friars even locked girls over the age of eight up in the dormitories in order to preserve their sexual purity. The mission work continued into the nineteenth century, as Spanish missionaries established schools for Indigenous persons.[14]

Catholic missionaries started to work in North America in 1611 with the arrival of the Jesuits. Jesuit missionaries mainly focused on work in New France, living among the local communities and recording their work in the *Jesuit Relations,* pamphlets, and letters sent by missionaries to France in the hopes of recruiting settlers and funding for the new colonial endeavor. Jesuit work in what would become the United States was largely sporadic, with itinerant priests traveling throughout the territory but never establishing long-term relationships.[15]

During the colonial era and the decades of the nascent nation, Catholic missionaries did not prioritize their work with Indigenous nations. There were too few priests and Sisters. Catholic priests were stretched to the limit, most constantly traveling to serve parishioners in several states. There were few Sisters to help them. The first group of Catholic nuns were the Carmelites in Maryland, established in 1790. However, this was a small group that was an enclosed order, largely dedicated to a life of prayer versus social services. The number of Catholic Sisters grew slowly, with the congregation of Catholic Sisters being Elizabeth Seton's Sisters of Charity, established in 1809. However, it was not until the 1820s through 1860s that the number of congregations of Sisters grew. During this era, those that existed focused on serving white, Catholic populations initially on the east coast but later further inland.[16] Given the lack of Catholic priests and Sisters, Catholic schools for Native children were not fully possible until the 1820s when there were enough Jesuit missionaries to request funding for a school; they opened St. Regis Seminary in 1824 in Missouri. (The original school only lasted a few years.)[17] However, there were too few permanent missionaries to have long-term missions as the Protestants did.

It was only in the 1830s that the nascent American Catholic hierarchy started to focus on Indigenous nations within the confines of the new nation. By then, there were more priests, often immigrants from Europe, to help with the various missions. In 1833, the Second Council of Baltimore placed the Jesuits in charge of work among the Indigenous nations in the West. The Jesuits focused on the Midwest, with few journeys into the Mid-South, West, or Southwest. Other groups, such as the Benedictines, joined this type of missionary work after the Civil War.[18] They offered education but focused more on religious conversion.

Other than a lack of manpower, there were two reasons for the relatively late start of Catholic missions. First was Protestant domination of assimilation practices. America simply was a Protestant nation. Another reason for the late start was the background of many Catholic missionaries: they were European-born, not American. There were few American-born priests or Sisters in the first few decades after the American Revolution. They were so few in number that they often wore themselves out traveling all over. Moreover, European missionaries did not feel the same nationalism that their Protestant contemporaries did, leading to a general introduction to European values but not overt American assimilation.[19]

From the perspective of output, the 1840s started the golden age of Catholic missions among the Indigenous tribes. Catholic periodicals glorified this era, reveling in the trials and adventures of Jesuit missionaries, most famously Pierre-Jean De Smet. De Smet was one of the many missionaries who traveled across the country, meeting with Indigenous communities. He wrote of his experiences as he tried to convert local Native leaders. Like many of his Catholic and Protestant predecessors, De Smet emphasized meeting Indigenous communities on a cultural middle ground and syncretic understanding of Christianity. De Smet was one of the most respected missionaries among Catholics and Protestants alike.[20] De Smet and his contemporaries reflected their colonial predecessors: religion was key to and infused the work of this new generation of missionaries.

While men tended to dominate Catholic missionary work before the nineteenth century, Catholic women had begun doing missionary work with Indigenous Americans in North America as early as the seventeenth century. Most notable is the work of Marie de L'Incarnation. Born in France, L'Incarnation joined the Ursulines in 1633. In 1639, she and a group of Ursulines arrived in Quebec to form their own community. They ran a school focused on teaching Indigenous girls the catechism. The Ursulines even translated their religious texts into the local language. Despite this early attempt at a school for Indigenous girls, it was not until the 1840s that American Catholic Sisters started to work fully in these types of missions.

As Catholic missionaries worked more and more with the Indigenous nations, they competed with Protestants. As Francis Paul Prucha wrote on the expansion of Catholic missions,

> Into this world of Anglo-Protestant missionaries, men and women who understood the signpost Conversion at the end of their road to mean the Indians' complete Americanization . . . came the Catholic missionaries. . . . They marched along a different road, from a different direction, to a different drummer. They, too, saw conversion toward which their road led, but for them it had a meaning somewhat different.[21]

Protestants focused on cultural assimilation, while Catholics focused on cultural syncretism, bringing Indigenous elements into Christian tradition.

Despite these different trajectories, Catholic and Protestant missionaries' goals largely aligned. Both believed in the mix of Christian and European traditions as key to assimilation. In his work on religion and Native American policy, Francis Paul Prucha suggested,

> For the Protestant conversion to take place, a total external transformation was deemed necessary, and the Anglo-Protestants demanded ultimately the obliteration of Indian culture in its entirety . . . . The Catholics were more likely . . . to accommodate themselves to the cultures they were seeking to make Christian.[22]

For Prucha, the key difference between Protestant and Catholic assimilation was cultural genocide versus a new syncretic belief system. This interpretation is slightly oversimplified, as Catholics were as likely to run and promote industrial schools as their Protestant counterparts. Indeed, as we shall see, Catholic Sisters were colonizers and imperial actors just as their Protestant counterparts.

U.S. INTERIOR POLICY BEFORE 1860

U.S. policy toward Indigenous persons reflected a belief that Christianity was a sure sign of citizenship. The government recognized the "Five Tribes," the Cherokees, Chickasaws, Choctaws, Creeks, and Seminoles, as allies and examples of how the Indigenous nations could become more like white Anglo-American cultures. These communities embraced not just white traditions, such as language, clothing, and slavery, but also converted to Christianity, elevating them in the minds of white politicians. Despite such beliefs in these communities as attaining a level of civilization, particularly regarding the Cherokee, the U.S. government treated the "Civilized Tribes" with the abandonment that characterized the antebellum era, leading to multiple ordered removals to free up land for white settlers.[23]

In the decades before the Civil War, U.S. policy toward Indigenous persons largely focused on trade, relocation, and assimilation. The First and Second Indian Trade and Intercourse Acts (1790 and 1793, respectively) focused on creating trading programs between white Americans and Indigenous persons. These policies led to the creation of factories, a form of trading posts. The factory system largely ended in 1822. The Second Indian Trade Act introduced the idea of education into white-Indigenous relations. The Act stated that the factories should have a white agent who would teach white agricultural practices. However, this practice was not standardized. The Department of War oversaw Indian policy at first, but the responsibility would shift to the Department of the Interior in 1847.[24]

While early assimilation endeavors were largely privatized, the U.S. government became involved in 1819. The Civilization Fund Act of that year delegated government funds to Indigenous education and assimilation for the first time in American history:

Be it enacted . . . that for the purpose of providing against the further decline and final extinction of Indian tribes, adjoining the frontier settlements of the United States, and for introducing them the habits and arts of civilization, the President of the United States shall be, and he is hereby authorized, in every case where he shall judge improvement in the habits and condition of such Indians practicable, and that the means of instruction can be introduced with their own consent, to employ capable persons of good moral character to instruct them in the mode of agriculture suited to their situation; and for teaching their children in reading, writing, and arithmetic, and for the performing of such other duties as may be enjoined, according to such instructions and rules as the President give and prescribe for the regulation of their conduct, in discharge of their duties. And be it further enacted, That the annual sum of ten thousand

dollars be, and the same is hereby appropriated, for the purpose of carrying
into effect the provisions of this act; and an account of the expenditure of the
money, and proceedings in execution of the foregoing provisions, shall be laid
annually before Congress.[25]

Private enterprises and government agents could apply for funding for Indigenous schools. However, they had to promote American values and teach a
certain type of curriculum. Funding from the Civilization Fund Act led to the
creation of 50 schools by the 1830s.[26]

The Civilization Fund Act originated in the belief that Indigenous Americans were dying out and that it was up to white Americans to save them,
at least as a cultural specimen of the past, demonstrating the march of
progress toward white civilized society. While the mission schools focused
on Christianization, the federally funded schools were designed to instruct
Indigenous persons in Euro-Americans' agricultural techniques. Superintendent of Indian Trade and later Secretary of the Office of Indian Affairs,
Thomas McEnney, linked such agricultural education to developing American nationalism. Influenced by Jefferson's view of America, which focused
on the self-sufficient small farmer, McEnney believed that such education
would allow these communities to survive and later become part of white
society. Later schools, however, would focus on industrialization, reflecting
the changing economy. By 1848, the Department of Indian Affairs specified
that all schools must be hands-on, teaching agriculture, industry, or manual
labor.[27]

Unlike later boarding and day schools, these early schools were meant to
be run with the permission of the local communities ("with their own consent"). Individual treaties might mandate the creation of a school, but the
local communities had more say in who ran the school. Moreover, school
attendance was not universally compulsory until the mid-twentieth century.
However, the government often proceeded without the input of the tribal
communities, relegating funding for schools without the permission of the
community leaders.[28]

In large part, there was little government oversight of these early schools.
The Department of War and the Department of the Interior focused more on
questions of trade and war. Religious and educational reformers merely had
to apply for money but did not need to follow any set guidelines; writing to
the Secretary of War was enough to secure funding. This lack of institutionalization led to a variety of situations. For example, the government did not
require teachers to have a four-year degree until 1930. It was only after the
Civil War that the government started to regulate Indigenous education, a
shift in policy and philosophy.[29]

CONCLUDING THOUGHTS

Separating missionary work from educational assimilation and white policies toward Indigenous persons in the pre–Civil War era is difficult. While vocational/industrial education was always part of the assimilationist agenda, religion was a major priority. As one history of Indigenous education notes, "Missionaries, in their ethnocentric zeal, assumed that once exposed to Christianity, 'civilization,' and the English language, Native people would be eager to change their lives 'for the better.'"[30] To the minds of those involved, be they Catholic or Protestant, there was no difference in mission: Christianity was the first step to Euro-American values of civilization. Later federal attempts at assimilation moved the focus from religion to rest primarily on labor.

Although not Protestant, Catholics believed in the mission of assimilation through religion and became active participants. The first group of Catholic Sisters, the Sisters of Loretto, started their school less than 30 years after the U.S. Congress passed funding for academic and industrial education as part of the Civilization Fund Act. The Jesuits and the Sisters established the school less than 20 years after the creation of the Bureau of Indian Affairs in 1824. It was part of a larger expansion of funding, from $10,000 in 1819 to $214,000 in 1842.[31] The Sisters of Loretto were part of a period of experimentation, reflecting larger themes and trends in antebellum American society. The Sisters' early attempts at assimilation and conversion would foreshadow practices that became standardized and mainstream in American policy and society.

NOTES

1. "Catholic Missionaries are Pioneers . . . ," *The Indian Advocate* (Sacred Heart, OK), October 1896, 111.

2. Carolus, "Early French Missionaries in America," *The Indian Advocate*, April 1897, 60–63; "Christianizing the Pueblos," *The Indian Advocate*, July 1894, 69–70; "The Coeur d'Alene Indians," *The Indian Advocate*, August 1903, 230–235; "Early Catholic Indian Missions in Canada," *The Indian Advocate,* April 1908, 101–107; "Early Missions," *The Indian Advocate*, January 1894, 5–8; "Father De Smet and the Montana Indians," *The Indian Advocate*, November 1902, 326–331.

3. One of the best overviews of this era is Daniel Walker Howe, *What Hath God Wrought: The Transformation of America, 1815-1848* (New York: Oxford University Press, 2007).

4. Jay P. Dolan, *The Catholic American Experience: A History from Colonial Times to the Present* (New York: Image Books, 1985), 101–221; Steven K. Green, *The Bible, the School, and the Constitution: The Clash that Shaped Modern*

Church-State Doctrine (New York: Oxford University Press, 2012), 11–44; Christine Leigh Heyrman, *Southern Cross: The Beginnings of the Bible Belt* (New York: Alfred A. Knopf, 1997); Judith Amanda Hunter, *Before Pluralism: The Political Culture of Nativism in Antebellum Philadelphia* (New Haven, CT: Yale University Press, 1991).

5. Ray Allen Billington, *The Protestant Crusade 1800-1860: A Study of the Origins of American Nativism* (New York: Quadrangle Book, 1964); Mark S. Massa, *Anti-Catholicism in America: The Last Acceptable Prejudice* (New York: The Crossroad Publishing Company, 2003), 18–39; Cassandra L. Yacovazzi, "'Down with the Convent!'": Anti-Catholicism and Opposition to Runs in Antebellum America," in *A Companion to Religious History,* ed. Benjamin E. Park (New York: Wiley Blackwell, 2021), 150–164.

6. David Emmons, *Beyond the American Pale: The Irish in the West, 1845-1910* (Norman, OK: University of Oklahoma Press, 2010), 6.

7. Debates over which public schools should use resulted in culture wars and, at times, physical violence in the East. See, for example, Hunter, *Before Pluralism*; Katie Oxx, *The Nativist Movement in America: Religious Conflict in the 19th Century* (New York: Routledge, 2013); Yacovazzi, "'Down with the Convent!" Anti-Catholicism and Opposition to Nuns in Antebellum America," in *A Companion to American Religious History*, ed. Benjamin Paker (New York: Wiley, 2021), 150–164.

8. See, for example, Henry Ganss, Letter to Katharine Drexel, 13 September 1892, St. Patrick's Archives, Carlisle, PA; J. A. Stephan, Letter to Rev. Sister Aquinata, July 31 1899, Pawhuska Correspondence, 1888-1904, AOSF.

9. Joel W. Martin, *The Land Looks After Us: A History of Native American Religion* (New York: Oxford University Press, 1999), 61–83; Jon Reyhner and Jeanne Eder, *American Indian Education: A History*. Second Edition (Norman, OK: University of Oklahoma Press, 2017), 4.

10. Martin, *The Land Looks After Us,* 61–83; Reyhner and Eder, *American Indian Education,* 28–37.

11. John Demos, *The Heathen School: A Story of Hope and Betrayal of the Early Republic* (New York: Alfred A. Knopf, 2014); Martin, *The Land Looks After Us,* 61–83; Reyhner and Eder, *American Indian Education,* 31–37.

12. Donald L. Fixico, *Bureau of Indian Affairs* (Santa Barbara, CA: Greenwood, 2012), 1–22, 69–86; Reyhner and Eder, *American Indian Education,* 44–63.

13. Reyhner and Eder, *American Indian Education,* 19–26.

14. Reyhner and Eder, *American Indian Education,* 19–26.

15. The *Jesuit Relations* were a series of letters, reports, and other chronicles largely written between 1632 and 1672 by Jesuit missionaries in Canada. They were sent to France and used as a propaganda tool to inspire laypersons to invest in France's new colony as well as encourage more missionaries.

16. Joseph G. Mannard, "'Our Dear Houses Are Here, There and Every Where': The Convent Revolution in Antebellum America," *American Catholic Studies* 128, no. 2 (2017): 1–27.

17. Mary Paul Fitzgerald, *Beacon on the Plains* (Leavenworth, KS: The Saint Mary College, 1939), 42–48.

18. William White Graves, *Life and Letters of Fathers Ponziglione, Schoenmakers, and Other Jesuits at Osage Mission. Sketch of St. Francis' Church. Life of Mother Bridget* (St. Paul, KS: W.W. Graves, 1916), 61; Joseph F. Murphy, *Tenacious Monks: The Oklahoma Benedictines, 1875-1975* (Shawnee, OK: Benedictine Color Press, 1974), 1–3; Reyhner and Eder, *American Indian Education*, 22–23.

19. Francis Paul Prucha, "Two Roads to Conversion: Protestant and Catholic Missionaries in the Pacific Northwest," *The Pacific Northwest Quarterly* 79, no. 4 (October 1988): 130–137.

20. On De Smet see, W. L. Davis, "Peter John De Smet: The Journey of 1840," *The Pacific Northwest Quarterly* 35, no. 1 (January 1944): 29–43; J. P. De Smet, "Father De Smet's Narrative Describing Upper Washington Territory, 1859," *The American Catholic Historical Researches* 12, no. 3 (July 1895): 102–106; J. P. De Smet, *Life, Letters and Travels of Father Pierre-Jean De Smet, S.J., 1801-1878* (New York: Francis P. Harper, 1905); J. P. De Smet, *Western Missions and Missionaries: A Series of Letters* (New York: James B. Kirker, 1863); John J. Killoren, *"Come, Blackrobe" De Smet and the Indian Tragedy* (Norman, OK: University of Oklahoma Press, 1994).

Also see Louis F. Burns, *Osage Missions Baptisms, Marriages, and Interments, 1820-1886* (Fallbrook, CA: Ciga Press, 1985), v–x; Fitzgerald, *Beacon on the Plains*, 65–75; Anna C. Minogue, *Loretto: Annals of the Century* (New York: The American Press, 1912), 129; Loretto Community, "Only One Heart: Loretto and Indigenous Peoples," *Loretto Community,* October 4, 2020, http://lorettocommunity.org/author/lorettocommunity/; John Mack, "Osage Mission: The Story of Catholic Missionary Work in Southeast Kansas," *The Catholic Historical Review* 96, no. 2 (April 2010): 262–281; Mark G. Thiel, "Catholic Ladders and Native American Evangelization," in *Native American Catholic Studies Reader: History and Theology,* ed. David Endres (Washington, DC: Catholic University of American Press, 2022), 27–58.

21. Prucha, "Two Roads to Conversion," 32.

22. Prucha, "Two Roads to Conversion," 34.

23. Ned Blackhawk, *The Rediscovery of America: Native Peoples and the Unmaking of U.S. History* (New Haven, CT: Yale University Press, 2023), 211–287; Ethan Davis, "An Administrative Trail of Tears: Indian Removal." *The American Journal of Legal History* 50, no. 1 (2008): 49–100; Sarah Dees, "Religion and US Federal Indian Policy," in *A Companion to Religious History,* ed. Benjamin E. Park (New York: Wiley Blackwell, 2021), 276–286; Jon T. Kilpinen, "The Supreme Court's Role in Choctaw and Chickasaw Dispossession." *Geographical Review* 94, no. 4 (2004): 484–501; Gregory D. Smithers, "The 'Pursuits of the Civilized Man': Race and the Meaning of Civilization in the United States and Australia, 1790s-1850s," *Journal of World History* 20, no. 2 (2009): 245–272.

24. Fixico, *Bureau of Indian Affairs,* 1–22, 69–86; Reyhner and Eder, *American Indian Education,* 44–63.

25. Fifteenth Congress, Session II, Chapter 85, March 3, 1819.

26. "Let All that is Indian Die," *Legal Review Native American Rights Fund* 38, no. 2 (Fall 2013): 1–9.

27. Fixico, *Bureau of Indian Affairs,* 1–22, 69–86; Reyhner and Eder, *American Indian Education,* 44–63.

28. Fixico, *Bureau of Indian Affairs*, 1–22, 69–86; Reyhner and Eder, *American Indian Education,* 44–63.

29. Fixico, *Bureau of Indian Affairs,* 1–22, 69–86; Reyhner and Eder, *American Indian Education,* 44–63, 168.

30. Reyhner and Eder, *American Indian Education,* 4. Also see Sarah Dees, "Religion and US Federal Indian Policy," in *A Companion to Religious History,* ed. Benjamin E. Park (New York: Wiley Blackwell, 2021), 276–286.

31. K. Tsiania Lomawaima, *They Called it Prairie Light: The Story of the Chilocco Indian School* (Lincoln, NE: University of Nebraska Press, 1994), 1–28.

Chapter 2

The Sisters of the Loretto and the Osage Missions in Kansas, 1847–1870

Being a member of the first group of Catholic Sisters to run an Indigenous school was not for the faint of heart. According to a letter from the 1940s, Sisters of the Loretto faced violence every day of their time working with the Osage in Kansas in the 1840s through the 1860s. Recalling a story from 80 to 90 years prior, the letter described how, when

> An Indian girl was ill and the parents came to see her. The squa [*sic*] thaought [*sic*] that the White Spirit was the cause of her illness and as she raised the knife the Indian man grabbed it and saved Mother Bridgets [*sic*] life and gave Mother the knife. Mother Bridget explained her illness and they parted good friends.[1]

This situation of an Indigenous person attacking one of the Sisters is common enough within the Sisters' records. A theme within the convent records and annals is that of the Sisters' fear of violence when they did something that challenged the Osage cultural norms, supplanting them with white values and practices. However, according to their archives, the Sisters ultimately prevailed in these power struggles. In doing so, the Sisters of Loretto's annals portrayed the Osage's acceptance of the Sisters' authority at the mission.

This chapter examines the first Catholic boarding school run by Catholic Sisters: the Osage Mission in Kansas. The Sisters started their school less than 30 years after the U.S. Congress passed funding for academic and industrial education as part of the Civilization Fund Act and more than 20 years after the creation of the Bureau of Indian Affairs in 1824. The Loretto school at Osage Mission was an early attempt at an assimilationist school, being the second one to be run by Catholics after the short-lived Jesuit school in 1820s Missouri. It was run without the support of a strong government bureaucracy or even a Catholic institution (such as the BCIM) that later schools would have.[2] To that end, the Sisters had to demonstrate how they established their own authority over the Osage community without the institutional support later schools would have. To do so, they constructed narratives that emphasized the Osage acceptance of supposed white cultural superiority.

These narratives were largely constructed for members of their own communities, Most of the archival sources were letters written between Lorettines. A few were memoirs, often in letter form, which tried to evaluate the community's past. Unlike other communities in this study, there were few letters preserved between the Sisters and the bishops or secular authorities. This suggests that the stories the Lorettines told were attempts at understanding their own history and their role within the larger world. As the Sisters reflected on their work, they created a sort of heroic narrative to demonstrate how they overcame adversity and ultimately brought white values to the Osage community.

There were some twentieth-century scholarship attempts that looked at the Lorettine's archival sources. The earliest book on the Sisters was published in 1916 by W. W. Graves, a Catholic scholar. One priest in the 1930s described the book as having "the authentic data," suggesting a level of perceived archival research.[3] In the 1930s and 1940s, a Sister Lilliana Owens did work on the Lorettine's mission in Kansas, publishing an article in 1947. According to archival letters, she appeared to have reached out to other Sisters for oral histories, though these would have been from the late nineteenth century, rather than the early era.[4] In 1955, Sister Mary de Sales Kelley defended a master's thesis on the archival material surrounding the Osage Missions. The thesis, however, reflected western bias, focusing on the supposed cultural backwardness of the Osage and Quapaw. Moreover, it suggested that the thesis was relative due to the "pertinence" of "the Indian Problem" in the 1950s, as "the conversion and education of the Indian is still as problem of the Catholic Church in the United States."[5] These texts, however, did not have a large audience, appearing to have been written for a limited Catholic one..

Despite writing on the Lorettos, such historians have largely downplayed the role of the Loretto Sisters in Kansas, focusing on the Jesuit missionaries. Even the sources within the archives tend to focus on the Jesuits. For example, an 1889 newspaper article from the Loretto archives wrote of the early mission that

> this little band consisting of Father Schoenmakers, Mother Concolia, Sisters Bridget, Mary and Vincentia were met by Father Bax and some dozen Indian boys. On the tenth the Sisters opened their school in a log house that had been built by Father Bax and his assistants.[6]

In such histories, the Sisters are designated helpmates to the Jesuits, rather than as autonomous actors. However, in this chapter, I place the Sisters of

Loretto as actors in their own right. Largely isolated within a foreign culture, these white women attempted to demonstrate their ability to succeed in their missionary work. While their annals tell of Indigenous resistance, the Sisters emphasized how these potential conflicts were ultimately resolved by Indigenous acceptance of white practices.

BACKGROUND

In the 1840s and 1850s, the United States was still defining the implications of Manifest Destiny; this was very much the early pioneer era. While the transportation revolution was beginning with the rise of railroads, steamboats, and canals, most settlers relied upon horses and walking in the West. There were railroads, but in the decades before the Civil War, they were regional; later, pioneers could travel cross-country by train. In addition to the limited transportation, there were also limits to long-distance communication. The telegraph was in its infancy, not fully maturing until the Civil War. Missionaries would have had to rely upon letters that could take months to arrive.[7] Given the lack of fast transportation and communication, the Sisters of Loretto and other missionaries were very isolated, both from their religious counterparts and government officials. They had to figure out how to run their schools and show their dominance over the local communities without government or military aid.

Prior to 1881, there were two groups of Osage, the Great Osage and the Little Osage, who were divided by geography and tradition. It was mainly the Little Osage in Kansas. In the era of exploration, the Osage initially had contact with the French and Spanish, playing one off the other to attempt to gain the upper hand in the evolving political situations. When the Louisiana Purchase of 1803 transferred that land to the United States, the Osage continued asserting dominance over other tribal nations through raiding parties. In 1825, the U.S. government forced the Osage onto a reservation (125 miles by 50 miles) in southern Kansas. This forced relocation led to hostilities between the Osage and other Indigenous communities, particularly the Cherokee, who laid claim to similar lands in Kansas and Missouri. Fighting between these various groups erupted, although it was sporadic, with the government intervening at various points. Both groups ultimately ended up in Oklahoma, with the Cherokee arriving first in 1838.[8]

By the 1820s and 1830s, the Presbyterians were the dominant settled missionaries in the Osage territory, with five functioning missions, while Catholics only sent a few itinerant missionaries. Even after the establishment of the Osage Catholic missions in 1847, Protestants still held sway over much of the area; by the Civil War there were Baptist, Episcopalian, and Society of

Friends (Quakers) missionaries in the area as well.[9] Evidence suggests that some of the Protestants did not view the Osage favorably. In 1827, a Presbyterian minister wrote of the Osage in disparaging tones, lamenting, "Vice reigns everywhere."[10] Later records (discussed below) suggest that Osage requested Catholic missionaries, suggesting a level of Protestant apathy.

French missionaries in the late 1600s were the first Catholics to meet the Osage. However, it was not until the Jesuits that the Osage began to have a long-term relationship with Catholic missionaries. The Jesuit records go back to 1750, focusing on the work of itinerant missionaries. Catholic missionaries did not initially prioritize the Osage, preferring to work more with the Pottawatomie before the 1840s. In the early decades of the nineteenth century, there were a few ministers to the Osage, primarily Louis DuBourg, Charles de la Croix, and Charles Van Quickenborne. Father Van Quickenborne was the first Catholic to celebrate mass in Southeast Kansas, at the location of the Osage Mission.[11]

According to various histories, DuBourg was one of the driving forces behind establishing a permanent mission. In 1823, he requested government funding for the Jesuit missions in Kansas and Missouri, petitioning Secretary of War John C. Calhoun for permission. Calhoun approved of the idea, and in 1824, the Jesuits opened a manual training school, St. Regis Indian Seminary, in Florissant, Missouri. According to a survey of the Catholic-run Native American Boarding Schools, St. Regis was the first Catholic-Run Boarding School. The school closed approximately eight years later. In 1829, Van Quickenborne wrote to President Andrew Jackson, requesting that the missionaries receive land to open a school for boys. Jackson agreed, so long as the Osage agreed. The affected community appeared to agree, but the question of where to establish the mission remained in the air.[12]

The next generation of missionaries had more luck establishing a permanent mission. According to one history, the Osage wrote to President Zachary Taylor and requested funding for a school in 1843, explicitly asking that Catholics run it. Given the Protestant presence, why they chose Catholics is unclear, but it could have been that the Protestants presented themselves as too busy to work with the Osage. Taylor agreed, but there was a missionary shortage. By this point, Father John Schoenmakers was the primary missionary to the region, although he was joined sporadically by other Jesuits. It was Father Schoenmakers who was the driving force behind the establishment of the Osage Mission. His intentions were unclear: he may have established a good relationship with the Osage, or he may have been responding to the reported Protestant neglect of the Cherokee, as one history suggested. Either way, it was under him that a long-term school came to be.[13]

Father Schoenmakers wanted to establish two schools: one for boys and one for girls. Schoenmakers wanted Jesuits to run the boy's school. For the girl's school, he needed women religious. The initial reason for this was practical; typically, female education had been relegated to female teachers. Catholic missionaries respected the use of Catholic Sisters in working with children. But, more than that, the priests believed that Catholic Sisters were vital to any such assimilationist educational endeavor. As one Jesuit wrote in 1847, since

> the surest prospect of advancing the work of civilization among the Indians chiefly depends on the education of the female children, we had formed the resolution to send out five or six Religious Lades (alias Nuns) who by vow and profession devote themselves to the education of girls.[14]

To aid him in his new endeavor, Schoenmakers recruited the Sisters of Loretto.

The Sisters of Loretto originated in Kentucky. Their motherhouse is 65 miles southwest of Lexington, near the Catholic enclave of Bardstown. Founded in April 1812 by a mix of lay women and a local priest, Father Charles Nerinckx, the Lorettos were slow to expand. Unlike some communities, such as the Sisters of St. Joseph (CSJs, discussed in chapter 7), they did not have a corresponding community in Europe from which to draw new members. Nor did they have long-established governing guidelines and community constitutions, which they had to build from the ground up.[15]

The community dedicated itself to the education of girls. There is evidence that Father Nerinckx wanted the Sisters to work with the Indigenous communities as early as 1824, going so far as to make a provisional contract with an agent for the Sisters to educate and "civilize" girls. However, nothing happened for 20 years. In the interim, the Loretto expanded past Kentucky, establishing missions and schools in Louisiana, Arkansas, and Missouri.[16]

Schoenmakers was honest in his request for help, telling the Lorettines that running the school would be difficult with little funding and the possibility of violence. Four Sisters agreed to come: Mother Concordia Henning, Sister Mary Petronella Van Prather, Sister Vincentia McCool, and Sister Bridget Hayden.[17] The party arrived in 1847. At that time, less than 150 Catholics were in the state (the number would rise after 1854, largely due to immigration from Germany and Ireland). The missions were initially under the jurisdiction of the newly elevated Archdiocese of St. Louis, but after 1851, the Apostolic Indian Territory East of the Rocky Mountains oversaw the missions.[18] All in all, they were isolated from other missionaries, both in terms of geography and resources.

THE SCHOOL

Opened on October 25, 1847, the Loretto's school at the Osage Mission was never as big as some federal schools but catered to a healthy number of students. The records don't contain the number of students per year, though in 1856, there were 40 students, and 2 years later, there were over 70. This number was about on par with the number of students at St. Andrew's school in Umatilla, Oregon, in the early 1890s (this school was situated on the Tulalip reservation). Most students at the Loretto's school were of mixed French-Osage heritage, unsurprising given Osage history. It may have been well respected by whites. Indeed, one report from 1849 recorded that "This is no doubt the best school in the Indian country, particularly the female department."[19]

When the Sisters arrived in 1847, there was not much government or Catholic support for their work. The original contract for the boys school stipulated that it was to be "the manual labor school . . . said school to be supplied with competent teachers, and the boys committed to their charge to be carefully instructed on Christian morality, the rudiments of plain English education, and in agriculture."[20] I did not find the specific contract for the girls' school; it may have been automatically included under the auspices of the boys' school. However, they appeared to have separate accommodations, with one report writing in 1855 that "the female department of our school counts 40 pupils and eight female attendants. For the accommodation of this large number they have one common refectory . . . one play room . . . and one common dormitory."[21] (See figure 2.1.)

Funding was always a concern. In the early 1850s, Father Schoenmakers wrote to the government, requesting funds for both the girls' school, under

Figure 2.1   Osage School for Girls. *Source: Courtesy of a Catholic Mission.*

the Lorettos, and the boys' school, run by the Jesuits. Schoenmakers noted that the boys' school was better funded than the girls' institution. His letters indicated that the schools typically received approximately $54 per student, which he requested be increased, citing medical costs he paid out of pocket. It is unclear if the medical expenses were for both schools or just the boys'. The cost of medicine is also confusing, since the Sisters ran their own infirmary. He claimed the school lost approximately $800 a year in out-of-pocket costs. However, it is unclear if he meant both schools or just one.[22]

The goal of the Lorettine's school was to teach the Osage and, after 1853, Quapaw girls what it meant to be a white woman; but not to gain equality through assimilation but rather to attain cultural and religious values. A 1916 history of the first superior, Mother Bridget, wrote,

> Osage girls who had roamed the prairies in scant attire were gathered into the schools and not only taught the elements of education, but were also trained to make their own clothing, after the style of the whites and to be modest, and refined young women, imbued with a desire to lead honorable Christian lives.[23]

The Sisters were on a mission to "civilize" through everyday habits such as clothing, but more importantly, through Christian tradition.

In addition to missionary work, the school was supposed to provide a manual and primary education. An unnamed Sister within the Loretto archives expands the previous description:

> School for these daughters of the red men had to be cleaning, cooking, sewing, laundry, making beds, and the everyday occupations of women in the home . . . .The 'four R's'—reading, 'riting, 'rithmetic, and religion—followed, then graduate organization into intermediate elementary divisions.[24]

While the "four R's" were part of the curriculum, it was manual training in white household traditions, "the everyday occupations of women in the home," that dominated the student's schedules. While this emphasis became common place in the post-bellum era, the goals of the school at the Osage Mission reflected developing educational reforms, particularly those targeting females, of the antebellum period.

Leading antebellum education reformer Catherine Beecher suggested that females would respond better to a more vocational education, focusing on domestic skills and limiting access to traditional academic subjects. Beecher argued that an advanced education would negatively affect the girls' emotions and bodies. She linked domesticity, particularly the capable running of a household, to U.S. citizenship, suggesting that American women were inherently suited for housekeeping skills. In her mind, other ethnicities must learn the habits of white American women. Beecher also connected domesticity to morality, suggesting that a true woman followed good Christian virtues by keeping a house and home clean and organized.[25]

Beecher's views on womanhood reflected the cult of domesticity of the nineteenth century, which linked white womanhood to the home and Christianity. Previously called the "separate spheres" mentality, at its most basic level, the cult of domesticity suggested that true womanhood lay in running a good home, keeping it as an oasis from the cares and evils of the world. According to this ideology, a true woman was to be a devout and active housekeeper, keeping her part of the world tidy. Beecher simply expanded that belief to suggest that there were more efficient methods by which women could maintain the sanctity of the home. Education, to her, was key to maintaining this standard of womanhood.[26]

While domesticity at the boarding schools would have been part of the broader trends in womanhood and female education in the 1840s, the goals of such a program changed over time. White reformers saw domesticity as key to any civilization program. There was the belief that the way to influence the entire community was through women and children. Reformers believed that girls who learned white domestic arts would bring white household habits to their reservations, thus instilling white values upon their families, kinship networks, and communities at large.[27]

While the education that focused on domesticity and manual training reflected the mindset of the antebellum period, its continuation after the Civil War represented an attempt to keep Indigenous persons in a secondary status. As discussed in the introduction, when the United States became more industrial, needing more workers for its factories and transportation systems, the Native American schools continued to promote a domestic education. Graduates were unable to participate and receive the benefits of the new economy.[28] However, at the time of the Lorettine's school in Kansas, that was not a concern. Their work better aligned with the goals of Beecher and other education reformers.

ASSERTING AUTHORITY

The Sisters were in a very precarious situation, being the minority in an unknown culture. Various sources suggest that the Loretto Sisters were uncomfortable living so close to the Osage. The Sisters were initially wary due to the "horrors of warfare with the Red Man" to quote a 1912 history of the Loretto.[29] The Jesuits confirmed that fear; in an 1895 letter, Rev. Paul Ponziglioni recalled that "The very name of the Osage was a terror all over the land, and not without a reason, for straggling warriors would frequently commit heavy depredations" on settlers and cargo units, noting the sporadic attacks that punctuated white expansion into Kansas. However, he stated that "the Osage would watch the Convent by day and by night, and the Sisters never have been exposed to any danger."[30] Despite such promises of protection, anxiety over such seemingly random attacks never truly abated.

Some later Sisters were unfamiliar with Native missionary work or even Native persons, leading to a level of aloofness. One history of the Sisters states that in 1860, two of the new Sisters of the mission "had never seen a copper-colored man and they were not a little afraid of him. . . . Good Mother Concordia said—Sister don't be afraid, neither he or any other Indian will ever hurt a Sister."[31] Indeed, sources suggest that Mother Bridget was the least afraid of the Osage and, of all the Sisters, the fondest of the students, with a source recording that "Mother Bridget had a great love for all her Indian girls, and she would often tell us how beautiful they were." The record suggested that while other Sisters were fond of the students, it was Mother Bridget who bonded with them most: "it did not take the new Sisters long to feel at home among the fine Indians, but they could never see in them all the beauty that Mother Concordia did."[32] Whichever, there appears to have been a level of hesitation in interactions between some of the Sisters and the Osage, which may have influenced the situations discussed below. Knowing they were strangers in a strange land, the Sisters had to find ways to prove to themselves that they had control over the situation, as well as how they came by it.

The Sisters of Loretto struggled to assert their authority over their charges. They wanted to show that they were in control, despite being vastly outnumbered by the local Osage community. This situation was common, as we shall see in later chapters. Two things make these instances unique: the Sisters had to assert themselves without the institutional support later schools had, and these moments had the potential to turn violent. While we shall see instances of violence later on, particularly with the CSJs at Fort Yuma, such cases typically reflected moments in which the Sisters interfered in tribal politics or spiritual matters. Such was not the case in Kansas. The events at the Osage Mission were backlashes to instances of cultural misunderstanding and assimilation. However, at least in the Sisters' records, their way won out and the Indigenous nations capitulated to their traditions and practices. Points of contention revolved around corporeal punishment as well as medicine. In later recounting these tales, Sisters used these moments to demonstrate their authority over the children at the school as well as the local Indigenous community.

Corporal Punishment

A key issue at the Lorettine school was that of corporal punishment. Within white society, canings and other forms of corporal punishment were common, particularly in schools. "Spare the Rod, spoil the child" (from Prov. 13:24) was a millennia-old practice taken to heart in many households and schools. Such behavior was starting to become controversial among social and educational reformers, particularly in the industrializing north, where it was suggested that corporal punishment was detrimental to development. Despite such arguments, the practice continued in schools until the end of the twentieth century.[33] At the time the Sisters ran the school, however, corporal punishment was still rather controversial, pointing toward questions of authority, particularly who had the authority to discipline the students.

Corporal punishment was quite common at the Indigenous boarding schools of the nineteenth and twentieth centuries. According to the Jesuit missionary J. J. Bax, the Osage knew of the propensity for physical punishment at white schools. In a letter to the famous missionary Pierre-Jean De Smet, Bax wrote that prior to the arrival of the Sisters, "The parents, full of prejudices against a 'school,' gave for excuse that the children who had been confided to the former missionaries (the Presbyterians) had learned nothing [and] had been whipped every day."[34] Bax's commentary suggests that the Osage did not approve of such discipline at the school, for the children ran away from the Presbyterians. Yet, there was a level of hypocrisy, as Bax noted that "the most efficacious correction that a father could employ against a child, was to threaten it with being sent to school," where they would be whipped.[35] The difference seemed to be who was the punisher: the white man or the Native one. Native upon Native, Bax suggests, was ok, but not white upon Native.[36]

Several instances that stand out in the Sisters' annals revolve around discipline, with the Sisters administering some sort of punishment. In either 1859 or 1860, the new mother superior, Bridget Hayden, found her life threatened over a matter of discipline:

> Mother Bridget Hayden succeeded Mother Concordia as superior of the mission and many and varied were her experiences. In the early days, when she was directress of the school, she was one day trying to conquer a stubborn Indian girl, when the father of the child appeared suddenly and unexpectedly. The child was glad to see her father at this moment, feeling it meant triumph for her; but when she saw her father take out his tomahawk, to use it against Sister Bridget, she was much frightened and, throwing herself between them, begged her father not to hurt Sister, that she had been a bad girl and Sister was only trying to correct her. The Indian at once replaced his tomahawk, assuring Sister Bridget that he would never hurt her for trying to make a good girl of his child.[37]

What was Mother Bridget doing that caused such a ruckus? The verb "conquer" suggests some form of corporal punishment, such as a spanking, caning, or whipping.

Key to this incident is the question of who was in charge of the student's behavior: the Sisters or the local community? The answer to this question determined who had the right to correct students' behavior. If it were the Sisters, they should have full control over determining the mode of redress for the girls' behavior. If the Native community, they have the right to fight back. Yet, that question had more meaning than just who was in charge of whom; it was a debate over whose culture won out in the battle of assimilation.

The use of the term "stubborn" suggests that the student was resisting assimilation. Upon seeing her punishment, the father initially assumes his control over his child, as if he is protecting her right to maintain her cultural values. However, he soon capitulates to the Sisters' authority. Faced with the threat of the death of one of her teachers, the student submits to the Sisters' authority, admitting that she had been misbehaving and that "Sister was only trying to correct her." Seeing his daughter admit that the Sister's punishment was supposedly justified, the father too submits to the Sisters' authority, promising "never to hurt her for trying to make a good girl of his child." He accepts the white definition of "good," which appears to mean submitting to white authority, rather than being "stubborn" and resisting assimilation.

In another incident, the Sisters threatened corporal punishment with a similar outcome. An anecdote recorded in 1911 tells of "The Incorrigible Pupil," who was a young girl named Pelagie who did not want to be at the school and resisted. The Sisters were frustrated, but despite all they did, things did not change. Finally, the proverbial straw that broke the camel's back occurred when Pelagie threw peaches at her classmates, hiding in a tree for three days. Frustrated,

> the Sisters declined having anything to do with the conquering of Pelagie; so the girls held Council as to the ways and means of accomplishing their object. It was decided that it was necessary to have the help of a Sister.

The girls and a Sister, M. Vincent White, snuck into Pelagie's room and

> Awaking her, the Sister addressed her thus; "Pelagie, you have been a bad girl and we have come to take some of the badness out of you with these hickory rods." Pelagie was up in a second pleading with them to spare her, that she would never again give them cause for complaint. She kept her promise.[38]

The threat of physical punishment was enough to help her change her mind.

Whether true or not, the story of Pelagie is significant because it was the students who wanted to turn to physical means in order to "conquer" Pelagie. Yet, they still never take that final step in doing so. Rather than taking matters into their own hands and censoring one of their own, they turn to the Sisters. By enlisting the help of Sister M. Vincent White, the female students were embracing the Sisters' authority. They are accepting that the Sisters hold control over their attitude, behavior, and body. The girls, according to the Sisters' narrative, have accepted white authority. The Sisters have succeeded in their goals.

In both stories, the Osage came to accept some form of corporal punishment from the white women as necessary. In the first incident, the student's father "assures Sister Bridget that he would never hurt her for trying to make a good girl of his child," while in the second, it is Pelagie's classmates who decide as a group to beat her in order to reform her. Canings and other forms of "conquering" students became accepted, a form of assimilation that enforced the Sisters' authority over the bodies of the students. In the decades that the Sisters ran the school, such supposedly corrective behavior was not unique, as they tried to enforce white views on "conquering" upon the bodies of their students.

Hair

Corporal punishment was not the only area in which the Sisters sought to assert their position of power over the bodies of the students; there were also cultural differences, which tended to revolve around medical care. One such instance was regarding hair. The question of hair was a continuing concern at all the Native American Boarding schools. School officials believed newly arrived students must have their hair cut, citing health reasons (particularly lice) and cultural reasons (white boys having short hair). Hair represented civilization to many of the white educators and reformers.

Hair had very different connotations for Native students. It could be a symbol of identity and family connection. Having one's hair cut could mean the death of family members or isolation from one's community. The Sisters of Loretto knew that hair had a special meaning to their children but seemed to have trivialized it, writing "Indians prize very highly a luxuriant growth of hair."[39] To the Lorettines, hair was more vanity ("a luxuriant growth of hair") than a sign of cultural and social identity. Moreover, the Sisters argued that there were certain instances that warranted the cutting of such a "luxuriant growth."

One instance demonstrates this cultural misunderstanding. An undated entry describes a young girl whose parents had dropped her off. The Sisters cut her hair "to treat the head, which badly needed treatment." Her parents heard and in great anger, they returned to the Mission. On seeing their girl

having a tar cap instead of her long hair, they were inconsolable. . . . They took out the tomahawk and asked for the Sisters who had treated their girl in such a manner, but the Sisters instead of appearing fled upstairs and locked herself in until the angry pair left the Mission.[40]

The Annals suggest that to the Native parents, the Sisters had overstepped their authority in order to touch the children's hair. However, the annals end on a happy note:

> After some months they came again to the Mission to see their daughter-This time they saw her a blooming girl . . . They were so pleased with the girl that . . . thanked the Sister many times for having saved the life of their daughter.[41]

The Sisters had won, at least for the moment, demonstrating that their practices were superior to those proposed by the girls' parents.

Later schools dealt with trichology (hair-related) situations similar to that of the Lorettines. Students simply did not want their hair cut and found ways to make that clear. For example, at Sisters of St. Joseph School at Fort Yuma, on the Arizona/California border, a newspaper article from 1890 suggested that the students rebelled, vandalizing school property. The reason: haircuts and physical discipline. As a result, "The Sister superintendent was compelled to promise not to cut their hair unless the boys consented and agreed also not to inflict corporal punishment."[42] In the Fort Yuma case, the Sisters compromised. With the Lorettines, the Annals argue that the Indigenous population submitted to white authority, within certain circumstances.

The question of hair also linked to white views of medicine. In addition to running the school, the Sisters started an infirmary open to the Indigenous nation. The Sisters and other missionaries justified the infirmary's cost with the belief that their medical care would lead to conversion. As Kenton Clymer wrote in his book on Protestant Missionary work in the Philippines, "having ministered to the physical needs of the people, they had better access to their homes for more direct evangelism."[43] This plan worked at least once:

> On one occasion, an old Indian woman visited the Mission, and when the Sisters asked her what she wanted, she said that she had heard of the 'Medicine woman' and had come a long way to see her and if she could cure her, she would embrace the faith of the Black robe Sisters . . . At the end of nine days, the poor woman's sores were entirely healed, and it was with a happy heart that Mother witnessed her baptism a few weeks later after having been duly instructed.[44]

The story must be taken with a grain of salt; the Sisters recorded that the old woman had an interpreter. However, if the story is to be believed, then the Sisters' success in their medical treatment of the woman was key to a conversion. In terms of belief and propaganda, the evidence would have helped emphasize the importance of religion within their missionary work. Moreover, it would have pointed toward the Sisters' ability to demonstrate their supposed religious and medical superiority over the Indigenous communities.

The Loretto recorded these instances to demonstrate their sense of cultural superiority and their belief in the righteousness of their work. The students' parents recognize a higher power to the symbol of hair: that of white medicine. The older woman converts, believing that Catholicism was the determining factor in her medical recovery. They accept that the Sisters' way is the best, even if it does involve undermining Osage beliefs and traditions. The Sisters had won out in this instance, gaining authority over the community through their so-called "civilized" practices.

White Values

Although actively promoting their own agenda through more aggressive means, Sisters appeared to protect the students in certain situations, particularly when doing so demonstrated their perceived cultural superiority. One history described an event when an Indigenous man and his wife came to the school. The wife asked for specific girl, who "appeared having on a nice new calico dress." The wife then informed the girl she was to be the man's second wife, at which "the girl drew back, braced herself up and said no, I cannot do it. Then the squaw grabbed the girls dress and was dragging her off by force." According to the source, Sister Vencentia came to the Sister "gave the dress three clips of her scissors then tore off the strip that the Squaw held and told the girl to run to the Fathers where she would be safe." Sister Vencentia then listened to the wife, before telling her (calmly according to the story) to leave, "Yes, you can yell now all you want, and when you get tired yelling leave here with what you have in her grip and be satisfied. The squaw never parted with the nice slice of calico torn from the girl's dress." Before leaving, the man thanked Sister Vencentia for saving the girl from a polygamous marriage.[45]

Whether true or not, the story is a metaphor for the driving goal of the school: the adoption of white, gender values. In the anecdote, the Sisters appear to be the rescuers of a girl who has assimilated to white ways from being returned to her former traditions. The student is wearing a dress made from calico and refuses to conform to the supposed custom of being a second wife. The girl is literally caught between two extremes: the supposedly uncivilized way of the wife, who is both physically and verbally forceful, and the civilization that the Sisters have imbued. The girl has been saved by the Sisters, who keep her ready for her presumed place in white society, symbolized by throughout her calico dress. The wife, however, has rejected civilization, demanding that the girl take part in a polygamous marriage, a Native tradition, which is held in contrast to the white tradition of monogamy. Indeed, she goes so far as to destroy the girl's dress, the sign of her acceptance of white culture and the Christian faith. The allegory for the extremes of civilization and supposedly "savagery" could not have been clearer.

The moral of all these incidents, whether the Sisters were victims or protectors, was that their way, that of white society, was superior to that of the Osage. In each story, the Osage parents capitulate to the Sisters, reportedly admitting that the Sisters knew better than they did. In the last story, even the students are assimilated, turning to the Sisters for protection against what were written to be barbarous ways. The Sisters were trying to show not only their authority over the students, but also that the Osage had accepted said authority. Whether this was the case or not, the Sisters were trying to demonstrate that they were in control of the situation and their students.

PUSHBACK TO AUTHORITY

Despite their emphasis on their authority through white culture, the Lorettines were aware that they were not always able to control their relationships with the local community. They appeared to use such incidents to emphasize the difference between their assimilated students and other Native communities. One example of this is an incident involving land ownership. According to the records, the Sisters worked with the local Jesuits, and the boy's school raised peaches. However, they were preparing to make peach preserves

> when at once a good number of squaws appeared. Each squaw was furnished with a sack. They told the religious that they came for those peaches, that the land was theirs and that everything that grew on it was theirs also—so they took the most and best of the peaches.[46]

Unlike other events in which the Sisters demonstrated their supposed cultural superiority and thus their authority over the students, in this case, the Indigenous women refused to bow down but instead pushed back against white control.

It is unclear when this event occurred, but clues within the source suggest the late 1850s or early 1860s. The Sisters recorded the events of the Civil War in their annals, writing about their (at times acrimonious) interactions with the armies. This event is not recorded alongside the events of the war. Anything after the Civil War becomes suspect: the Sisters ceased to work with the Osage by 1870, although they remained in the Osage Mission, running a school for white girls. In the years after the Civil War, the U.S. Army started to relocate the Osage to Oklahoma. Some communities took longer to leave than others, but the process was largely complete by 1870. Thus, it is logical to conclude that the peach incident happened either in the tumultuous years leading up to or through the American Civil War.

The incident reflected Osage's response to the U.S. government's redistricting of Osage land. As one history of the Osage described, the communities "in effect were moved ahead of white settlement, until in 1854 they became surrounded, an enclave, and there was an impasse."[47] In the 1840s and 1850s, the U.S. government started to redefine so-called "Indian Territory," with the northern parts becoming states and territories, even if previous treaties had designated them to specific tribal nations. Part of this re-allotment came from debates over the Missouri Compromises of 1820 and the Compromise of 1850, which divided slave states from the so-called free states. While dividing the United States in two, these two political acts did not consider the Indigenous peoples already living on that land.[48]

The 1850s and 1860s were a turbulent time in Osage/white relations. In March 1858, *The Washington Union* reported the spread of violence in Kansas:

> We continue to hear rumors of violence committed or threatened on the Osage. We counsel all good citizens of all parties to report their grievances to the proper officers . . . and not to believe too many of the rumors that are afloat.[49]

Just over ten years later, *The Emporia News* from Emporia, Kansas, reported that members of the Osage nation were involved in a murder (of whom it is not stated) but that travelers to the area should not worry about any violence or "hostilities."[50]

One of the contributing factors was the Kansas-Nebraska Act of 1854. High school students or those who suffered through a United States survey course in college may remember the act as a leading cause of the Civil War, as it opened Kansas territory up for white settlement, allowing white settlers to choose whether Kansas would enter the Union as a slave or free state. Critics called this practice "squatter sovereignty"; a term that seems apt when examining the law's little-explored impact on Indigenous nations. White settlers confronted the Osage and other Indigenous persons determined to claim Native land for themselves. Violence exploded between enslavers and so-called free-soilers (those who wanted to bring Kansas into the Union as a free state). In addition to fighting among themselves, white setters found themselves at odds with Indigenous Americans as white encroachment expanded throughout Kansas. White settlers quickly reached out to Congress, asking the governing body to send the army to remove the Osage, an act that occurred after the Civil War.[51]

The Civil War worsened the land-situation for Osage communities in Kansas. With the increase of white-on-white violence, the Osage found themselves caught between rival factions as early as 1854 but with increasing intensity after 1861. On top of the fighting, the 1862 Homestead Act promised land surveyed in the 1840s and 1850s to white families moving West, so long as they had not joined the Southern States in rebellion. Migration increased after the Civil War ended.[52]

The Osage had no say in the policies governing these white encroachments on their land. At first, these political changes may not have been important; decrees from far-off Washington, D.C. may have seemed inconsequential until the arrival of armed white settlers, determined to claim the Osage lands for themselves. White squatters would inform the local Indigenous communities of new laws, surveys, and territorial lines, expecting the Osage to vacate the land immediately. Some communities rebelled through violence. It appears that other communities took other forms of rebellion.

In the case of the Sisters at the Osage Mission, rather than take more overt action: the Osage's response was to reclaim peaches from their land. The historical context indicates that the Sisters and the Osage found themselves amid land politics, specifically white expansionism. Given these circumstances, it is not surprising that the Osage women reacted the way they did to the Sisters planting on what could arguably be their land. Unlike other stories the Sisters told, in this one, the Indigenous women do not back down. In this matter, at least, they would not fully respect or respond to the Sisters' authority.

We might wonder why the Sisters' recorded this incident, as it did not fully support their narrative of cultural authority over the local Indigenous communities. There are no set reasons, but we might speculate. One would be simply a matter of truth; it happened and the Sisters were simply recording facts. Another rationale might fit into the larger theme of the archival sources: perhaps the peach incident served as a demonstration of the difference between students who had assimilated to white society, and those who had not. The Sisters and their students are the ones peacefully picking peaches. They are following in a domestic activity, a white one (as the act of canning suggests). It is those not associated with the school who attack this rather tranquil community. The Sisters suggest this attack is without provocation. Thus, these probably hungry women became examples of non-civilized persons, the proverbial savage. The Sisters may have allowed for this narrative deviation of assumed authority in order to demonstrate the difference between "civilized" students and "uncivilized" women.

Despite the peach incident, histories of the Lorettines in Kansas did attempt to emphasize the good relations between the Sisters and local communities. A 1916 history of the Osage Missions in Kansas wrote,

> The Indians held the Sisters in the highest esteem and were always ready to protect them from harm. It is said that for years the Indians believed that the Sisters came down direct from the abode of the Great Spirit for their especial good.[53]

Written in the style of a hagiography, the history extolled the Sisters' good relationship with the Osage, creating the image of the perfect mission school. A memoir from the Loretto archives was more realistic, stating that the Osage students struggled to adapt. However, it too viewed the past through prover-bial rose-colored glasses, writing, "After the Indian girls had been with the Sisters for a few months, they gradually settled down and became fond of work and study."[54] The children in the land incidence seem to take on similar characteristics, being docile and working with the Sisters on their task.

The behavior of the students and those who "held the Sisters in the highest esteem" blatantly contradicted the behavior of the Indigenous women who demanded the peaches. The source is careful not to mention whether the Sisters knew these women, referring to them generically as "squaws." There are potentially three meanings behind this omission: (1) the author did not know and was going on hearsay; (2) the Sisters did not believe these women were from the communities with whom they worked; or (3) the Sisters did not want to admit there was an uprising against their authority. Whatever the reason, the meaning behind this incident is clear: these women have not accepted the Sisters' authority. They are supposedly of a lower stratum of persons than with whom the Sisters had worked and assimilated. Whatever the reason, given the limitations on this source, such analysis is pure speculation.

CONCLUSION

The Sisters of Loretto were not trying to prove to the world how they sur-vived and came to gain control in Kansas. They were creating a narrative of heroism and cultural superiority to help members of their own congregation understand these uncertain years. The stories often portray Indigenous per-sons as "backward," rushing to respond to a perceived slight with a violent solution. However, by the end, the Indigenous people appear to accept that the Sisters' so-called "civlilized" ways, ultimately assimilating not only to white culture but white power structures. The supposed Osage affirmation of white values demonstrated the Sisters' control over the Osage.

In the late 1860s and early 1870s, the U.S. government had forcefully removed the Osage to Oklahoma. The Loretto Sisters remained at Osage Mis-sion, running a girls' school. Several histories suggest that the Osage were miserable with the move and requested that the Loretto, or other Catholic missionaries, accompany them to run new schools. In 1878, Father Schoen-makers, who had worked with the Osage in Kansas, wrote that the Osage council

unanimously asked for Catholic Schools . . . along with the Quakers school pro-vided the Catholics build their own school improvements; of course these terms will not be accepted, as Catholic priests cannot live among the Osages without some means of support.[55]

In the 1880s, the Sisters of St. Francis began to work with the Osage in Pawhuska, Oklahoma. The Sisters of Loretto would take over the school in Oklahoma in 1915, "[rejoicing] that [their] Indians are once more under the care of Loretto," according to one archival source.[56]

We will return to the Osage in chapter 6, focusing on the work of Sisters of St. Francis (OSFs) with them after 1880. There was a different political and social situation at the turn of the century in Oklahoma. Rather than stories of the hiccups associated with being one of the first Catholic mission schools run by Sisters, the OSFs' sources emphasize their own struggles to solidify their control over the Osage students, particularly when facing competition with the federal schools.

NOTES

1. Mary Stegman, Letter to Mother Olivette, 30 January 1940, LHC, Osage Mission, St. Ann's, St. Francis Correspondence; RG-Sch VII Box II-5.

2. K. Tsiania Lomawaima, *They Called it Prairie Light: The Story of the Chilocco Indian School* (Lincoln, NE: University of Nebraska Press, 1994), 1-28.

3. Father J. M. Fox, C. P., Letter to Sister M. Lilliana, December 3, 1931, LHC, Osage Mission, St Ann's, St Francis correspondence/research S Lilliana Owens, RG-SCH, VII Box II-6; William Whites Graves, *Life and Letters of Fathers Ponziglione, Schoenmakers, and Other Early Jesuits at Osage Mission: Sketch of St. Francis' Church. Life of Mother Bridget* (St. Paul, KS: W.W. Graves, 1916).

4. Sister M. Augustine, Letter to Dear Sister, November 20, 1934, LHC, Osage Mission, St Ann's, St Francis correspondence/research S Lilliana Owens, RG-SCH, VII Box II-6; C.J. Brown, Letter to Rev Sister M. Lillian, May 7, 1931, LHC, Osage Mission, St Ann's, St Francis correspondence/research S Lilliana Owens, RG-SCH, VII Box II-6 ; Father J.M. Fox, C.P, Letter to Sister M. Lilliana, December 3, 1931, LHC, Osage Mission, St Ann's, St Francis correspondence/research S Lilliana Owens, RG-SCH, VII Box II-6; Sister M. Wilfrid, Letter to Sister Lillians, May 12, 1934, LHC, Osage Mission, St Ann's, St Francis correspondence/research S Lilliana Owens, RG-SCH, VII Box II-6. Owen's research was published as Sister M. Liliana Owens, "The Early Work of the Lorettines in Southeastern Kansas," *Kansas History: A Journal of the Central Plains* 14, no. 3 (August 1947): 263–276.

5. Sister Mary de Sales Kelly, "A Study of the Osage Mission Schools Based on United States Archival Material 1847-1870" (MA Thesis, Catholic University of America, Washington, DC, August 1955), iii.

6. John R. Brunt, "Some Early History of the Osage Mission," *The Journal*, Osage Mission, 14 February 1889. Located in LHC06G Kansas 2–3.

7. Daniel Walker Howe, *What Hath God Wrought: The Transformation of America, 1815-1848* (New York: Oxford University Press, 2007).

8. These two groups differed due to political allegiances and geography. The Osage's language, Dhegiha Siouan, is similar to that of the Quapaws, Kansas, and

Omaha-Poncas. Initially, this language group originated in the Great Lakes region before expanding south. Their lineage practices are patrilineal, with approximately 24 clans. John Joseph Mathews, *The Osages: Children of the Middle Waters* (Norman, OK: University of Oklahoma Press, 1961), 95–174, 528, 537, 545, 566, 721; Blue Clark, *Indian Tribes of Oklahoma: A Guide* (Norman, OK: University of Oklahoma Press, 2009), 232–246; Janet Berry Hess, *Osage and Settler: Reconstructing Shared History though an Oklahoma Family Archive* (Jefferson, NC: McFarland & Co., Publishers, 2015), 11–38.

9. Louis F. Burns, *Osage Missions Baptisms, Marriages, and Internments, 1820-1886* (Fallbrook, CA: Ciga Press, 1985), v–x; Mary Paul Fitzgerald, *Beacon on the Plains* (Leavenworth, KS: The Saint Mary College, 1939), 31–40, 59; Willis Glenn Jackson, "Missions Among the Kickapoo and Osage in Kansas, 1820-1860" (MA Thesis, Kansas State University, Manhattan, KS, 1965), 1–45; Anna C. Minogue, *Loretto: Annals of the Century* (New York: The American Press, 1912), 129; Loretto Community, "Only One Heart: Loretto and Indigenous Peoples," *Loretto Community,* October 4 2020, http://lorettocommunity.org/author/lorettocommunity/; John Mack, "Osage Mission: The Story of Catholic Missionary Work in Southeast Kansas," *The Catholic Historical Review* 96, no. 2 (April 2010): 262–281; Mathews, *The Osages,* 68.

For primary sources, see "To Iowa Yearly Meeting of Friends," *The weekly Oskaloosa Herald* (Oskaloosa, Iowa), September 25, 1879; "The Men of Vermont," *The Caledonian* (St. Johnsbury, VT), May 9, 1862; "A Plea for Less Bigotry," *Pittsburg dispatch* (Pittsburg, PA), June 23, 1889; "Report on the Committee of Indian Affairs," *The Weekly Oskaloosa Herald* (Oskaloosa, IA), September 20, 1877; "Two Old Texans," *The Dallas Daily Herald* (Dallas, TX), January 17, 1885.

10. Benson Prixley, quoted in William White Graves, *Life and Letters of Fathers Ponziglione, Schoenmakers, and Other Jesuits at Osage Mission. Sketch of St. Francis' Church. Life of Mother Bridget* (St. Paul, KS: W.W. Graves, 1916), 128.

11. Clark, *Indian Tribes of Oklahoma,* 232–246; Hess, *Osage and Settler,* 11–38; Fitzgerald, *Beacon on the Plains,* 31–40, 42–48; Graves, *Life and Letters,* 94–96; Thomas Kinsella, *A Centenary of Catholicity in Kansas, 1822-1922 ; the History of our Cradle Land (Miami and Linn Counties) ; Catholic Indian Missions and Missionaries of Kansas ; The Pioneers on the Prairies : Notes on St. Mary's Mission, Sugar Creek, Linn County; Holy Trinity Church, Paola, Miami County; Holy Rosary Church, Wea; Immaculate Conception, B.V.M., Louisburg; St. Philip's Church, Osawatomie; Church of the Assumption, Edgerton, Johnson County; to Which is Added a Short Sketch of the Ursuline Academy at Paola; the Diary of Father Hoecken, and Old Indian Records* (Kansas City, MO: Casey Printing, 1921), 33–54; Mathews, *The Osages,* 525–538.

12. Clark, *Indian Tribes of Oklahoma,* 232–246; Hess, *Osage and Settler,* 11–38; Fitzgerald, *Beacon on the Plains,* 31–40, 42–48; Graves, *Life and Letters,* 94–96; Kinsella, *A Centenary of Catholicity in Kansas,* 33–54; Mathews, *The Osages,* 525–538.

13. Burns, *Osage Missions,* v–x; Graves, *Life and Letters,* 14; Minogue, *Loretto,* 129; Loretto Community, "Only One Heart: Loretto and Indigenous Peoples," *Loretto*

Community, October 4, 2020, http://lorettocommunity.org/author/lorettocommunity/; Kinsella, *A Centenary of Catholicity in Kansas,* 33–54; Mack, "Osage Mission," 262–281; M. Liliana Owens, "The Early Work of the Lorettines in Southeastern Kansas," *The Kansas Historical Quarterly* 15, no. 3 (August 1947): 263–276.

14. J. Van de Velde, S. J. Letter to W. Medill, 27 July 1847, LHC, Osage Mission, St. Ann's, St. Francis historical data & memoirs RG-SCH, VII Box II-8.

15. Joan Campbell, *Loretto: An Early American Congregation in the Antebellum South* (St. Louis, MO: Bluebird Publishing, 2015), 56–157; John J. Glennon, "Introduction," in *Loretto Centennial Discourses 1812-1912* (St. Louis, MO: B. Herder, 1913), iii–v; Hogan, "Sister Servants: Catholic Women Religious in Antebellum Kentucky", 50–100; Hannah O'Daniel, "Southern Veils: The Sisters of Loretto in Early National Kentucky" (PhD Dissertation, University of Louisville, Louisville, KY, 2017), 42–49; M. Liliana Owens, "The Pioneer Days of the Lorettines in Missouri, 1823-1841," *Records of the American Catholic Historical Society of Philadelphia* 70, no. ¾ (December 1959): 67–87; M. S. Ryan, "Loretto and Its History," in *Loretto Centennial Discourses 1812-1912, au. Sisters of Loretto* (St. Louis, MO: B. Herder, 1913), 38–49.

16. Campbell, *Loretto,* 56–157; Glennon, "Introduction," iii–v; Hogan, "Sister Servants," 50–100; O'Daniel, "Southern Veils," 42–49; Owens, "The Pioneer Day," 67–87; Ryan, "Loretto and Its History," 38–49.

17. Burns, *Osage Missions,* v–x; Graves, *Life and Letters,* 14, 62–77; Minogue, *Loretto,* 129; Loretto Community, "Only One Heart: Loretto and Indigenous Peoples"; Mack, "Osage Mission," 262–281; Owens, "The Early Work of the Lorettines," 263–276.

18. Graves, *Life and Letters,* 62–64.

19. John Richardson, quoted in *Annals of Osage Mission,* 33; Fitzgerald, *Beacon on the Plains,* 103; Sisters of Loretto, Letter to J.G. Sanders, July 10, 1929, LHC, Osage Mission, St. Ann's, St. Francis Correspondence; RG-Sch VII Box II-5; Sister Mary Ioo, Letter to Joseph Caruana, May 22, 1891, Corresp 1890-1904, Sisters of St. Francis Archives, Philadelphia, PA; W.W. Graves, *Annals of the Osage Mission,* 32.

20. Thomas H. Harvey, "Contract for the Osage Mission, 1847," reproduced in Mary Paul Fitzgerald, *Beacon on the Plains* (Leavenworth, KS: The Saint Mary College, 1939), 242.

21. Father Schoenmaker, quoted in *Annals of Osage Mission,* 38.

22. John Schoenmakers, Letter to George Merripenny, October 1, 1855, reproduced in Graves, *Life, and Letters,* 190–192; John Schoenmakers, Letter to the Honorable Secretary of the Interior, October 1, 1854, reproduced in Graves, *Life and Letters,* 189.

23. Graves, *Life and Letters,* 281–282.

24. Unknown author, "Loretto Academy, Florissant, Missouri, and Osage Mission, St. Ann's Kansas," 2, LHC, Osage Mission, St. Ann's, St. Francis historical data & memoirs RG-SCH, VII Box II-8.

25. Catherine E. Beecher, *A Treatise on Domestic Economy for the Use of Young Ladies at Home and School* (New York: Harper & Brothers, 1845).

26. Although some historians have stopped using the idea of "separate spheres mentality," I would argue it encompasses the nineteenth century mindset just as

equally as the cult of domesticity. There are far too many books to list on antebellum nineteenth-century gender roles. Bruce Dorsey, *Reforming Men and Women: Gender in the Antebellum City* (Ithaca, NY: Cornell University Press, 2002); Nancy Isenberg, *Sex and Citizenship in Antebellum America* (Chapel Hill, NC: University of North Carolina Press, 1998).

27. Tabatha Toney Booth, "Cheaper than Bullets: American Indian Boarding Schools and Assimilation Policy, 1890-1930," in *Images, Imaginations, and Beyond Proceedings of the Eighth Native American Symposium,* ed. Mark B. Spencer (Durant, OK: South-Eastern Oklahoma State University, 2009), 46–56; Diane Glancy, *Fort Marion Prisoners and the Trauma of Native Education* (Lincoln, NE: University of Nebraska Press, 2014); Caitlin Keliiaa, "Unsettling Domesticity: Native Women and 20th-Century US Indian Policy in the San Francisco Bay Area" (PhD Dissertation, University of California, Berkeley, Berkeley, CA, 2019); K. Tsianina Lomawaima, "Domesticity in the Federal Indian Schools: The Power of Authority over Mind and Body," *American Ethnologist* 20, no. 2 (1993): 227–240; Robert Trennert, "Educating Indian Girls at Nonreservation Boarding Schools, 1878-1920," *Western Historical Quarterly* 13, no. 3 (July 1982): 271–290; Carolyn A. Weber, "Caught between Catholic and Government Traditions: Americanization and Assimilation at St. Joseph's Indian Normal School," *American Educational History* 40, no. 1–2 (2013): 75+; Amanda J. Zink, *Fictions of Western American Domesticity: Indian, Mexican, and Anglo Women in Print Culture, 1850–1950* (Albuquerque, NM: University of New Mexico Press, 2018).

28. Lomawaima, *They Called it Prairie Light,* 65.

29. Minogue, *Loretto,* 129.

30. Paul M. Ponziglione, Letter to Mr. E.B. Park, July 21, 1895, Kansas, Osage Mission, Rev. Paul Ponziglione Letters Box 3-2.

31. Unknown author, "Osage Missions," 1, LHC, Osage Mission, St. Ann's, St. Francis historical data & memoirs RG-SCH, VII Box II-8.

32. Sister Mary Edith Laughlin, "Some Recollections of Mother Bridget Hayden The Osages," 4, LHC, Osage Mission, St. Ann's, St. Francis historical data & memoirs RG-SCH, VII Box II-8.

33. For example, A. P. S., "Corporal Punishment," *The Maine Normal* 1, no. 6 (1867): 249–256; M. T. B., "Corporeal Punishment As a Means of School Discipline," *The Connecticut Common School Journal and Annals of Education* 3 (11), no. 5 (1856): 138–142; Neanias, "Modes of Corporeal Punishment in Schools," *The Connecticut Common School Journal and Annals of Education* 3 (11), no. 5 (1856): 142–143; W. M. A. Stearns, "School Discipline," *The Massachusetts Teacher (1858-1871)* 18, no. 3 (1865): 73–84.

34. J. J. Bax, Letter to John De Smet, June 1 1850, reproduced in Pierre-Jean De Smet, *Western Missions and Missionaries: A Series of Letters* (New York: James B. Kirker, 1863), 358.

35. J. J. Bax, Letter to John De Smet, June 1 1850, reproduced in De Smet, *Western Missions,* 358.

36. For example, David Wallace Adams, *Education for Extinction: American Indians and the Boarding School Experience 1875-1928* (Lawrence, KS: University Press of Kansas, 1995); Celia Haig-Brown et al., *Tsqelmuncwic: The Kamloops*

Indian Residential School- Resistance and Reckoning (Vancouver: Arsenal Pulp Press, 2022); Susan D. Rose and Jacqueline Fear-Segal, *Carlisle Indian Industrial School: Indigenous Histories Memories and Reclamations* (Lincoln, NE: University of Nebraska Press, 2016).

37. "Osage Mission," unknown date, pg 1, LHC, Osage Mission, St. Ann's, St. Francis historical data & memoirs RG-SCH, VII Box II-8.

38. M. Vincent White, "The Incorrigible Pupil, 1911, 2, LHC, Osage Mission, St. Ann's, St. Francis historical data & memoirs RG-SCH, VII Box II-8.

39. Unknown author, "Osage Missions," 3, LHC, Osage Mission, St. Ann's, St. Francis historical data & memoirs RG-SCH, VII Box II-8.

40. Unknown author, "Osage Missions," 3, LHC, Osage Mission, St. Ann's, St. Francis historical data & memoirs RG-SCH, VII Box II-8.

41. Unknown author, "Osage Missions," 3, LHC, Osage Mission, St. Ann's, St. Francis historical data & memoirs RG-SCH, VII Box II-8.

42. "Civilizing the Yumas. Noble Work of Catholic Missionaries Among the Indians," *Staunton Vindicator* (Staunton, Virginia), September 12, 1890.

43. Kenton Clymer, *Protestant Missionaries in the Philippines, 1898-1916: An Inquiry into the American Colonial Mentality* (Chicago, IL: University of Illinois Press, 1986), 18.

44. Sister Mary Edith Laughlin, "Some Recollections of Mother Bridget Hayden The Osages," 4, LHC, Osage Mission, St. Ann's, St. Francis historical data & memoirs RG-SCH, VII Box II-8.

45. "Osage Mission Anecdotes," 20–23, Kansas, Osage Mission, Memoirs of Sisters & Pupils, Box 3-1.

46. Unknown author, "Osage Missions," 3, LHC, Osage Mission, St. Ann's, St. Francis historical data & memoirs RG-SCH, VII Box II-8.

47. Mathews, *The Osages,* 650.

48. Fitzgerald, *Beacon on the Plains,* 96–97; Roy Gittinger, "The Separation of Nebraska and Kansas from the Indian Territory," *The Mississippi Valley Historical Review* 3, no. 4 (1917): 442–461; Ronald E. Grim, "Mapping Kansas and Nebraska: The Role of the General Land Office," *Great Plains Quarterly* 5, no. 3 (1985): 177–197; Mathews, *The Osages,* 585–692.

49. "From the Fort Scott Democrat, March 4th," *The Washington Union* (City of Washington [D.C.]), March 23, 1858.

50. "An Account of the Late brutal murder . . . ," *The Emporia News* (Emporia, Kan.), May 29, 1868.

51. Unfortunately, very little research has been done on the impact of the Kansas-Nebraska Act and Indigenous nations. Fitzgerald, *Beacon on the Plains,* 96–97; Gittinger, "The Separation of Nebraska and Kansas from the Indian Territory," 442–461; Grim, "Mapping Kansas and Nebraska: The Role of the General Land Office," 177–197; Mathews, *The Osages,* 585–692.

52. Fitzgerald, *Beacon on the Plains,* 96–97; Gittinger, "The Separation of Nebraska and Kansas from the Indian Territory," 442–461; Grim, "Mapping Kansas and Nebraska: The Role of the General Land Office," 177–197; Mathews, *The Osages,* 585–692.

53. Graves, *Life and Letters,* 274-275.

54. Laughlin, "Some Recollections of Mother Bridget Hayden The Osages."

55. Father Schoenmakers, Letter to Sister M. Cosina, March 8 1878, L.C.H., Kansas Osage Mission Rev. John Schoenmakers, SJ box 3-3.

56. Laughlin, "Some Recollections of Mother Bridget Hayden The Osages," 1. Also see Minogue, *Loretto,* 134; Mathews, *The Osages,* 686–687.

Chapter 3

Native American Boarding Schools and Institutional Efforts after the Civil War

In 1859, W. S. Harney, brigadier general commanding, assistant adjutant general in the Headquarters of the Army in New York City, wrote to General Scott, stationed in Oregon:

> From what I observed of the Indian affairs of this department, the missionaries among them possess a power of the greatest consequence in their proper government, and one which cannot be acquired by any other influence. They control the Indian by training his superstitions and fears to revere the religion they possess, by associating the benefits they confer with the guardianship and protection of the Great Spirit of the whites. The history of the Indian race on this continent has shown that the missionary succeeded where the soldier and civilian have failed; it would be well for us to profit by the lessons its experience teachers in an instance which offers so many advantages to the white as well as the red man, and adopt the wise and humane suggestion of Father De Smet.[1]

Frustrated by increasing tensions between the United States agents and local Indigenous nations, as well as the perceived lack of failure of the assimilation processes so far, Harney believed that the best way to proceed was to build upon the work of the previous generations of missionaries. His thoughts reflected the greater institutionalization of U.S. government assimilation attempts in the latter half of the nineteenth century.

The period leading up to and after the Civil War created dramatic changes in American life. The Civil War tore the nation apart, while attempts at Reconstruction only served to increase racial and class tensions. Americans expanded westward, spurred on by the 1862 Homestead Act and the rise of the railroads. The nation started to flex its imperialist muscles, working to gain more influence in the Americas and the Pacific. Conceptions of race, based upon fallacious pseudo-science, became ingrained in everyday life.[2]

The federal government began to bureaucratize, in order to weed out the corruption of the early decades. Caught in the middle of all these changes were the Native American boarding schools, which went from a mishmash of loosely related experiments to a relatively conforming, institutional network, complete with increasing government oversight.

Key to understanding the Native Boarding Schools is the imperialist mind-set of the late nineteenth-century, which influenced policies and programs both at home and abroad. Spurred on by the Monroe Doctrine, which placed the United States as the protector of the Americas, as well as ideas of Manifest Destiny and American superiority, various businesses and government agencies attempted to assimilate those within their orbit of influence, focusing on Christianity and labor. This practice was not only true for Americans working abroad, but also those working with minorities within the United States, whom Americans viewed with suspicion as an uneducated "other," on par with supposedly uncivilized groups abroad. Education programs both at home and abroad were similar, leading to cultural genocide both at home and abroad.[3]

Religious groups jumped on the imperialist bandwagon, believing they had a moral obligation to convert non-whites to Christianity. As Kenton Clymer wrote in his study on imperialism in the Philippines, the "ideological compatibility between church and state found practical expression in the missionary efforts to further the national purpose and in the close relations many of the missions enjoyed with the government."[4] However, in certain situations, such as the Philippines and among Catholic tribes, Protestant missionaries had to contend with the fact that they were trying to convert those already Christian. Moreover, many Protestant missionaries argued that Catholicism was not a form of Christianity, being more likely to have syncretic views and practices that incorporated Indigenous beliefs.[5]

While American missionaries had already begun this process with the Indigenous nations in the decades before the American Revolution, what changed after the Civil War was the government's support of this work. It also began to recognize the religious diversity within the missions, focusing on a more secular education with religious extracurricular activities. In the 1860s and 1870s, the U.S. government expanded funding and oversight of Christian Indigenous missions. However, it started to veer away from said support by the turn of the century.

EARLY CHANGES IN FEDERAL POLICY

The 1860s marked a transitional period in the history of Native American Boarding Schools. By the end of the Civil War, most government officials agreed that oversight of the Native American reservations was corrupt. Prospective agents used political connections to gain appointments, using the position to access funding meant for the tribal communities. Governmental attempts at reform began in 1867 and 1868, with various peace commissions meant to examine conditions on the reservations as well as the various treaties. With the election of Ulysses S. Grant in 1868, the Department of the Interior underwent dramatic changes. Grant appointed Ely S. Parker, who was of Seneca origin, to be the commissioner of Indian Affairs; Parker was the first ever Native person to hold that post. In addition to placing Parker in a position of influence, Grant created the Board of Indian Commissioners, hoping to have educated and well-meaning persons oversee the reservations and schools.[6]

In 1869, Grant's Peace Policy went into effect. The policy placed the reservations and schools in the hands of religious communities, relieving them from corrupt laypersons. Grant believed that religious communities, in particular the Quakers, were particularly attuned to the needs of Indigenous persons and were more likely to put their needs first. The Peace Policy gave out contracts to various religious denominations, including the Episcopalians, Presbyterians, Quakers, Methodists, and Catholics. Grant and other federal officials cemented the importance of religious institutions by inviting representatives to attend conferences on education in the 1870s.[7]

Grant's Peace Policy faced pushback, with multiple attempts to repeal the act and dissolve the peace commissions. While some, such as the Catholics, Episcopalians, and Quakers, lauded the policy as promoting religious freedom and liberty, critics suggested that certain groups (mainly Catholics) dominated white representation on the reservations, leading to a bias against other groups. Other dissenters pointed to the rising violence in the West, as several Indigenous groups tried to maintain their historic lands in the midst of increased white expansion.[8] These debates would influence policy changes in the 1870s onwards.

THE BCIM

Catholics decided they needed to protect their interests in the scramble for government contracts. This conclusion led to the creation of the BCIM. The BCIM originated from the work of General Charles Ewing. Ewing worked hard in the 1860s to help Catholic missionaries navigate the changing political scene. He advocated religious freedom and Indigenous persons having a choice in choosing which (but not whether a) religious denomination worked with them. He challenged the authority of the local reservation agents, particularly when they clashed with Catholics working on the missions. He also worked to provide a variety of supplies to Catholic missions, such as wine to missions in Alaska. Catholic clergy supported Ewing's work, recognizing his influence through his personal political connections.[9]

In 1872, there was a meeting between the Board of Indian Commissioners and various missionary societies, which no Catholic attended. (The well-known meeting's organizers had asked legendary missionary Pierre-Jean DeSmet to attend, but he was traveling abroad fundraising. They asked no other Catholic.) As more meetings occurred in the nation's capital, Catholic bishops and clergy demanded to have a say but realized they needed representation. In January 1874, the Archbishop of Baltimore, J. Roosevelt Bayley, wrote to the Secretary of the Interior that in response to the "erroneous information sent to the Department, and they feel that it would be a great advantage to them and agreeable to the Department if some one fully acquainted with the whole matter" work as an intermediary between the government and the Catholic missions, as well as oversee the Catholic missions. To that end, the committee appointed Charles "to act as Commissioner on the part of the Catholic Bishops for this purpose."[10] Ewing's appointment began the BCIM.

The BCIM advocated for Catholic participation in these federal missions. As a report from 1895 wrote, Catholics "agreed upon the necessity of having a civil agent at Washington, who should there represent them before the United States Government in all that concerned the interests of Catholic Indians."[11] The organization's goals also included "to direct the administration" of Catholic missions, "to secure . . . the remain of those agencies to which Catholic missionaries were justly entitled," "to protect the religious faith and material interests of all Catholic Indians," and "to procure for Indians moral and practical Christian teachers"[12] Through their advocacy, Catholics tried to negotiate a space in Protestant-dominated spaces, particularly the federal boarding schools.

Despite having government funding, Catholic missions were still perpetually underfunded. The BCIM worked to fundraise in order to make up the difference. There were consistent yearly fundraisers. For example, in St. Cloud, Minnesota, local parishes collected funding for Indigenous and African American missions the first Sunday of Lent. The fundraisers supported the missionary work of religious groups at home and abroad, hoping to supplement staff and supplies. Some of the smaller missions relied upon these funds.[13] The BCIM also worked with wealthy philanthropists, such as Katharine Drexel.[14]

Protestants protested the influence of Catholic missionaries. Even before the creation of the BCIM, Protestant missionaries complained that Catholics received 50% of the funding in 1872. Catholics retorted that they worked with less than half the number of Indigenous persons than the Methodists did. Under the direction of the BCIM, Catholic missionaries gained more schools. By 1886, there were 50 contract religious schools; Catholics ran 36 of these. Catholics were able to run so many schools in part because there was interest among missionaries as well as supposed support from the local Indigenous communities, who requested Catholic educators over Protestant ones.[15]

Coinciding with the rise of Catholic influence in the boarding schools was a rise of anti-Catholic sentiment in the United States. Inspired by the rise in immigration, the increase in parochial schools, and renewed fears about the power of the papacy, the elections of 1884 and 1892 focused on ways to limit Catholic involvement in every aspect of American life. Relations between the BCIM and the Department of Indian Affairs deteriorated. Thomas Jefferson Morgan, the Commissioner of Indian Affairs between 1889 and 1893, wanted to decrease the number of Catholic contract schools. He changed policies toward Catholics; rather than the BCIM negotiating for all Catholic schools, Morgan required that each school make its own contract. Morgan started to restrict the curriculum, using any deviation from his standards as an excuse to defund the Catholic missions. He also sent students from the Catholic schools to federal schools, again decreasing government funding. By 1892, the BCIM and the DIA were barely on speaking terms, and the BCIM had hired a lawyer to support their interests.[16] We shall see this situation play out on a local level in chapter 6.

By the turn of the twentieth century, the federal government began to defund the religious schools. Although affected by this policy change, Protestant missionaries and educators ultimately supported the decision to do so and withdrew their applications for funding. Protestants hoped that without federal support, Catholics would lose any influence they might have had with the Indigenous nations. Government officials also hoped that Indigenous students would join public schools, no longer creating a need for the boarding schools. That did not happen.[17] This change will be explored more in chapter 5.

Although impacted by this era of increasing bureaucracy, Catholic Sisters' work remained central to federal and Catholic attempts at assimilation. In the 1860s to the 1890s, they continued to open and run schools throughout the United States. There was no set pattern to these schools, in terms of geography; the Catholic Sisters simply went where the local bishops called them. As we shall see in the next chapters, Catholic Sisters ran these schools in order to promote set ideas of white civilization and authority. To demonstrate their ability to do so, they created narratives that focused on their control of Indigenous bodies, education, identity, and politics.

NOTES

1. W.S. Harney, Letter to General Scott, 3 June 1859, in P. J. De Smet, "Father De Smet's Narrative Describing Upper Washington Territory, 1859," *The American Catholic Historical Researches* 12, no. 3 (July 1895): 102–106.

2. For example, Richard Edwards et al., *Homesteading the Plains: Toward A New History* (Lincoln, NE: University of Nebraska Press, 2017), 91–127; Eric Foner, *The Second Founding: How the Civil War and Reconstruction Made the Constitution* (New York: W.W. Norton & CO., 2020); H. G. Hopkins, *American Empire: A Global History* (Princeton, NJ: Princeton University Press, 2018); Jessica M. Kim, *Imperial Metropolis: Los Angeles, Mexico, and the Borderlands of American Empire, 1865-1941* (Chapel Hill, NC: University of North Carolina Press, 2019); Richard White, *Railroaded: The Transcontinentals and the Making of Modern America* (New York: W.W. Norton & Company, 2011); Richard White, *The Republic for Which It Stands: The United States During Reconstruction and the Gilded Age, 1865-1896* (New York: Oxford University Press, 2017).

3. For example, Adams, *Education for Extinction*; Kenton Clymer, *Protestant Missionaries in the Philippines, 1898-1916: An Inquiry into the American Colonial Mentality* (Chicago, IL: University of Illinois Press, 1986), 153; Eittreim, *Teaching Empire*; Clifford Trafzer et al., eds., *Boarding School Blues: Revisiting American Indian Educational Experiences* (Lincoln, NE: University of Nebraska Press, 2006); Harold Fischer-Tiné et al., eds., *Spreading Protestant Modernity: Global Perspectives on the Social Work of the YMCA and the YWCA, 1889-1970* (Honolulu, HI: University of Hawai'i Press, 2021).

4. Clymer, *Protestant Missionaries,* 153.
Also see Grabill, *Protestant Diplomacy and the Near East*; Marty, *Righteous Empire*; Moran, *The Imperial Church*; Newson, "Pan-Protestantism and Proselytizing"; Reeves-Ellington et al., *Competing Kingdoms*; Stuart, "Beyond Sovereignty?," 103–125; John Wolffe, "Protestant–Catholic Divisions in Europe and the United States: An Historical and Comparative Perspective," *Politics, Religion & Ideology* 12, no. 3 (2011): 241–256.

5. Clymer, *Protestant Missionaries in the Philippines,* 1–8, 93–113; Eittreim, *Teaching Empire,* 1–24.

6. Rahill, *The Catholic Indian Missions and Grant's Peace Policy, 1870-1884,* 25–37, 294, 305; Reyhner and Eder, *American Indian Education,* 64–87.

7. Roxanne Dunbar-Ortiz, *An Indigenous Peoples' History of the United States* (Boston, MA: Beacon Press, 2014), 144–151; Jennifer Graber, "'If a War It May Be Called': The Peace Policy with American Indians," *Religion and American Culture* 24, no. 1 (2014): 36–69; Rahill, *Catholic Missions and Grant's Peace Policy,* 25–37, 294, 305.

8. Rahill, *Catholic Missions and Grant's Peace Policy,* 294, 305.

9. Rahill, *Catholic Missions and Grant's Peace Policy,* 92.

10. J. Roosevelt Bayley, Letter to Secretary of the Interior, January 2 1874, reproduced in *Catholic Missions and Grant's Peace Policy,* 118.

11. Charles Ewing, *Circular of the Catholic Commissioner for Indian Missions to the Catholics of the United States* (Baltimore, MD: John Murphy & Co., 1874), 5.

12. Charles Ewing, *Circular for the Catholic Commissioner,* 8.

13. "Collections for Indian and Negro Missions and for the Propagation of our Holy Faith," *The Diocese of St. Cloud: Official Record and Messenger* (St. Cloud, MN), February 1891, Vol. 1 No. 2, NDA; "Official," *The Diocese of St. Cloud: Official Record and Messenger,* June 1891, Vol. 1 No. 6, NDA; James D. White, "Essay: The Life of Theophile Meerschaert," in *Diary of a Frontier Bishop: The Journals of Theophile Meerschaert, e*d. James D. White (Tulsa, OK: The Sarto Press, 1994), 19–20.

14. Prucha, *The Churches and the Indian Schools, 1888-1912,* 41–52; Rahill, *Grant's Peace Policy,* 119–168.

15. Reyhner and Eder, *American Indian Education,* 88–119.

16. Reyhner and Eder, *American Indian Education,* 88–119.

17. Reyhner and Eder, *American Indian Education,* 88–119.

Chapter 4

Authority, Narrative, and Performance at the Sisters of the Holy Child Jesus Missions in Avoca, Minnesota, 1884–1890

In November 1885, the Sisters of the Holy Child Jesus' (SHCJ's) Catholic Indigenous mission at Avoca, Minnesota, the Academy of the Holy Child, gave "little 'Musical Entertainment' to greet our dear Mothers" who were visiting from out of state. The community's annals proudly recorded that

> the children's refectory having been decorated with flags . . . etc and "a squaw's" blanket with pipes of peace and tomahawk and all arranged properly— . . . An addition was made in the Indian language, and two children dressed in their Indian costume sang and danced the "Omaha dance."[1]

No image exists of the performance; however, an image from a similar one in 1909 from the Carlisle Indian Industrial suggests how these students may have looked (figure 4.1). The tone of the entry suggested that the Sisters were proud of this performance. To them, it demonstrated the role the Catholic Sisters took in the creation of narratives about supposed tribal and civilized identities. Through these performances, the Sisters demonstrated their authority over the students, crafting narratives of successful assimilation.

In his essay on relationships between Cherokee public speakers and Christian missionaries, Joel Martin uses the idea of performance within a political agenda. He characterizes public talks on Cherokee sovereignty as a form of performance, that is, "highly charged signify- ing [*sic*] events intentionally designed to touch hearts but also to confront ideologies and prejudices and to produce solidarity . . . ."[2] My understanding of the school performances at the Avoca school relies upon a similar interpretation. The SHCJs hosted a variety of student productions and exhibits with the intent of demonstrating their ability at assimilators. These performances created a mythical narrative of the students' life before school, before emphasizing how well the students

Figure 4.1   Female Students at the Carlisle Indian Industrial School in Ethnic Dress, Circa 1909. Perhaps this was similar to how the students dressed at Avoca during the "Little Entertainment." *Source: Image courtesy of the Cumberland County Historical Society.*

had acclimated to white, Christian culture. In doing so, the SHCJs hoped to "produce solidarity" among the audience, or rather a level of support and pride for the Sisters' mission.

In analyzing performance, this chapter relies upon previous studies on the perceptions and portrayals of Indigenous performance and authenticity, both in popular culture as well as at the schools. Paige Raibmon's ground-changing *Authentic Indians* looked at white cultural perceptions and biases that led to various Native performances at World Fairs and other meeting places in the Northwest. Her work challenged the narratives of "authenticity," or rather, what represented true Indigenous culture and beliefs, noting how this concept reflects perceptions of others rather, than of Native persons' truth.[3] Other studies have also analyzed cultural authenticity in the social, political, and entertainment spheres, coming to similar conclusions as Raibmon.[4]

Equally important to this current study is John R. Gram's article on performance and assimilation at the Boarding Schools in the American Southwest. Gram focused on moments of public performance, such as parades and holidays, or rather "moments intended for consumption by both the student body and local citizens—as agents of assimilation." Gram argued that these performances demonstrate Indigenous persons as part of a narrative of "progress," rather than remaining remnants of a by-gone era while at the same time trying to legitimize certain supposed authentic aspects of their own culture (such as cultural myths that could be easily incorporated into the Anglo-Saxon mentality). Moreover, like Raibmon, he linked these performances to identity-making, noting the ethnic binary that white citizens saw dividing them from Indigenous students.[5]

This chapter builds upon Raibmon's and Gram's work in two ways. First, it explores the use of performance, trying to tease out the various meanings. In doing so, this study looks at private and semi-public performances: that is, those by visitors to the convent, as well as the community at large. Second, my work examines a small Catholic school, rather than one of the larger boarding schools or other areas of performance (such as the World's Fairs) that tend to dominate the historiography. Most importantly, this chapter intertwines questions of authority with narratives of assimilation, which the Sisters controlled through the performances at the Avoca School.

It is important to note that performance culture was not unique to Catholic schools catering only to Native children. The white children at Avoca learned and performed choral music from the early months of the school in 1883.[6] However, it takes on a different meaning when viewed through the lens of race and assimilation. The performances by Indigenous students focused on demonstrating their acculturation to white values while also demonstrating their mythologized past. Based on the existing records, the Indigenous students either performed supposed scenes of "Indigenous life" or demonstrated a supposed Catholic religiosity through song and show. All aspects of these performances would have been staged, seeking to prove how well the Catholic Sisters had accomplished their goals of religious and cultural education.

While not as big or well known as other schools, the case study of the Academy of the Holy Child in Avoca gives us another insight into the Catholic missions for Native students. The Avoca missions have not usually been noted in larger histories of Minnesota or those of Catholic Sisters, although they are included in the list of schools run by Catholics on the Catholic Truth and Healing website.[7] Part of this is due to a lack of sources; I have not been able to find many primary sources outside of the SHCJ archives, even in the Bureau of the Catholic Indian Missions collections (the BCIM oversaw Catholic missions throughout the country.) Avoca gives us a sneak-peak into one of the smaller, more intimate communities. For context, I have made small comparisons between Avoca and the Carlisle Indian Industrial, one of the biggest examples of the assimilationist projects.

BACKGROUND

Minnesota has historically been a vibrant borderland, hosting various Native communities and European powers prior to the American Revolution. Various groups came together to trade furs and other goods. Bands of Assiniboine, Crees, and Ojibwe were the main negotiators of trade, controlling interactions along the Great Lakes. However, it was often a place of warfare, with various Native and European nations fighting among themselves and against each other. After the American Revolution, the Treaty of Paris of 1783 divided the Minnesota region between United States and Spanish claims. The Louisiana Purchase of 1803 placed the area in American hands, leading to increased westward expansion.[8]

The nineteenth century was a period to dramatic Native displacement within the Minnesota region. A 1825 Treaty set divisions between lands for white settlers and lands for the Dakota, Ho-Chunk, Iowa, Menominee, Odawa, Ojibwe, Potawattomi, and Sac and Fox. In 1837, both the Dakota and Ojibwe cede tracks of land. By 1851, Dakota had lost most of their land in southern Minnesota. Fighting between the United States and Dakota in 1862 led to the federal government nullifying all treaties regarding Dakota claims to land in Minnesota. The 1862 Homestead Act allowed for over ten million acres to be opened to homesteaders. In 1863, Congress also demanded the sale of Ho-Hunk lands, resulting in their forced removal to South Dakota.[9]

Technological change also influenced settler colonialism. The expansion of the railroad, led on by federal funding such as the Pacific Railroad Act in 1862, opened up not just the southern part of the state, but linked Minnesota to the East and West Coasts through lines joining the Transcontinental Railroad. Trains allowed not only for transportation but also the easy removal of raw materials and goods. Railroads popped up in the settlements in the southern portions of the state. New settlements established new industries, focusing on mining as well as mills and factories. White settlers quickly flocked to former Native homelands, hoping to make their fortunes.[10]

By the time of Catholic missionary work, primary Native nations were bands of Ojibwe and Dakota. While they continued to trade with Americans, they found themselves increasingly isolated within the new politics of the era. Desperate to have more control over the natural resources needed for trade, the Ojibwe and Dakota often clashed with each other in a series of battles and wars. Tensions also rose between the Native populations and white settlers. Questions of race and citizenship became increasingly based around skin tone, with whites viewing Native population as a lesser people. This belief contributed to the rise of white missionaries and educational endeavors in Minnesota.[11]

EARLY CATHOLIC MISSIONARY WORK

Catholic missionary work in Minnesota dates to the colonial era, with French priests working among members of the Great Lakes tribal nations. While such attempts were largely sporadic, the decades prior to the Civil War saw organized Catholic attempts to work with various Indigenous nations. For example, in 1852, the Sisters of St. Joseph (the SSJs) traveled from St. Louis to Minnesota, staffing a school at Long Prairie.[12] They had set up other schools in the Diocese of St. Paul for white children but had interest in missionary work among the Native populations. The SSJs primarily worked with the Ho Chunk, teaching an English education. There was talk about adding an industrial curriculum, but it is unclear whether that happened before the short-lived venture ended. The mission was riddled with competition from Protestant missionaries, who advocated for the closure of the school and raised concerns over clerical staffing and finances. The SSJs left within a year.[13]

Starting in the late 1870s, Catholic missionaries ran eight schools in Minnesota. The SHCJs were not the only women's congregation to do such work; others included Benedictine Sisters, the Sisters of Mercy (SMs), and the Sisters of St. Joseph of Carondelet (CSJs). They worked with the tribal bands of the Chippewa, Ojibwe, and Sioux, among others.[14] Despite the vibrant missionary scene in Minnesota, it was the promise of work with immigrants that originally brought the SHCJs to Avoca.

Located southwest in Minneapolis, Avoca was originally one of several settlements for Irish immigrants in Minnesota; another one was Currie, a local village that served as the Murray County Seat. Under the auspices of the National Colonization Society and the Irish-American Colonization Company, Catholic reformers and clergy, such as John Ireland, John Lancaster Spalding, and John Sweetman, worked to bring Irish Catholics from poor urban environments out to new colonies in Minnesota. Of these three, John Ireland was the most persistent and devoted in his mission. These were to be Catholic havens, where Ireland and other Catholic reformers believed that immigrants could learn industrial and agricultural skills in order to become independent, self-supporting Americans.[15]

Located in southwest Minnesota, the Avoca colony was one of the most important. A pamphlet for the Catholic Colonization Bureau described Avoca in glowing terms. Stating that the colony dated back to 1878, the propaganda celebrated the rapid growth of Avoca, from a place "twenty miles from any railroad station. No railroad, no depot, no market nearer than twenty miles"[16] to one that by 1880 had "five general stores, three hotels, two grain elevators, [a] railroad depot," and more.[17] This would have been similar to the community that SHCJs entered in 1883.

THE SHCJS ARRIVE

The SHCJ originated in England. Their founder, Cornelia Connelly, was born in the United States but traveled to England in order to pursue a religious vocation. She founded the SHCJs in 1846 with the intent to send Sisters to the United States, but due to budget constraints and other concerns, the first Sisters did not arrive until 1862 (despite the misgivings of the clergy about having a group of migrant Sisters during the middle of the Civil War). The congregation settled within the diocese of Philadelphia and started parochial schools, although their motherhouse remained in Pennsylvania. The community focused on education, not only for immigrant children, but also people of color. Their work took them throughout the United States, including Minnesota.[18]

The SHCJs joined the Avoca mission to work with these immigrant students. Initially, five Sisters traveled as part of this mission. Upon arrival, the Sisters cleaned and prepared their new abode for religious life (such as setting up an altar), as well as organizing the school and dormitories for students. The Sisters stated that there was immediate interest in their school. In a letter from June 1883, the Sisters reported that they had "applications for the school by persons of every age, & condition." There were also soon requests for private lessons. When faced with financial responsibility, the letter stated that one "father will sell a cow rather than that she [a potential student] miss the opportunity of improving herself."[19] They soon began to offer music lessons and religious lessons for local children: "to day [sic] the Sisters gave their first instruction to the children from the surrounding farms who had not made their first Communion."[20] The language of "from the surrounding farms" suggests that the children with whom they worked were white rather than Indigenous.

However, due to the presence of the District and parochial schools, the school was not an immediate success.[21] The Sisters ran a day school for local children and appear to have had a few boarders. They expressed concern for the lack of boarders, from which they would receive their main income; in November 1883, they wrote, "we have still only six boarders in the Convent—we are still praying for more children[.]"[22] Without more students, the school could close and the SHCJs could be recalled to Pennsylvania, depriving Ireland of labor.

The solution to have them remain came in the form of expanding the Sisters mission to include Native girls. In March 1884, Bishop Ireland informed them that he had plans to send "Fifty Indian Girls" but was waiting on the government contract to be completed and signed. The Sisters expressed their excitement, reporting in July that the contract was finally ready. However, students did not arrive until the fall of that year.[23] (See figure 4.2.)

Figure 4.2   The Sisters of the Holy Child Jesus School in Avoca, Minnesota, Approximately 1888. *Source: Courtesy of the Murray County Historical Society.*

While seemingly a shift in direction from immigrant education to Native education, Ireland's goals regarding immigrant and Native students were similar. Ireland wanted immigrants to become upstanding citizens of the United States, which he believed was only possible through education. As discussed in the introduction to this book, Catholics and other reformers had a long history of providing practical training to orphans and immigrants, in the hope of making them wage-earners and contributing members of society. Such schools often had a punitive aspect, being reform schools for those who were in legal trouble. Industrial schools, no matter what type, were common in the east, such as St. Mary's Industrial School in Baltimore, Maryland (1866–1950) and St. Mary's School for the Deaf in Buffalo, New York (established in 1853).[24]

Educational organizations in England and elsewhere often mirrored those institutions designed for Native persons in the United States, such as an Industrial training school, most infamously the Carlisle Indian Industrial School. Like schools for white and immigrant students, the Native industrial schools provided not only a basic education but also a practical background in farming, while others promoted industries. The Native schools were meant to assimilate Native persons into white capitalist traditions, focusing on the person becoming an active and contributing member of society through their individual productivity, creating a labor force. In many ways, these industrial training schools were part of the same assimilationist plan, no matter the background of the students within.[25]

In addition to education, religion was a key part to these assimilationist plans for immigrant and Indigenous students, although there were differences. Ireland and other Catholic officials hoped that schools for Catholic immigrants would help them maintain their Catholic faith, while schools for Native students focused more on conversion, along with continuing education for those who already held Catholic beliefs. In either case, Catholic reformers hoped to challenge the dominant culture, which equated Protestantism with American citizenship and Catholicism with foreign intervention. They wanted to prove unequivocally that Catholics, be they Indigenous or immigrant, were as worthy of a place within the body politic as any Protestant.[26] While receiving government funding, the Avoca school was more intimate, similar to localized missionary attempts at conversion and assimilation in the decades prior to the American Civil War.[27]

Despite these similarities, there was a difference in the perception of immigrants versus Native students. Assimilation programs wanted immigrants to become citizens, while the government and many white persons relegated Native persons to perpetual wardship. Immigrants were supposed to fully embrace the dominant white culture, proving their allegiance to their new country and reaping the rewards it brought. The government, and many reformers, believed that no matter their skills, Indigenous persons would be the perpetual other. Yes, there were programs that promoted citizenship through assimilation, such as the Dawes Act of 1887 (which promoted the end of the reservation system in an attempt to teach Native persons the values of private property and white culture), but such a process was viewed as the goal of a lifetime, compared to the quicker Americanization for immigrants.[28]

OJIBWE

Most of the students who attended the Avoca school were Ojibwe. The Ojibwe are part of the Anishinabeg culture, a sub-group within Algonquin culture. The Anishinaabe were historically located in the Great Lakes area, particularly between Lake Huron and Lake Superior. They are divided into three groups, called the Council of Three Fires: the Ojibwe, the Odawa, and the Potawatomi. The Ojibwe were primarily located along the shores of Lake Superior, settling around Sault Ste. Marie in northern Minnesota. The Council of Three Fires was linked together but had local autonomy to pursue trade and alliances. They were often bound together in their diplomatic relations with the nearby Dakota, with whom they had several wars as well as moments of alliance.[29]

There were early Ojibwe interactions with the French in the 1600s. Jesuit missionaries recorded interactions with them in the infamous *Jesuit Relations*.

It was the French who gave the Ojibwe the name of "Chippewa," presumably a bastardization of a French alliteration. The two groups participated in the fur trade, with the British joining in competition and later dominance. The first permanent white settlements in Ojibwe territory came between 1819 and 1825, as the army built forts. Civilians quickly came into the area, and the government demanded that the Ojibwe sell some of their land. Facing economic disaster from the loss of the fur trade, the Ojibwe agreed. From then on, the Ojibwe signed away most of their lands through a series of treaties. Slowly, the U.S. government required the Ojibwe bands to move onto reservations, with most of the relocation occurring between 1854 and 1867. With the land cessions and forced removal, Minnesota became a territory in 1849 and a state in 1858.[30]

Assimilation was part of the Ojibwe-white relations. Protestant and Catholic missionaries worked hard to find common ground with the Ojibwe, focusing on religious-cultural traditions to create a syncretic form of belief.[31] However, the Catholics appeared to make little headway with the Ojibwe prior to 1900. Indeed, *The Indian Advocate*, a periodical run by Benedictine monks in Oklahoma, noted that in the 1870s, there were less than 100 Catholics among the Ojibwe, while by 1903, there were nominally 3,000 to 4,000 converts.[32] After 1900, there were multiple signs of increased conversions. Missionaries made sure to give lessons, hold mass, and print Catholic literature both in English as well as Ojibwe dialects.[33] By the 1910s, Ojibwe Catholics had co-fraternities and attended Catholic Congresses and Conventions.[34] Most importantly, the second Indigenous Catholic priest was Ojibwe.[35] However, the first students to arrive at the school were still years away from such a transformation.

The SHCJs responded to their Ojibwe students in a rather expected way, being rather perplexed by the differences in culture. In January 1885, the Annals started recording their responses to the students themselves. One entry dated January 22 stated, "The children seem strange, but of course that is to be expected."[36] The use of the term "strange" is interesting. The probability would be that these students did not speak English or had not adopted any Euro-American tendencies, such as white styles of clothing. An entry from four days later stated that all but four of the students did not speak English, noting that the children were still "strange."[37]

The records, incomplete as they are, do not record moments of extreme punishment or trauma. The Sisters' descriptions of the Native children under their care developed, from generic to specific. By 1889, the Sisters recorded the Native students' names, something missing from their earlier years. They also expressed a preference for certain traits, writing on September 18 that their enrollment numbers were low since "the other children have disappointed us."[38] What these disappointments were is unclear, though we might assume that, like the Lorettines, the SHCJs had students who resisted assimilation. Overall, the SHCJs records demonstrate that performance played a major part in the Sisters' interactions with their students, from initial encounters throughout their tenure, which ended in August 1890.

PERFORMANCE

Performance was a key aspect at the Native American boarding schools, creating what Elizabeth Outka termed the "commodified authentic." These were Native items and traditions that white persons commodified and created a new market for, even if just a performance market, based on the paradox of a "hybrid that fused (or promised to fuse) artifice and authenticity" in an attempt to create a "nostalgic evocation" of the past, while still being "tantalizing modern."[39] While Outka's model mainly focuses on English traditions, it remains an apt model to understand the Indigenous schools. Traditions at these schools created an imagined past, placing it carefully within limits that white audiences would have known. As John R. Gram notes in his study on schools in the American Southwest, these performances would have acted out an acceptable imagined past for Indigenous students, but one that would have been fading as students gained white values and traits.[40]

Entertainers and government officials used performances to promote certain narratives. Entertainers, particularly those associated with the Wild West Shows, created performances that emphasized the supposed "savagery" of Indigenous culture, with the caveat that this culture was something of the past. Government officials, particularly those at the United States Office of Indian Affairs, attempted to produce a narrative of civilizing— that is, one from savagery to "productive citizenship"—under the various government policies (such as the schools and allotment programs). These performances were to be anthropological in nature, meant to educate rather than entertain.[41]

The Indigenous children at the Avoca school participated in a wide variety of performances. Some of these reflected the Catholic nature of the school, while others were based upon displays of supposed authentic ethnic traditions. Some of the performances were not recorded, merely hinted at. For example, shortly after the student's arrival in 1884, the Sisters proudly recorded, "The Indian children children [*sic*] continue giving great satisfaction. Many people come from the surrounding colonies to see the children."[42] It is unknown what happened at these moments; however, the students would probably have been encouraged to either demonstrate their new knowledge or exhibit some aspect of their background.

Performance of a Mythological Past

On the one hand, the Sisters used performance as a way to showcase the mythological backgrounds of the students, which the Sisters would overcome in order to create a "civilized" person. Indigenous students were part of theatrical events. The most detailed one comes from the beginning of this chapter, during which students gave

> little "Musical Entertainment" to greet our dear "Mothers" who were visiting from out of state. The community's annals proudly recorded that "The children's refectory having been decorated with flags . . . etc and "a squaw's" blanket with pipes of peace and tomahawk and all arranged properly—. . . An addition was made in the Indian language, and two children dressed in their Indian costume sang and danced the "Omaha dance."[43]

The goal of the performance would have been to introduce members of the SHCJs community who were not familiar with the Omaha, Ojibwe, and Lakota cultures to a taste of this "exotic" culture. The Mothers would have been familiar with some of the basic stereotypes, such as "squaw's blanket . . . and tomahawk" and "the Omaha dance," allowing this performance to reinforce their already held views. The second reason would have been the language of cooperation and assimilation. The symbolism of "the pipes of peace" would have given the whole event the feeling of a mini-peace conference, or perhaps a diplomatic union. The "entertainment" would have been a not-so-subtle way to demonstrate the baseline for measing the progress the students would make on their path toward white, civilized society.

The point of these performances was to be part of the commodified market. The performances demonstrated the myth of the "noble savage," suggesting a mythologized past. Despite the violent imagery of the tomahawk, the performance would have been tamed, all choreographed and planned. The audience was safe, looking upon an imaged past with possibly eager eyes. The message was clear: the past had been tamed, and the students were now primed for assimilation.

Items made by students were also apparently of interest to visitors, with one 1884 visitor "asking for specimens of the Indian children's work. She went over the convent and seemed much pleased with everything."[44] However, the Annals do not state what these items were. Were they examples of white-style handiwork, such as sewing or embroidery? Or were these supposed Native crafts? The meaning of either, however, would have been the same as the entertainment performances: demonstrating their adoption of white cultural values or creating a so-called "Indigenous identity," such as a supposedly traditional doll.

There was at least one instance when the children produced items for profit, participating in the ethnic consumerism of the late nineteenth century. In October 1888, the Annals reported that a local priest brought a doll "to be dressed by the Indians, for the Pipestone Fair." The doll was to be sold for fundraising. There was no hiding the reason behind this request: "He will get much more for it, if they dress it."[45] Whether this was the first time the girls received such a request is unknown; however, it is obvious that the local priest knew its commercial benefit due to its origin as Indigenous-made.

While the students were actors in various entertainments, public or private, they also performed their assumed identities through the manufacturing of items. Given the emphasis on an industrial or practical education at these schools, such performance is not surprising. Such an activity was more behind-the-scenes, rather than overt demonstration of assimilation and imagined identity. Yet, the result was the same: a portrayal of what white culture deemed to be "authentically" Native. In the late nineteenth-century, there was a burgeoning consumerism that was obsessed with items that represented this imagined world, from the World's Fairs to the Wild West Shows. In creating goods for sale, Native persons were able to play into white stereotypes of their cultural distinction and cultural assimilation.[46]

The students at the Avoca school were not the only ones to display their handiwork. At the Sisters of St. Francis' school in Oklahoma, the students had a school exhibition in which they demonstrated their "art, needle work" as well as examples of their classwork.[47] The Lorettines's school at Bernalillo in New Mexico "sent specimens of the INDIAN GIRLS' work in drawing, needle-work, plain sewing, etc. to the Columbian Exposition in Chicago Where [sic] received recognition and were awarded many prizes," as the Annals recorded.[48] This moment reflects the historic and modern commercialization of Indigenous beliefs and supposedly authentic goods. In each of these moments, the question of agency comes up. When studying groups such as the Society of the American Indian, we can see some Indigenous persons using these supposed authenticities to promote Indigenous claims to citizenship.[49]

Performance as Progress

The Sisters also used performance in order to create a sense of progress on the road to assimilation. For example, in June 1886, the Sisters included "'Pictures' of Domestic Economy" as part of their entry that month.[50] The Sisters do not record what exactly the children did at this exhibition, but one might assume that the students demonstrated their progress toward assimilation, demonstrating white gender domestic roles such as cooking, sewing, and housekeeping.

The Sisters also emphasized music as part of the assimilation process. This was white music, Christian music, rather than music from a mythologized native past. The Annals recorded in June and July 1888 that "the pastor of Avoca . . . gave books to the children who formed 'the Church Choir'." It then stated that the next month: "The Choir went to Currie [*sic*] as desired."[51] Music also seems to be a theme in the student experience, not just at Avoca but at other schools as well, such as the St. Louis School in Oklahoma, run by the Sisters of St. Francis, as well as the Carlisle Indian Industrial School.[52]

Musical performances were not unique to the Avoca school. Students at the Osage Mission in Kansas (chapter 2) sang Christmas Carols, embracing a Judeo-Christian holiday tradition, while those at the St. Louis School in Oklahoma (chapter 4) had students sing the "Battle Hymn of the Republic" on the anniversary of Lincoln's birth in 1909, demonstrating their supposedly assumed patriotism through the celebration of a former president and place within the body politic. The Carlisle Industrial School also had a strong music culture, with students performing vocal and instrumental concerts both at the school and in the town. There were also religious music groups, such as the Holy Name Society and a Catholic orchestra, which worked with local Catholic priests and religious women.[53]

On a larger level, these performances would have been familiar to those who attended the World's Fairs and expositions, held throughout the United States and Europe at the height of the imperialist era through the twentieth century. At these expositions, European and American powers sought to demonstrate not only their superiority over other countries, but also over those whom they colonized. Colonized subjects, such as Indigenous persons in the United States and Canada, would perform various stylized aspects of their culture to an audience. Historian Robert Rydell placed these performances within the context of the colonizer and colonized, demonstrating that imperialism "provided the bedrock on which modern times and modern progress depended" by juxtaposing the supposed "primitiveness" of the Indigenous persons with the perceived "modernity" at the rest of the fair. [54]

The Native American Boarding Schools had a special place at the World's Fairs and Expositions. While various tribal nations would perform imagined forms of the past, the boarding schools would emphasize how Indigenous students could be assimilated. The first such attempt was at the 1893 Columbian Exposition in Chicago, at which Congress sponsored an exhibit of a school. The Exposition school had a rotating group of students from schools across the country (although most of the burden soon fell upon the shoulders of the flagship school, the Carlisle Indian Industrial School.) Students would continue their studies, while fairgoers could observe them. The exhibit did not do well, but it did set the stage for future exhibits at later World's Fairs.[55]

There is evidence that the missionaries at Avoca were aware of the connection between their work and the World's Fairs. After the SHCJ left, performances continued. In 1893 (the same year as the Columbian Exposition), the Minneapolis newspaper *The Irish Times* reported:

> There was a fine entertainment given by the Indian girls at the convent school at Avoca on the evening of June 26, which drew words of praise from the Passionist missionary, Father Michael . . . He had visited the World's Fair and had seen the exhibit of the U.S. Indian school there, and it was his opinion that the exhibit of the pupils of Avoca convent compared favorably with it. He complimented the Sisters and scholars on their work.[56]

That the Sisters' work and the student's performance replicated, and exceeded, the proceedings at the World's Fair should not be surprising. If anything, it demonstrates a cultural awareness of accepted portrayals and performances by Indigenous persons at the school.

Missing from the Record

Despite the documentation of these performances, much is unrecorded. One important omission is that of the students' clothing during the recitals and plays. What is symbolic of their past or a demonstration of their roles as students of the school? John R. Gram's history of Southwestern boarding schools notes that during larger performances, female students would wear representations of white domesticity, specifically aprons. Images from the Carlisle Indian Industrial School also demonstrate this emphasis on white clothing. It is possible that students at Avoca wore such styles. However, it is also possible that students wore clothing to symbolize their ethnic heritage. At Carlisle and schools in the Southwest, there were performances in which students wore clothing that represented their background.[57]

This emphasis on costume during performances might seem off topic, but it helps us understand the meaning of these performances. As Joan Fitzpatrick Dean's analysis of pageantry suggests, "Costumes, uniforms, and other distinctive clothing . . . disclose the cultural if not political identity of those individuals who played central roles."[58] Should the students have worn uniforms that reflected white social mores, the message would have been that they were on the path to assimilation, embracing the ideals of their instructors. Such was the case at Carlisle, such as when female students dressed as Puritans during a 1909 performance (see figure 4.3).

If the students at Avoca wore ethnic costume, the meaning could be more complicated. As Gram notes, ethnic clothing could represent a mythological

Figure 4.3   Female Students at the Carlisle Indian Industrial School Dressed as Puritans During a School Performance. *Source: Image courtesy of the Cumberland County Historical Society.*

American past, which white society was embracing. However, it would also have signaled supposed "savagery," or rather a promise of assimilation but not there yet. Such was the cast at other Native performances, such as those at the various World's Fairs and expositions (discussed in further detail below). While not as grandiose as the parade and holiday celebrations described in John R. Gram's history of Southwestern boarding schools, these performances linked the white consumer with the Indigenous child.[59]

At the school in Avoca, the students' performances acted as a type of product. The records are unclear as to whether the Sisters actively advertised or sold these performances of supposed Indigenous culture or acculturation. However, their annals are full of examples of people coming specifically to see the children's performances, suggesting that word was spreading.[60] The children would have been unable to benefit from these performances. Instead, it was the Sisters who reaped the rewards and demonstrated their success as cultural assimilators.

FINAL YEARS OF SHCJ

In October 1889, the Sisters sent a letter to the Mother General, discussing the reasoning behind the Sisters leaving Avoca. They emphasized that the decision was largely due to Archbishop Ireland, who was watching government funding and suspected that the government would lower or cease to fund the school. Moreover, they mentioned diocesan changes. The Diocese of St. Paul divided into the Diocese of St. Paul of Minnesota and the Diocese of Winona-Rochester in 1889, resulting in a new hierarchy. The Sisters apparently wanted to stay with Bishop Ireland, rather than the newly appointed Bishop Joseph Cotter of the latter diocese. Bishop Ireland suggested that it was a good time for the Sisters to reevaluate their missions and leave. However, the letter then tried to focus on the Sisters' larger missions and the impact it would have: "I forgot to say Dr. Ireland said he *advised* us to give up Avoca, as our teaching was better suited to a larger place."[61]

The Sisters of St. Joseph (CSJs) took over in 1890.[62] The CSJs arrived in August 1890 and seemed ready to get to work (the SHCJs' Annals record that they were "eager for us to go").[63] However, there are very few records detailing the CSJs time in Avoca. Most of the CSJs' sources on their tenure at the school come from communication with the BCIM and focus on the practical matters. The Sisters seemed worried about enrollment and attendance, dedicating next to nothing to describe their charges, so we do not know if the practices under the SHCJs continued or not. It is probable that at least the musical performances persisted, as they provided a link between the school, the Catholic Church, and the community, demonstrating the imagined identities described above. Faced within continuing declines in enrollment, the Avoca School closed in September 1894, with the students being sent to federal schools at Pipeline and Flandreau.[64]

CONCLUSION

The Sisters in Avoca used the student performances to create a narrative of success. Their ability to supposedly effectively assimilate their children demonstrated their authority at the school. Others found this narrative appealing. When Bishop John Lancaster Spalding of Peoria, Illinois, visited the school in September 1888, he was "astonished to see the children so 'civilized'."[65] The SHCJs' school in Avoca, Minnesota, had succeeded in their quest.

Yet, that success came with an unwritten cost. How much did Indigenous students resist the Sisters' narratives? How much did they understand about the meaning of the performances? Moreover, how much did the students' internalize versus how much was an act? The Sisters presented one narrative of control and success; however, at what cost?

In the last chapter, we will better see the cost. At Fort Yuma, the CSJs authorized a narrative of control that resulted in the deposition of a local Quechan leader. However, the Sisters saw their actions as justified, for they had only been there to help the school. Their quest for authority over Indigenous persons and success in their mission resulted in political chaos.

NOTES

1. Nov 8, 1885, SHCJ Annals, Vol I, 100, SHCJA.

2. Joel W. Martin, "Crisscrossing Projects of Sovereignty and Conversion: Cherokee Christians and the New England Missionaries during the 1820s," in *Native Americans, Christianity, and the Reshaping of the American Religious Landscape*, ed. Joel W. Martin and Mark A. Nicholas (Chapel Hill, NC: University of North Carolina Press, 2010), 71.

3. Paige Raibmon, *Authentic Indians: Episodes of Encounter from the Late-Nineteenth-Century Northwest Coast* (Durham, NC: Duke University Press, 2005).

4. For example, David R. M. Beck, *Unfair Labor? American Indians and the 1893 World's Columbian Exposition in Chicago* (Lincoln, NE: University of Nebraska Press, 2019); Craig N. Cipolla, "Native American Historical Archaeology and the Trope of Authenticity," *Historical Archaeology* 47, no. 3 (2013): 12–22; Susan Hegman, "Native American "Texts" and the Problem of Authenticity," *American Quarterly* 41, no. 2 (June 1989): 265–283; Louellyn White, "White Power and the Performance of Assimilation: Lincoln Institute and Carlisle Indian School," in *Carlisle Indian Industrial School: Indigenous Histories, Memories, and Reclamation*s, ed. Jacqueline Fear-Segal and Susan D. Rose (Lincoln, NE: University of Nebraska Press, 2016), 106–123; Shamoon Zamir et al., "Native Agency and the Making of 'The North American Indian': Alexander B. Upshaw and Edward S. Curtis," *American Indian Quarterly* 31, no. 4 (2007): 613–653.

5. John R. Gram, "Acting Out Assimilation: Playing Indian and Becoming American in the Federal Indian Boarding Schools" *American Indian Quarterly* 40, no. 3 (2016): 251, 254.

Also see Jeffrey Alexander, "Cultural Pragmatics: Social Performance between Ritual and Strategy," *Sociological Review* 22, no. 4 (December 2004): 527–573; David Glassberg, *American Historical Pageantry: The Uses of Tradition in the Early Twentieth Century* (Chapel Hill, NC: University of North Carolina Press, 1990); L. G. Moses, "Indians on the Midway: Wild West Shows and the Indian Bureau at World's Fairs, 1893-1904," *South Dakota State Historical Society* 21 (1991): 206–229; L. G. Moses, *Wild West Shows and Images of American Indians 1883-1933* (Albuquerque, NM: University of New Mexico Press, 1999).

6. October 18, 1883, SHCJ Annals, Vol. 1, 39; Nov 8, 1883, SHCJ Annals, Vol. 1, 44.

7. "Catholic-Operated Native Boarding Schools in the United States pre-1978," Catholic Truth and Healing, accessed May 30, 2023, https://ctah.archivistsacwr .org/.

8. Mary Lethert Wingerd, *North Country: The Making of Minnesota* (Minneapolis, MN: University of Minnesota Press, 2010), 1–74.

9. Kasey R. Keeler, *American Indians and the American Dream: Policies, Place, and Property in Minnesota* (Minneapolis, MN: University of Minnesota Press, 2023), 27–65.

10. Keeler, *American Indians,* 27–65.

11. Wingerd, *North Country,* 75–231.

12. Chapter 7 also examines the SJSs from the St. Louis Motherhouse. However, there I use the abbreviation CSJs. The original community of SJSs were French missionaries, who looked to their leadership in the mother country during their first several decades of existence in the United States. Under the leadership of the St. Louis house, several communities of Sisters plans to become a separate community from their French counterpart in 1860. This led to the splintering of the community in the United States. Those who remained under the leadership of St. Louis became the Sisters of St. Joseph of Carondelet (the CSJs) in 1877. Those who became autonomous congregations are known as SSJs. However, in 1852, this division had not occurred, which is why I use SSJs here. For more on the SSJs and CSJs see Elisabeth C. Davis, "The Disappearance of Mother Agnes Spencer: The Centralization Controversy and the Antebellum Catholic Church," *American Catholic Studies* 130, no. 2 (2019): 31–52; Elisabeth Davis, "We Know Not God's Designs in Permitting a Separation: Women Religious, the Consolidation Controversies, and the Nineteenth Century American Catholic Church," *Journal of Religious History* 47 (December 2023): 566–585; Mary M. McGlone, *Anything of Which a Woman is Capable: A History of the Sisters of St. Joseph in the United States, Vol. 1* (St. Louis, MO: Bookbay, 2017); Mary McGlone, *Called Forth by the Dear Neighbor: A History of the Sisters of St. Joseph in the United States Volume 2- from 1860-2010* (St. Louis, MO: Federation of the Sisters of St. Joseph, 2020).

13. Helen Angela Hurley, *On Good Ground: The Story of the Sisters of St. Joseph in St. Paul* (Minneapolis, MN: University of Minnesota Press, 1951), 30–64.

14. "Catholic Truth and Healing," Minnesota, accessed June 1, 2023, https://ctah .archivistsacwr.org/list/cat/minnesota/.

15. Malcolm Campbell, "Immigrants on the Land: Irish Rural Settlement in Minnesota and New South Wales, 1830-1890," *New Hibernia Review* 2, no. 1 (Spring 1998): 43–61; Emmons, *Beyond the American Pale*; Anita Talsma Gaul, "'Living in Perfect Harmony": A Multiethnic Catholic Parish on the Minnesota Prairie, 1881-1910," *Journal of American Ethnic History* 30, no. 1 (Fall 2010): 37–71; James P. Shannon, "Catholic Boarding Schools on the Western Frontier," *Minnesota History* 35, no. 3 (September 1956): 133–139; Alice E. Smith, "The Sweetman Irish Colony," *Minnesota History* 9, no. 4 (December 1928): 331–346.

16. Catholic Colonization Bureau, *Catholic Colonization in Minnesota. Colony of Avoca, Murray County, Southwestern Minnesota* (St. Paul, MN: The Pioneer Press, 1880), 5.

17. Catholic Colonization Bureau, *Catholic Colonization in Minnesota,* 7.

18. Radegune Flaxman, *A Woman Styled Bold: The Life of Cornelia Connelly, 1809-1879* (London: Darton, Longman, and Todd, 1991); Roseanne McDougall and Emily Siegal, "The Life of the Society of the Holy Children Jesus in the United States, 1862-Present: An Ecclesial Perspective," *American Catholic Studies* 132, no. 4 (2021): 95–117.

19. Sister St. Augustine, Letter to My Dearest Sisters, June 10, 1883, SCHJA.

20. SHCJ Annals, June 22, 1883, 19.

21. M.F. Borgia, Letter to My Dear Sisters, July 1883, SCHJA.

22. Nov 18, 1883, SHCJ Annals, Vol I, 47.

23. July 10, 1884, SHCJ Annals, Vol 1, 70; August 16, 1884, SHCJ Annals, Vol 1, 74.

24. Marvin Lazerson, "Understanding American Catholic Educational History," *History of Education Quarterly* 17, no. 3 (1977): 297–317; Ellen Richardson, "Catholic Women as Institutional Innovators: The Sisters of Charity and the Rise of the Modern Urban Hospital in Buffalo, N.Y., 1848-1900" (PhD Dissertation, State University of New York at Buffalo, Buffalo, NY, 1996), 60–65.

25. Dominic E. Gerlach, "St. Joseph's Indian Normal School, 1888-1896," *Indian Magazine of History* 69, no. 1 (1973): 1–42; R. Bruce Harley, "The Founding of St. Boniface Indian School, 1888-1890," *Southern California Quarterly* 81, no. 4 (Winter 1999): 449–466; Tanya L. Rathbun, "Hail Mary: The Catholic Experience at St. Boniface Indian School," in *Boarding School Blues: Revisiting American Indian Educational Experiences,* ed. Clifford E. Trafzer et al. (Lincoln, NE: University of Nebraska Press, 2006), 155–173; James P. Shannon, "Catholic Boarding Schools on the Western Frontier," *Minnesota History* 35, no. 3 (September 1956): 133–139.

26. For example, Campbell, "Immigrants on the Land," 43–61; Elisabeth C. Davis, "To Keep the Catholics Intact: The Catholic Experience at the Carlisle Indian Industrial School, 1883-1918," *U.S. Catholic Historian* 40 (Fall 2022): 1–20; Jay P. Dolan, *Catholic Revivalism: The American Experience 1830-1900* (Notre Dame, IN: University of Notre Dame Press 1978); Shannon, "Catholic Boarding Schools on the Western Frontier," 133–139.

27. Deborah Dawson Bonde, "MISSIONARY WAYS IN THE WILDERNESS: Eliza Hart Spalding, Maternal Associations, and the Nez Perce Indians," *American Presbyterians* 69, no. 4 (1991): 271–282; Linda Clemmons, "'Our Children Are in Danger of Becoming Little Indians': Protestant Missionary Children and Dakotas, 1835-1862," *Michigan Historical Review* 25, no. 2 (1999): 69–90; Linda Clemmons, "'We Find It a Difficult Work': Educating Dakota Children in Missionary Homes, 1835-1862," *American Indian Quarterly* 24, no. 4 (2000): 570–600.

28. E. G. Emily Conroy-Krutz, *Christian Imperialism: Converting the World in the Early American Republic* (Ithaca, NY: Cornell University Press, 2015), 85–88, 110–114; Eittreim, *Teaching Empire*; Cristina Stanciu, *The Makings and Unmakings of Americans: Indian and Immigrants in American Literature and Culture, 1879-1924* (New Haven, CT: Yale University Press, 2023).

29. "The Anishinaabe (Ojibwe, Saulteaux)," *Gladue Rights Research Database,* accessed February 12, 2024, https://gladue.usask.ca/anishinaabeg; Loriene Roy, "Ojibwe," *Gale Encyclopedia of Multicultural America*, edited by Gale, 3rd ed., Gale,

2014. Credo Reference, https://search.credoreference.com/articles/Qm9va0FydGl jbGU6NDIzMjQ0OOA==?aid=239563; Anton Treuer, *Ojibwe in Minnesota* (St. Paul, MN: Minnesota Historical Society, 2010), 1–31; William W. Warren, *History of the Ojibway People* (St. Paul, MN: Minnesota Society Press, 1984).

30. "The Anishinaabe (Ojibwe, Saulteaux"; Roy, "Ojibwe"; Treuer, *Ojibwe in Minnesota*, 1–31; Warren, *History of the Ojibway People.*

31. Michael David McNally, *Ojibwe Singers: Hymns, Grief, and a Native Culture in Motion* (Oxford: Oxford University Press, 2000).

32. "Catholic Chippewas on the Persecution in France," *The Indian Advocate* (Sacred Heart, OK), September 1903; "The Chippewa Indians of Minnesota," *The Indian Advocate*," August 1903.

33. "Catholic Congress at Red Lake; History of Mission from Formation," *The Catholic Bulletin* (St. Paul, Minn.), June 30, 1917; "Church Notices," *The Cook County Herald* (Grand Marais, Minn.), May 25, 1907; "Indians at Cass Lake," *The Bemidji Daily Pioneer* (Bemidji, Minn.), July 11, 1914; "Local Affairs," *The Superior Times* (Superior, Wis.), February 4, 1882.

34. "Catholic Congress at Red Lake; History of Mission from Formation"; "Chippewa Catholics Hold Meeting," *The Irish Standard* (Minneapolis, MN), July 21, 1917; "Chippewa Convention Closes," *G34rand Rapids Herald-Review* (Grand Rapids, Itasca County, Minn), July 4, 1917; "Chippewa Societies," *The Catholic Bulletin* (St. Paul, Minn.), July 18, 1914; "Diocese of Crookston," *The Catholic Bulletin* (St. Paul, Minn.), July 4, 1914; "Indians at Cass Lake," *The Bemidji Daily Pioneer* (Bemidji, Minn.), July 11, 1914; "Indians Crows Lake Cass," *The Ely Miner* (Ely, Minn.), July 17, 1914; "Sixth Annual Chippewa Convention Closed Tuesday," *The Bemidji Daily Pioneer* (Bemidji, Minn.), June 27, 1917; "Society," *The Bemidji Daily Pioneer* (Bemidji, Minn.), July 12, 1913.

35. "Catholic Indians," *The Catholic Bulletin* (St. Paul, Minn.), December 30, 1916; "Father Gordan Here Sunday," *The Daily Ardmoreite* (Ardmore, Okla.), April 19, 1916; "Haskell Priest An Indian," *The Topeka State Journal* (Topeka, Kansas), August 30, 1915; "Indian Priest to Run for Congress," *The Bemidji Daily Pioneer* (Bemidji, Minn.), July 13, 1918; "Local and Personal," *The Tomahawk* (White Earth, Becker County, Minn.), January 15, 1904; "Rev. Philip B. Gordon, Chippewa Indian Priest at Catholic University, has been Specially Designated by Cardinal Gibbons for Missionary and Lecture Work Among Red Men," *Evening Star* (Washington, D.C.), May 15, 1915; "Strong Appeals Made for Indian," *Tulsa Daily World* (Tulsa, Indian Territory [Okla.]), September 30, 1915.

For more on Father Philip Gordon, see Tadeusz Lewandowski, *Ojibwe, Activist, Priest: The Life of Father Philip Bergin Gordon, Tibishkogijik* (Madison, WI: University of Wisconsin Press, 2019).

36. January 22, 1885, SCHS Annals, Vol I, 84.

37. January 26, 1885, SHCJ Annals, Vol I, 89.

38. September 18, 1889, SHCJ Annals, Vol II, 60.

39. Elizabeth Outka, *Consuming Traditions: Modernity, Modernism, and the Commodified Authentic* (New York: Oxford University Press, 2009), 4.

40. Gram, "Acting Out Assimilation," 251–272.

41. Moses, "Indians on the Midway," quote on page 206.

42. Sept 9, 1884, SHCJ Annals, 75–76.

43. Nov 8, 1885, SHCJ Annals, Vol I, 100.

44. Oct 21, 1884, SHCJ Annals, Vol I, 79.

45. Oct 18, 1888, SHCJ Annals, Vol II, pg. 45.

46. Beck, *Unfair Labor,* 135–166; Melissa Rinehart, "To Hell with Wigs! Native American Representation and Resistance at the World's Columbian Exposition," *American Indian Quarterly* 36, no. 4 (2012): 403–442; Carolyn A. Weber, "Caught between Catholic and government traditions: Americanization and assimilation at St. Joseph's Indian Normal School," *American Educational History* 40, no. 1–2 (2013): 75+.

47. Chronicles, June 7, 1909, Pawhuska Chronicles--May 1908-October 1909, AOSF.

48. Bernalillo Annals, 1893, LHC, LHC06.l.A.01.012 Annals, 1875-1966 (All Schools) Bernalillo, Bx 1–12, Loretto Heritage Center, Loretto, KY.

49. E. G. Lisa Adlred, "Plastic Shamans the Astroturf Sun Dances: New Age Commercialization of Native American Spirituality," *American Indian Quarterly* 24, no. 3 (Summer 2000): 329–352; George Pierre Castile, "The Commodification of Indian Identity," *American Anthropologist* 98, no. 4 (1996): 743–749; Alexandra Harmon, Colleen O'Neill, and Paul C. Rosier, "Interwoven Economic Histories: American Indians in a Capitalist America," *The Journal of American History* 98, no. 3 (2011): 698–722; Doreen E. Martinez, "Wrong Directions and New Maps of Voice, Representation, and Engagement: Theorizing Cultural Tourism, Indigenous Commodities, and the Intelligence of Participation," *American Indian Quarterly* 36, no. 4 (2012): 545–573; Vera Parham, "'These Indians Are Apparently Well to Do': The Myth of Capitalism and Native American Labor," *International Review of Social History* 57, no. 3 (2012): 447–470; Michelle Wick Patterson, "'Real' Indian Songs: The Society of American Indians and the Use of Native American Culture as a Means of Reform," *American Indian Quarterly* 26, no. 1 (2002): 44–66.

50. June 30 1886, SHCJ Annals, 114.

51. July 22 1888, SHCJ Annals, Vol. II, 43.

52. For St. Louis School, see Annals, June 12, 1908, 12–13, AOSF; Annals, December 23, 1908, 30, AOSF.

For Carlisle, see "Catholic Indians Sang Carols," *The Carlisle Arrow,* January 19, 1912; "General School News," *The Carlisle Arrow,* February 13, 1914; "General School News," *The Carlisle Arrow,* January 19, 1912; "Local Miscellany," *The Arrow,* March 27, 1908; "Man-on-the-band-stand," *The Red Man and Helper,* November 20, 1908; "General School News," *The Carlisle Arrow,* April 28, 1911 "Local Miscellany: Items of Interest Gathered by our Student Reporters," *The Arrow,* December 7, 1906; "Local Miscellany: Items of Interest Gathered by our Student Reporters," *The Arrow,* December 14, 1906.

53. Sister Mary Edith Laughlin, "Some Recollections of Mother Bridget Hayden The Osages," 5–6, LHC, Osage Mission, St. Ann's, St. Francis historical data & memoirs RG-SCH, VII Box II-8; Chronicles, February 12, 1909, Chronicles 1908-Pawhuska Chronicles--May 1908-October 1909, AOSF; "The Holy Name Society," *The Carlisle Arrow,* June 2, 1916, CISDRC; "General School News," *The Carlisle Arrow,* October 23, 1908, CISDRC; "General School News," *The Carlisle Arrow,* October 28, 1910, CISDRC.

54. See Robert W. Rydell, *World of Fairs: The Century-of-Progress Expositions* (Chicago, IL: The University of Chicago Press, 1993), 62. Also see David R. M. Beck, *Unfair Labor? American Indians and the 1893 World's Columbian Exposition in Chicago* (Lincoln, NE: University of Nebraska Press, 2019), 4; Gertrude M. Scott, "Village Performance at the Chicago World's Columbian Exposition 1893" (PhD Dissertation, New York University, New York, 1991).

55. J. Kent McAnally, "The Haskell (Institute) Indian Band in 1904: The World's Fair and Beyond," *Journal of Band Research* 31, no. 2 (1996): 1; Christine M. O'Bonsawin, "The Nonparticipation of Canadian Indians in the Anthropology Days of the 1904 St. Louis Olympic Games," in *The 1904 Anthropology Days and Olympic Games: Sport, Race, and American Imperialism*, ed. Susan Brownell (Lincoln, NE: University of Nebraska Press, 2008), 217–242; Linda Peavy and Ursa Smith, ""Leav[ing] the White[s]...Far Behind Them": The Girls from Fort Shaw (Montana) Indian School, Basketball Champions of the 1904 World's Fair," in *The 1904 Anthropology Days and Olympic Games: Sport, Race, and American Imperialism*, ed. Susan Brownell (Lincoln, NE: University of Nebraska Press, 2008), 243–277; Robert A. Trennert, "Selling Indian Education at World's Fairs and Expositions, 1893-1904," *American Indian Quarterly* 11 (1987): 203–220.

56. "The Northwest," *The Irish Standard*, (Minneapolis, Minn), July 8, 1893.

57. Sally J. McBeth, "Indian Boarding Schools and Ethnic Identity: An Example from the Southern Plains Tribes of Oklahoma," *Plains Anthropologist* 28, no. 100 (1983): 119–128; Louellyn White, "White Power and the Performance of Assimilation," 106–123.

58. Joan Fitzpatrick Dean, *All Dressed Up: Modern Irish Historical Pageantry* (Syracuse, NY: Syracuse University Press, 2014), 5.

59. Glassberg, *American Historical Pageantry*; Gram, "Acting Out Assimilation," 25–273.

60. For example, October 18, 1883, SHCJ Annals, Vol 1, 39; November 8, 1883, SHCJ Annals, Vol 1, 44, October 21, 1884: SCHS Annals, 79; September 26, 1888, Vol II, 44.

61. Emphasis in original text. Sister Mary Walburga, Letter to Mother General, October 1889, SHCJA.

62. Unlike the SSJs discussed earlier in this chapter, this group was under the new congregation of St. Louis, hence the shift to CSJs.

63. Quote from August 20 1890, SHCJ Annals, Vol II, 72. Also see August 13, 1890, SHCJ Annals, Vol I, 71.

64. "Avoca Mission," Bureau of Catholic Indian Missions, Series 1-1, Microfilm 20, Marquette University Libraries, Marquette WI (MUL); "Pipestone Daily Star, 30," *The Madison Daily Leader* (Madison, S.D.), September 1, 1894.

65. Sept 26, 1888, SHCJ Annals, Vol II, 44.

Chapter 5

Rise of Anti-Denominationalism, 1880–1918

A February 1896 edition of *The New North-West,* published in Montana, presented a dramatic scene in Washington, D.C., as the House debated appropriations for the Native American Boarding Schools. The key point was whether the "sectarian schools" would continue to receive funding. Representative William S. Linton of Michigan had argued the case for cutting funding for the Catholic contract schools, suggesting that "The Roman Catholic church would take care of itself. It was powerful enough. It had a right to, but not with public money."[1] Linton's suggestion was challenged by members of the Democratic party, however ultimately carried. However, given pushback, Congress sought a compromise, trying to phase out funding over a year or two, versus an immediate cut.[2] The age of non-sectarian education at the Native American Boarding schools had begun.

Linton's and his allies' call for the defunding of the Catholic contract schools reflected anti-Catholicism sweeping the country brought on by the waves of immigration, that brought in more Catholic immigrants from southern Europe. A report of Linton's achievement published in the Dakota Territory's *Union County* wrote that "the only sectarian schools to which the money now goes are the Roman Catholics." It then described funding for the sectarian schools as "unrepublican, undemocratic and un-American."[3] A June 1896 article on the debates over defunding made the link between immigration and defunding the schools even more explicit, denoting that Linton and his supporters ran on a platform of "absolution freedom from all public schools from sectarian influence. . . . for the absolute separation of church and state . . . for stringent immigration laws."[4] The link between sectarian schools and the Catholic Church was clear: to support the sectarian school was to support Catholics, both of which, was un-American.

Linton's crusade to cut funding for the "sectarian schools" reflected a new era of the boarding school era as the federal government slowly began to defund the religious contract schools at the turn of the twentieth century. While Linton and his allies tried to push for a full defunding of the school, there was only partial defunding in the years that followed the sensational debates in the House as Catholics and their allies successfully campaigned for the continued support of the contract schools.[5] Although affected by this policy change, Protestant missionaries and educators ultimately supported the decision to do so and withdrew their applications for funding. Protestants hoped that without federal support for religious education, Catholics would lose any influence they might have had with the Indigenous nations. Government officials hoped that Indigenous students would join public schools, no longer creating a need for the boarding schools. That long-term plan did not happen.[6]

Corresponding with the secularization of governmental policy, the nature of education changed. Rather than including Christianity as a sign of "civilization," the federal government turned its focus mainly to industrial labor. Inspired by technical schools, such as Booker T. Washington's work at the Tuskegee Institute, white educators believed in Washington's views on racial progress, arguing that Indigenous persons could slowly climb up the racial ladder, step by step, until they achieved a level of equality to other races through financial self-sufficiency.[7]

Like many of the programs at Tuskegee Institute and other similar ventures, Indigenous students' vocational training did not include up-to-date trades, but rather started with menial work. White educators of Indigenous persons, or even Black students, never truly sought to create equality, but rather an engineered dependence. The students learned trades that did not reflect the increasing industrialization of the country, such as new factories or technologies. Instead, these programs focused on agriculture and housekeeping; only rarely did an Indigenous student become part of the professional trades.[8]

Despite the increasing emphasis on a nondenominational education, educators continued to believe in some form of Christianity as fundamental to the assimilation process; it just was a secondary or tertiary focus. As the superintendent of the Haskell's Indian Industrial School, H. B. Peairs, maintained, "A really civilized people cannot be found in the world except where the Bible has been sent and the gospel taught; hence we believe that the Indians must have as an essential part of their education, Christian training."[9] A newspaper from McConnellsburg, Pennsylvania, echoed this sentiment in 1909: "Christianity grows as the knowledge and love of Bible grow. But what if the convert cannot read?"[10] Despite changes in federal policy, religious training and education were key to the assimilation process. It was just to be secondary, adjacent to the main goals of the school.

While preaching secularization, federal rules regarding the boarding schools emphasized the need to respect a variety of Christian beliefs. According to the 1898 *Rules for the Indian School Service,* Pratt and other federal school officials needed to allow for religious differences: "Pupils shall be encouraged to attend churches and Sunday school of their respective denominations."[11] Church attendance was "encouraged"; it was not a mandatory part of the day as it would have been in years past. In 1913, the commissioner of Indian affairs, Cato Sells, emphasized this continuing need for religious diversity, writing to the superintendent of Carlisle Moses Friedman, that "The Office [Bureau of Indian Affairs] wishes to do all that it properly can to further the religious training, regardless of the denomination to which they belong."[12] Based on these rules, superintendents of the federal boarding schools had to allow for the religious education of Catholic students.

IMPACT ON CONTRACT SCHOOLS

Holding on to their belief in the importance of education in everyday life, Catholics found themselves moving against the tide, continuing to promote religion over a more hands-on education. *The Indian Advocate* wrote in 1899 that "Religion is a mollifying influence, the purifying ingredient, the basis of any worthy civilization and pre-eminently raises rational being above all other creation on this earth."[13] To that end, missionaries still created and ran industrial boarding schools and day schools, with religious education to be at the center of these communities.

The Church hierarchy supported this continuing mission. The Third Plenary Council of Baltimore, a meeting of the nation's clergy in 1884, cemented support for the schools, emphasizing the importance of the gospel.[14] Pope Pius X affirmed this sentiment in 1908: "Of one thing We feel assured, namely, that the Indians will not be deprived of the blessings of salvation nor of the advantages of Christian education."[15] Catholic missionaries truly believed that religious education should preempt a vocational one. As a 1953 history of Catholic missions wrote,

> The lack of religious instruction in federal Indian schools rendered them insufficient for a people who for centuries had been steeped in the superstition of crafty medicine men. The Indian might be instructed, but the education of the whole man was not achieved.[16]

However, this was difficult to accomplish in the face of rising anti-denominational education.

The effects of the government's emphasis on a nondenominational education soon became evident. As early as 1895, it was clear that secular policies would lead to cuts in funding for the Catholic schools.[17] In 1900, the BCIM sent a circular to all superintendents of schools under its purview announcing that "The Indian Appropriate Bill has passed both Houses of Congress. It contains no provision for the education of Indian children in contract schools next year. Consequently all Government aid for your schools will cease on the 30th of next June."[18] The schools discussed in this book were affected by this new decree. The circular advised the heads of schools that the BCIM would do what it could to support them but advised them to start looking for alternative funding from private means or the local dioceses.

Catholics saw the rise of defunding as an attack on Catholics themselves. *The Indian Advocate* expounded this sentiment forcefully in 1897:

> When the Protestants though that Grants "peace policy" was to benefit them, all the chief sects among them approved of it and took part in it; but as soon as time provide their missions were sterile, that the Indians preferred the Catholic "blackgowns" to their preachers; and that the Catholics were taking in the whole field, and getting control of the expenditure of the bulk of the money set aside . . . they discovered that the constitution . . . the separation of Church and State, etc., etc., all prohibited sectarian appropriations.[19]

Catholics believed that their work made other groups jealous, thus threatening the Protestant majority. As the Catholic priest assigned to the Carlisle Indian Industrial School wrote in 1904, what were Catholics to do as "Bigotry and fanaticism invaded the halls of Congress and the Senate."[20]

Some Catholics saw the defunding of the schools as part of a secularization of the government and of American society. *The Indian Advocate* made the connection between the rise of a secular society and the fall of civilization. It suggested that the lack of belief will lead to lawlessness: "Now, put such a man—and we have enough of them—put such a man in a State, a city, in your own neighborhood. What guarantee have you for his good conduct?" In a rhetorical exercise, *The Indian Advocate* suggested that the unbeliever would be "bound by the civil law only when and in so far as the restraint I thus put upon myself is less annoying than would be the visitations of the law."[21] The periodical was later editorialized in 1910:

> We pride ourselves on the successful separation of church and state; but the truth is, we have established religion, for the support of which all the people are heavily taxed. Our richly endowed established religion is that of Agnosticism, and Aggressive Atheism.[22]

Catholics believed that with the rise of secularization, civilization in general was boomed.

With the changing political circumstances, Catholic missionaries struggled to run their boarding schools on limited funds. In a 1904 editorial for the Benedictine periodical, *The Indian Advocate,* Father Ganss wrote:

> But suddenly our whole work was confronted by an expected danger . . . While we Catholics were living in a state of false and delusive security . . . a stealthy, insidious influence was undermining our work. Bigotry and fanaticism invaded the halls of Congress and the Senate . . . and clamored that no more appropriations should be given to sectarian or denominational schools.[23]

What was to be done? As *The Indian Advocate* stoutly proclaimed in 1896, "Catholics work for the salvation of the Indian and not for the appropriations of the government."[24] However, funding was still an issue in order for the schools to stay open. Catholics had relied upon donations distributed by the Ladies Catholic Indian Missionary Society for decades, but it was not enough.[25] As Ganss wrote, "At this critical moment, when no help was in view and the closing of our schools and abandonment of their pupils seemed imminent, God in His infinite mercy sent an angel of hope."[26] The solution, at least for now, was funding provided by Katharine Drexel.

The work of the Catholic educators would never have been able to do so without their patron, Katharine Drexel. Drexel was responsible for providing the economic support that the local clergy and Catholic students needed. Her work helped fund the building of schools, the hiring of teachers, and the day-to-day needs. She worked not just with the Catholic schools but with the federal schools. Drexel had a strong presence at the Carlisle Indian Industrial School, funding the religious communities that worked with students there, paying for student outings, and paying for Catholic students to attend college. The Catholic missions would have failed without her intervention.[27]

Despite Mother Drexel's intervention, the situation remained dire. In early 1917, the Minnesota periodical *The Tomahawk,* which claimed to focus on Indigenous voices and issues, recorded a plea for funding for the local schools. It stated that the Ojibwe at the White Earth Reservation

> respectfully request and petition [the government] to enter into a contract with the Bureau of Catholic Indian Missions . . . for the care, maintenance and education of ten (10) children of the Chippewa tribe at St. Mary's Mission Boarding School, Red Lake Research, Minnesota, for the fiscal year ending June 30, 1918, to be paid for as you may determine out of our trust and treaty funds.[28]

Throughout this whole time, the federal government had slowly been acquiring or closing the Catholic schools. In his 1915 speech, Ketcham noted that the government had bought Catholic schools, with the promise of replacing the teachers with civil servants and allowing Catholics to continue to practice their faith. Ketcham noted that there was some propaganda suggesting that Catholics were abandoning the schools; he argued that Catholics "had acted with sincerity and relied on the good faith of the government; she has, however, endeavored to protect her Indian schools and secure that fairness of treatment which she had a right to respect."[29]

As the government took over Catholic schools, they kept on some of the teachers, stating they would replace these teachers with civil servants. This led to a minor crisis in 1912 that revolved around the clothing of Catholic Sisters. Catholic Sisters on the schools wore their habits, symbolizing their faith and devotion. However, as government contractors, they were not supposed to promote a certain religion. Government officials tried to order the Sisters to not wear their habits when teaching. The Sisters refused. The whole affair ended in a tense stand-off, with the Sisters continuing to wear what they felt was their right. However, the whole situation led to more Catholic schools being taken over by government officials or closed.[30]

CASE STUDY: POLITICKING OVER RELIGIOUS STUDY AT THE SCHOOLS

The impact of these debates influenced the everyday experience of the Catholic Sisters at the schools. One example comes from the Sisters of St. Francis, the OSFs, in Oklahoma. Chapter 6 goes into detail with the OSFs missions. What follows here is merely a brief overview of how the disputes over religious education affected the OSFs. The OSFs found themselves caught in a variety of politicking, particularly within the circle of Catholic missionaries. While they had taken religious vows, which should seclude them from real-world politics, the Sisters understood that their contract to work with the Osage specified they provide a secular education. Unlike the Benedictines, they ran government-funded institutions and had to follow specific guidelines. The Sisters found themselves caught between the ideals of missionary work and the reality of receiving governmental funding.

At the very basic level, the expectations of the local priests did not match the reality of the Sisters' daily lives. There seems to have been a question of authority. In 1899, Father Joseph A. Stephan from the BCIM wrote to the school's superior,

> Therefore, you owe it to yourself and to the pupils entrusted to your care to have it thoroughly understood by all that you are the head of the St. Louis School, and as such empowered to decide all matters connected with the

management of the school, and that your authority on the premises must be respected.[31]

Oddly, this comment reflects the Sisters' relationship with local priests rather than the local Osage community. Stephen was suggesting that the Sisters had to stand their ground against the local priests, who demanded they provide a more religious education.

Documents also suggest that the local clergy were more interested in the religious nature of the Sisters' lives and the role of religion in the schools. In May 1907, one of the Sisters wrote to Bishop Theophile Meerschaert, the bishop of Oklahoma, stating that the local priest, Father Edwards, had been

interfering too much in the affairs of Sisters . . . He is subjecting them to all kinds of petty annoyances and persecutions . . . [and] has repeatedly deprived certain Sisters of Holy Communion for a whole week.[32]

It is not clear why Father Edwards was "interfering" in the Sisters' lives, though supplementary evidence suggests that the Sisters' daily routine was not as austere as he might have hoped. A few months later, one of the Sisters at the Pawhuska school wrote to Mother Aloysia, stationed in Pennsylvania, that Father Edwards had "deprived [her] of Holy Communion" after "the priest had complained that the children did not behave while the Sisters Received [the sacraments]."[33]

The interference of the clergy reflected a larger question on the role of religion within the mission schools. Although funded by the Department of the Interior and overseen by the BCIM, other Catholics within Oklahoma felt they had a say in the school's running. The OSFs reported in 1899 that Bishop Meerscheart said it was part of their duty to catechize students. According to them, he likened the school to a parochial school in the city, under the bishop's supervision and geared toward religious education, although Meerscheart later refuted the Sisters' claims.[34] Father Stephan, the director of the BCIM, replied that this was not the case: "So far as the Government is concerned, what is most desired is that the pupils attending the school should receive a good common school education and practical training in certain industrial branches named in the contract."[35] The Sisters had to respect their contract, rather than the wishes of the local clergy.

There is evidence that the Sisters also worked with the Catholic students at the local federal school. Oklahomaources do not fully describe how many Catholic students were there during the Sisters' tenure, although in 1906, one of the Sisters recorded 77 students from the government school who attended Mass with the Sisters.[36] The Sisters suggested that the federal school was unwilling to allow the Sisters to visit; an entry from May 1908 described a confirmation for students from the Sisters' school and the local federal school, which the Sisters said that the federal school had "reluctantly" allowed the students from their school to attend.[37] However, the federal school officials were required to do so by common practice and federal law.

To provide better context of the role of the OSFs at the local federal school, we can turn to the Catholic influence at the federal schools, which comes from the Carlisle Indian Industrial School. Founded by Richard Henry Pratt in 1879, the Carlisle School recognized the need to include religion in its industrial education. In his history of the school, Pratt stated that

> the co-operation of the different churches and Sunday schools in Carlisle was sought, especially for those who had come from various missionary influences at their homes. . . . A Sunday school was established on the school grounds for the girls, small boys and larger boys who were not sufficiently advanced to profitably attend Sunday schools with the white children.[38]

Religion, while tangential, was still to be part of the experience. However, Pratt viewed Catholicism with suspicion. He claimed that Catholic reservation and contract schools were not following federal guidelines for the schools, focusing on "proselytizing" versus education.[39] Pratt's anti-Catholicism permeated the school. One of the local priests to Carlisle described the situation as where "prejudice and bigotry are dying a prolonged and resisting death."[40] Due to federal regulations, Pratt could not bar Catholics from the school.

It was due to the work of the local parish priest, Henry Ganss, that Catholics even had a presence at Carlisle. After much negotiation, the Industrial School's administration granted him permission to work with these students in approximately 1883. His work was to be limited to religious sacraments and education among students who already identified as Catholic. Ganss, and later parish priests, became staples at the Industrial School, participating in school activities such as graduation, running student music programs, and providing support staff.[41] Ganss later requested and was joined in his work by three groups of Catholic women religious: the Sisters of St. Joseph (the SSJs,1901–1902), the Sisters of Mercy, (the SMs,1902–1903/possibly 1906), and the Sisters of the Blessed Sacrament (the SBSs,1906–1918).[42]

Each of these groups had a historical connection to working with Indigenous communities. The SJSs had been working on missions since the 1850s. The final chapter of this book examines their work in California. Prior to 1918, various congregations of the SMs ran or worked on boarding schools in Arizona, Minnesota, New York, North Dakota, and Oklahoma. Indeed, it was a community of the SMs (not the one at Carlisle) who ran a school in Ogdensburg, New York, which several members of the Mohawk St. Regis attended before arriving at Carlisle. And, the SBSs had been partly founded by Katharine Drexel specifically to work with Indigenous communities and the African American community.[43]

Father Ganss did not mince words when telling the Sisters that they faced an uphill battle. Aware of Pratt's anti-Catholic stance, Ganss wrote to the SJSs that "In view of the first light which will beat on the Sisters coming here . . . it is to be suggested that you send earnest prudent . . . and cultured teachers."[44] The Sisters would not receive much assistance from the school's administration; they would be on their own (with the support of the local priest) in trying to save the souls of the local students.

Following federal policies, Catholic Sisters at the federal schools did not provide a secular education, as they did at their own schools. In addition to providing a religious education, Ganss and the Catholic Sisters stationed in Carlisle created various religious and social clubs and events for Catholic students. The Sisters oversaw the Girls Holy Name Club and the "The Girl's Catherine Tekakwitha Society." They also ran various musical groups, such as choirs and orchestras. The Sisters also attended to Catholic students who were in the hospital. Catholic Sisters also helped plan student weddings, holiday parties, and other celebrations.[45]

There is some evidence to suggest that the students and staff at the federal school appreciated the Sisters; however, such records were created by Catholics themselves. When the SJSs arrived in 1901, they reported that "the older girls flocked around us and told us of their joy to see Sisters once again. The majority seem to be from Wisconsin and quite a number had been at school with our Sisters."[46] Even the administration appeared to support the Sisters; the SSJs reported that despite their concerns about a possible Catholic backlash, "the Sisters will be all right and wish Major Pratt as friendly as he is all will in time be satisfactorily arranged."[47]

Despite outward cordiality, school officials worried about the Catholic influence over students. In October 1909, Moses Friedman, the superintendent at Carlisle, sent the Bureau of Indian Affairs the "Rules Governing Catholic Students at the U.S. Indian Industrial School, Carlisle, PA."[48] Section XV emphasized that

> The Chaplain and Sisters pledge themselves to correspond sympathetically and work in full harmony with the rules of the school. . . . They promise in nowise to interfere with the workings of the School. In short, it will be their constant and sacred endeavor to assist the school officials to elevate the school to the highest degree of education efficiency.[49]

This rule emphasized that the Catholics working at Carlisle must align their goals with those of Carlisle, putting aside any other loyalties or beliefs. Despite working with the local Catholic clergy to accommodate the spiritual needs of the Catholic students, school officials worried that Catholics might subvert the school's goals. They therefore limited the Catholic missionaries' influence to specific types of religious instruction, and nothing else.

It is possible that the situation was similar in Oklahoma. The OSFs had already struggled with encouraging religion at the local federal school. In addition to taking care of the students at their own school, the Sisters were also in charge of the religious education of Catholic students at the local federal school. Such a situation was not unique to Oklahoma; Catholic Sisters also took charge of children's religious education at the Carlisle Indian Industrial School (previously discussed). The 1898 *Rules for the Indian School Service* stated that "Pupils shall be encouraged to attend churches and Sunday school of their respective denominations." Based on these rules, superintendents of the federal boarding schools had to allow Catholic students to receive a Catholic religious education. This declaration reflected a long-standing accommodation of Catholic belief, albeit reluctantly.

In the midst of secularizing educational policies, Catholic Sisters were caught between their roles as missionaries and educators. When in charge of a single school, as with the case of the OSFs, they struggled to find balance between the contradictory requirements set upon them by the federal government and the local clergy. However, when only affiliated with a school, such as the various communities that were with the Carlisle School, these women were free to fully follow their religious vocation.

CONCLUSION

Although affected by this policy change that heralded the age of "non-sectarian" schools, Protestant missionaries and educators ultimately supported the decision to defund the "sectarian schools" and withdrew their applications for funding. Protestants hoped that without federal support, Catholics would lose any influence they might have had with the Indigenous nations. Government officials also hoped that Indigenous students would join public schools, no longer creating a need for the boarding schools. That did not happen.[50]

Throughout this era of bureaucracy and impacted by the resulting changes, Catholic Sisters' work remained central to federal and Catholic attempts at assimilation. Throughout the 1860s to the early decades of the 1900s, they continued to open and run schools throughout the United States. There was no set pattern to these schools in terms of geography; the Catholic Sisters simply went where the local bishops called them. As we shall see in the next chapters, Catholic Sisters ran these schools to promote set ideas of white civilization and authority. To demonstrate their ability to do so, they created narratives that focused on their control of Indigenous bodies, education, identity, and politics.

NOTES

1. "For Sectarian Schools: Linton of Michigan Made Speech Against Appropriations," *The New North-West* (Deer Lodge, Montana), February 28, 1896.

2. "In Congress," *Arizona Republican* (Phoenix Arizona), June 6, 1896; "The Legislative Grind," *The Valentine Democrat* (Valentine, Nebraska), April 30, 1896; "The National Capital," *The Islander* (Friday Harbor, Washington), April 30, 1896; "Sectarian Schools," *The Frontier* (O'Neill City, Nebraska) April 30, 1896; "St. Louis Convention," *The American* (Omaha, Nebraska), July 3, 1896.

3. "Nor More Public Funds: Indian Catholic Schools Will Get No Public Money in the Future," *Union Country Courier* (Elk Point, Union County, D.T.), March 5, 1896.

4. "Deep Incensed," *Abilene Weekly Reflector* (Abilene Kansas), June 25, 1896.

5. See for example, "Championed by Mr. Vest," *The Guthrie Daily Leader* (Guthrie, OK), April 18, 1897; "Editorial and Local," *The Indian Advocate,* April 1899, 39; "The Indian Bill," *Marietta Daily Leader* (Marietta, OH), March 1, 1899; "Indian Education," *The Saint Paul Globe* (St. Paul, Minn.,) December 9, 1898; "Indian School Appropriation," *The Nebraska Advertiser* (Nemaha City, Nebraska), May 12, 1899; "National News," *The Progress* (Shreveport, LA), February 20, 1897; "Run Two Years Longer," *The Silver Blade* (Rathdrum, ID), April 25, 1896.

6. Reyhner and Eder, *American Indian Education*, 88–119.

7. Reyhner and Eder, *American Indian Education,* 88–119; Stancui, *The Making and Unmakings of Americans*, 81–115.

8. K. Tsianina Lomawaima, "Domesticity in the Federal Indian Schools: The Power of Authority over Mind and Body," *American Ethnologist* 20, no. 2 (1993): 230.

9. H.B. Peairs, quoted in Adams, *Education for Extinction*, 164.

10. "Home Mission Schools," *The Fulton County News* (McConnellsburg, PA), July 23, 1908.

For more on mission schools as well as the relationship between education, religion, and assimilation, see Conroy-Krutz, *Christian Imperialism*, 85–88, 110–114; Eittreim, *Teaching Empire*.

11. Office of Indian Affairs, *Rules for the Indian School Service* (Washington, DC: Government Printing Office, 1898), 25. According to Prucha, this rule was present in the 1894 and 1900 edition of the *Rules*. Prucha, *The Churches and the Indian Schools, 1888-1912*, 249, footnote 5.

12. Cato Sells, Letter to Moses Friedman, October 31, 1913, CISDRC.

13. "Religion is the mollifying influence . . . ," *The Indian Advocate,* January 1899, 12.

14. Peter Guilday, *A History of the Councils of Baltimore (1791-1884)* (New York: The MacMillan Company, 1932), 221–252; Rahill, *The Catholic Indian Missions and Grant's Peace Policy*, 325–341.

15. Pope Pius X, Apostolic Letter of Pius X in Commendation of the Society for the Preservation of the Faith Among Indian Children," April 3, 1908, reproduced in "The Indian Sentinel," 1910, AOSF, Pawhuska Correspondence, 1904–1911.

16. Rahill, *Catholic Missions and Grant's Peace Policy,* 25.

17. "The Future Indian Educational Policy of the Government," *The Indian Advocate,* April 1895, 32; "The Present Congress . . . ," *The Indian Advocate,* April 1896, 48.

18. The Bureau of Catholic Indian Missions, Circular to Superintendent of Catholic Indian Contract Schools, April 23, 1900, LHC, LHC06.D.03.002 Indian Industrial School Correspondence, 1890–1936, Bernalillo, BC 3-2.

19. "Says the *Catholic Review,*" *The Indian Advocate,* October 1897, 108.

20. Henry Ganss, "Our Work for the Indian," *The Indian Advocate,* May 1904.

21. "Unbelief and Citizenship," *The Indian Advocate,* August 1909, 273.

22. "We Pride Ourselves . . . " *The Indian Advocate* (Sacred Heart, OK), February 1910, 483.

23. Henry Ganss, "Our Work for the Indian," *The Indian Advocate,* May 1904.

24. "Mgr. Steven . . . ," *The Indian Advocate,* October 1896, 109.

25. "Evangelization of the Red Man," *The New York Herald* (New York [N.Y.]), October 11, 1875.

26. Henry Ganss, "Our Work for the Indian," *The Indian Advocate,* May 1904.

27. Amanda Bresie, "Mother Katharine Drexel's Benevolent Empire: The Bureau of Catholic Indian Missions and the Education of Native Americans, 1885–1935," *US Catholic Historian* 32 (2014): 1–24; Margaret McGuiness, *Katharine Drexel and the Sisters Who Shared Her Vision* (Mahwah, NJ: Paulist Press, 2023).

On Drexel's role at Carlisle see Catholic Students Receive Medals," *The Arrow,* April 20, 1908, CISDRC; "Concerning our Entertainments," *The Carlisle Arrow,* January 29, 1909, CISDRC; Sister Mary Paul, Letter to My Very Dear Mother, January 12, 1901, ASSJP; J. W. Shanahan, Letter to Mother Clemens, November 4, 1900, ASSJP; "Indians at St. Joseph's College," *The Red Man and Helper,* October 23, 1903, CISDRC; James A. MacAlister, Letter to Katharine Drexel, circa 1890–1899, CIRDRC.

28. "Red Lake Indians Want Catholic School," *The Tomahawk* (White Earth, Becker County, Minn.), May 17, 1917.

29. William Ketcham, reproduced in "Plea for the Catholic Indian Schools," *The Irish Standard* (Minneapolis, Minn), February 20, 1915.

30. Such laws on religious garb at schools started at the state level. For example, *The Indian Advocate* editorialized against a Pennsylvanian law outlawing religious garb in 1896 suggesting that "it is not enforced against Dunkards, Quakers, and other peculiar people employed in the public schools of that state. It is only used against Catholics." "Although the Religious Garb Bill . . . ," *The Indian Advocate,* April 1896, 43. Also see Prucha, *The Churches and Indian Schools,* 189–205.

31. J. A. Stephan, Letter to Rev. Sister Aquinata, July 31, 1899, AOSF, Pawhuska Correspondence, 1888-1904.

32. Mother M. Aloysia, Letter to Theophile Meerschaert, May 15, 1907, AOSF, Pawhuska Correspondence, 1904–1911.

33. Sister M. Olivia, Letter to Mother M. Aloysia, September 22, 1907, AOSF, Pawhuska Correspondence, 1904–1911.

34. There was also a dispute over who owned the school lands, with Meerschaert allegedly claiming the local diocese did. Meerschaert also claimed he had said no such thing. J. A. Stephan, Letter to Rev. Sister Aquinata, July 31, 1899, AOSF, Pawhuska Correspondence, 1888–1904; Theophile Meerschaert, Letter to Monseigneur Stephan, September 7, 1899, AOSF, Pawhuska Correspondence, 1888–1904; J.A. Stephan, Letter to Rev. Sister Aquinata, September 16, 1899, AOSF, Pawhuska Correspondence, 1888–1904.

35. J. A. Stephan, Letter to Rev. Sistere Aquinata, July 31, 1899, AOSF, Pawhuska Correspondence, 1888–1904.

36. St. Louis Indian School, Pawhuska Oklahoma Visit, October 29, 1906, AOSF, Pawhuska Correspondence, 1904–1911.

37. May 17, 1908, Annals, 3.

38. Richard H. Pratt, *The Indian Industrial School, Carlisle, Pennsylvania: Its Origins, Purposes, Progress, and the Difficulties Surmounted* (Carlisle, PA: Cumberland County Historical Society, 1979), 18–19.

39. The Red Man, June, July, & August 1894, CISDR.

40. H. G. Ganss, Letter to Mother M. Clemens, November 17, 1900, ASSJP.

41. Davis, "To Keep the Catholics Intact," 1–20; Prucha, *The Churches and the Indian Schools,* 39, 162–184; SBSS Annals, 57, SBSS, AADP; G. Ganss, *History of St. Patrick's Church* (Philadelphia, PA: D. J. Gallagher & Co., 1895), 35–215; Gardner Digital Library, *St. Patrick's Catholic Church,* accessed November 8, 2022, http://gardnerlibrary.org/encyclopedia/st-patrick%E2%80%99s-catholic-church; Linda V. Itzoe, *Highway of Missionaries: An Illustrated History of the Diocese of Harrisburg* (Strasbourg: Editions du Signe, 2006), 35, 94.

42. Davis, "To Keep the Catholics Intact," 1–20; Prucha, *The Churches and the Indian Schools,* 39, 162–184; SBSS Annals, pg. 57, SBSS AADP.

43. School Records for Catherine Sawati, CISDRC; School records for Hattie Sawati, CISDRC; School Records for John Sawati; School records for Josephine Sawati, CISDRC; School records for Mary Sawati, CISDRC; School records for Thomas Sawati, CISDRC; Bresie, "Katharine Drexel's Benevolent Empire"; McGlone, *Anything of Which a Woman is Capable,* 113–117; Sr. M. Georgiana Rockwell, *St. Katharine's Hall: Carlisle, Pennsylvania- The Unfolding Apostolate of the Sisters of the Blessed Sacrament-1906-1918* (Bensalem, PA: Sisters of the Blessed Sacrament, 1980).

44. H.G. Ganss, Letter to Mother M. Clemens, 17 November 1900, ASSJP.

45. "Catherine Tekakwitha Notes," *The Carlisle Arrow,* February 28, 1913; "General School News," *The Carlisle Arrow,* October 23, 1908; "General School News," *The Carlisle Arrow,* October 28,1910; "General School News," *The Carlisle Arrow,* February 24, 1911; "George Bearsarms," *The Red Indian and Helper,* January 9, 1903; "The Girls' Holy Name Society," *The Carlisle Arrow,* February 20, 1914; "The Girls Holy Name Society," *The Carlisle Arrow,* October 10, 1913; "The Girls Holy Name Society," *The Carlisle Arrow,* November 14, 1913; "The Girls' Holy Name Society," *The Carlisle Arrow,* February 20, 1914; "The Girls' Holy Name

Society," *The Carlisle Arrow,* September 19, 1913; "The Girls' Holy Name Society," *The Carlisle Arrow,* October 17, 1913; "General School News," *The Carlisle Arrow,* February 25, 1916; "The Holy Name Society," *The Carlisle Arrow,* June 2, 1916. All from CISDRC.

46. Sister M. Paul, Letter to Very Dear Mother, January 9, 1901, ASSJP.

47. Sister Mary Paul, Letter to My Very Dear Mother, January 9, 1901, ASSJP.

48. Moses Friedman, Letter to J.H. Dortch, October 29, 1909, CISDRC.

49. "Rules Governing Catholic Students at the U.S. Indian Industrial School, Carlisle, PA," 1908, CISDRC.

50. Reyhner, *American Indian Education,* 88–119.

Chapter 6

Constrictions on the Sisters of St. Francis and the Pawhuska Mission, Oklahoma, 1887–1915

In the Fall of 1902, things looked grim at the St. Louis School for Osage Indian Girls in Pawhuska, "Indian Territory" (today Oklahoma). Run by the Sisters of St. Francis of Philadelphia (the OSFs) since 1887, the school administrators were frustrated with contracts stuck in limbo between the Sisters and the Department of the Interior. To add to the problem, school enrollment was down and the Sisters worried they would lose their contract and funding. Things only got worse in November when Sister Gerard, the superior at the school, wrote to Father Joseph A. Stephan, the head of the BCIM, that the local "Agent has taken 11 children that were enrolled here and placed them in the Government School."[1] The following month, she wrote again, stating that after the Sisters sent law enforcement officers after a truant student, the local Marshall returned the student to the federal school rather than their school.[2] Not only did the Sisters have administrative issues, but they now had to contend with the government officials transferring their students to the federal school without notice or permission. Would the OSFs be able reclaim it since they would be going against the U.S. government? After all, the success of their mission was now in jeopardy.

Chapter 2 examined how the Sisters of Loretto worked to establish their authority over the Osage communities with whom they worked. In the 1840s through 1860s, the Sisters worked to establish their authority as being higher than those of the parents, who wanted a role in the student's education and behavior. By the 1880s, the Osage had worked with Catholic missionaries for several decades. They were a known entity, who the Osage appeared to have acknowledged had authority over the students. However, in Oklahoma, the Sisters faced a challenge from another authority: the federal government and federal boarding school. Faced with this new threat, the Sisters had to find a way to take control over who made decisions for these students.

Like the Sisters of Lorettos' school, the OSFs' was a contract school. Contract schools were not run by government agents but other educators, particularly religious communities. They received funding from the federal government through a yearly round of contract renewals. Religious denominations ran most, if not all, of these schools, with Catholics dominating the greater majority. While contract schools had existed since the 1820s, it was only in the era after the Civil War that these contracts became more formalized, employing set renewal processes. Politics interfused these proceedings, reflecting the tides of anti-Catholic backlash at the end of the nineteenth century, as previously discussed in chapter 5.

BACKGROUND

The geography of "Indian Territory" changed multiple times in the nineteenth century.[3] While the U.S. government concentrated on removing eastern Native nations west after the Louisiana Purchase of 1803, it was not until 1830 that it defined "Indian Territory" in terms of specific geography and administration. The original "Indian Territory" comprised modern-day Oklahoma, Kansas, Nebraska, and parts of the Dakotas. In 1844, the government determined that the Platt River, which corresponded with the infamous line in the Missouri Compromise that divided slave states from free states, would be the territory's northern border. The geographical borders shrank further after the Kansas-Nebraska Act of 1854, which created a new southern line of Kansas. In 1889, the government opened the area to white (and Black) settlement, further limiting the lands "granted" to Indigenous persons. The land would be further divided with the creation of new states; Oklahoma became one in 1907.[4]

In the 1870s, the Osage bought land in Oklahoma, although some of the community remained in Kansas. However, violence from white settlers forced most remaining to move to "Indian Territory." Following the purchase, the nation was land-rich in Oklahoma, with their new reservation totaling approximately 1,460,000 acres.[5] There was a white perception that the Osage were a prosperous nation. A 1904 article from the Oklahoma paper, *The Chickasha Daily Express*, described the Osage as "The richest of the Indian tribes" due to an abundance of oil and natural gas on their reservation.[6] The Osage did have access to these resources, although white settlers raced to the reservation to stake their claim. The tribe even made money by leasing some of their land to Texas ranchers.[7]

In the late 1880s and throughout the 1890s, there was public outrage about the perceived wealth of the Osage. An 1898 article in the Maysville, Kentucky, *Daily Public Ledger* was derisive of the Osage:

The Osage Indians are the richest community in the world. They number but 1,729 souls . . . they own 1,500,000 acres of valuable land; have $9,000,000 in trust with the Government . . . They have so much money that they are lazy, idle and in a state of rapid degeneration.

The *El Paso Daily Herald* reported that same year that "there is no more striking example of the corrupting influences of wealth and idleness."[8] Unsurprisingly, newspapers reported in 1899 and 1900 that several families might file for bankruptcy due to their spending habits.[9]

Despite these perceptions, the Osage struggled in a variety of ways. The Osage were unused to the climate in Oklahoma and struggled to live off the land. They did not start to consistently receive money from the government until 1879. Like other nations, the government required parents to send their children to one of the assimilationist schools, either the Pawhuska federal school (established in 1874) or one of the two Catholic schools.[10]

There were multiple other concerns. One of the most prevalent was a conflict with the Cherokee, who controlled most of what became Oklahoma. An 1871 letter from a Catholic missionary described,

The poor Indians have sold all their land & now are wandering on the cherokee's [*sic*] lands without a home: the Agent built them a saw mill in the "Indian Territory" but the cherokees [*sic*] sent them an injunction forbidding them to cut saw timber on the cherokee [*sic*] lands.[11]

It took time to work out the question of whose territory was whose and who controlled what resources.

Like so many others, the Osage struggled to remain autonomous from the U.S. government. In 1881, the Osage in Oklahoma established their constitution, forming a representative government. However, the Bureau of Indian Affairs did not approve and, in 1900, dismantled and replaced it with a new internal government that would remain largely under the control of agents from the Bureau of Indian Affairs. The Osage also worked hard to keep communal lands but were forced to acquiesce to U.S. government interference. In 1906, they gave up most of their land, dividing the rest into land allotments. They were one of the last tribal nations to do so. The process took several years due to legal and tribal challenges to the system, particularly the equality of the divisions. In 1909, *The Vinita Daily Chieftain* reported that each person would receive 660 acres of land, of which they might sell 500 acres. Most of the former Osage and Cherokee lands became the state of Oklahoma.[12] It was this situation that the Catholic missionaries re-acquainted themselves with the Osage.

EARLY MISSIONARIES TO INDIAN TERRITORY

Catholics did not immediately prioritize the "Indian Territory." Some Jesuit missionaries and itinerant priests from St. Louis and Little Rock visited the area. Other groups, such as the Quakers, set up their own missions.[13] Even Father William Ketcham, who oversaw the Bureau of Catholic Indian Missions, admitted the slowness of their effort in "Indian Territory," writing in 1903 that if the Catholic Church "seems to have been slow in taking an active part in the missionary and educational field offered by the 'Indian Territory,' this tardiness was due to circumstances over which she had no control."[14] Missionaries initially worked with the Choctaws and Chickasaws, later expanding their work to the Apache, Cherokee, Comanche, Quapaw, and Osage (whom the government had forcefully removed from Kansas).[15]

Given their previous relationship with Catholic missionaries in Kansas, the Osage requested that the government grant these same groups permission to work with them again in Oklahoma. In 1878, Father John Schoenmakers, who had worked with the Osage in Kansas, wrote that the Osage council

> unanimously asked for Catholic Schools they could have them, along with the Quakers school, provided the Catholics build their own school improvements; of course, these terms will not be accepted, as Catholic priests cannot live among the Osages without some means of support.[16]

They received little.

The Benedictines were the initial long-term missionaries to the area, arriving in 1875. Benedictine Felix DeGrasse founded the original mission that worked with the Osage in Oklahoma. This location was also the home of a federal boarding school for Osage girls (founded 1874), which could house up to 180 students.[17] The priest lived an itinerant life, traveling most of the Osage reservation. Soon, the Benedictines started campaigning for a mission school, receiving funding from the Society for the Propagation of the Faith (an organization that funded religious missionary work worldwide), parishes in France and Katharine Drexel. A newspaper article from 1893 described this first mission as "a house for two priests, a boarding school for seventy-five children and a convent for seven Sisters. . . . Our school was crowded to its utmost capacity and giving full satisfaction to the Indians."[18]

The Benedictine Sisters joined the fathers, running a school for girls. Other communities soon joined them, including the Sisters of St. Francis, the Sisters of Loretto, the Sisters of the Blessed Sacrament, the Sisters of St. Joseph, and the Sisters of Mercy. Key to the success of the Catholic missions were the railroads. By 1891, three railroads traveled through Oklahoma Territory, running north to south and limiting quick east to west travel. Catholic missionaries and authorities, such as the bishops, used railroads to visit all the missions.[19]

To laud their work, the Benedictines actively wrote to the Society for the Propagation of the Faith, an organization that had overseen Catholic missionary work since 1822, detailing their daily lives and requesting funds.[20] They also published a monthly paper, *The Indian Advocate,* between 1888 and 1910. Produced and published near Shawnee, Oklahoma, the goal of the *Advocate* was to document "the progress of civilization in 'Indian Territory,' by promoting the spiritual as well as temporal welfare of the Indian race."[21] The periodical praised the work of the missionaries, not only the Benedictines but other communities stationed at the schools and reservations.

Catholic missionaries ultimately ran a total of 14 schools for Native children in Oklahoma. Of these, the OSFs ran five: St. Elizabeth School in Purcell (1888–1948), St. John's School in Hominy Creek (operated by the Sisters 1888–1907; open 1888–1913), St. Joseph's Academy in Chickasha (1899–1968), St Louis School for Osage Indian Girls in Pawhuska (run by the OSFs 1887–1915; operated 1887–1949), and St. Patrick Indian Mission in Anadarko (1892–1965). This chapter focuses only on the St. Louis School for Osage Indian Girls.[22] (See figure 6.1.)

The Sisters of St. Francis originated in Pennsylvania, in the diocese of Philadelphia, in 1855. Established by three women and commissioned by the Bishop of Philadelphia, John Neumann, the community worked with the

Figure 6.1 Image of St. Louis School for Girls. *Source: Courtesy of Oklahoma Historical Society.*

rising number of immigrants to the city. The Sisters expanded their social work, creating schools and hospitals for those within their care. The community expanded quickly, establishing institutions in Delaware, Maryland, New York, and Rhode Island. It was under the persuasion of Katharine Drexel and Father Stephan of the BCIM (introduced in chapter 5) that the Sisters decided to expand westward, coming to Oklahoma in 1887. The original missionaries came from the house at Glen Riddle.[23]

The Sisters of St. Francis established the St. Louis School for Osage Girls in late 1887. The school was well situated, located just west of Pawhuska, the home of the Osage government since 1872. The boarding school initially contained 4 Sisters and 85 students. The school catered mainly to Osage students, with whom the Sisters of Loretto (the second group to work at the school) would have been familiar, after their work on the Osage Mission in Kansas (see chapter 2 for more analysis).[24] Like other schools in this book, the OSFs provided a variety of education courses. A 1910 school profile in *The Indian Sentinel* reported that, in addition to music and "a thorough grammar-school training," students took courses "in the domestic arts, such as sewing dressmaking, baking, cooking, housekeeping, and laundering."[25]

As with most schools, we have little information about the students and what happened after they left the school. A 1910 profile of the school reported that "one of the former pupils of the School, a mixed-blood, is now a Franciscan nun, belongs to the faculty of the school, and is a successful instructor."[26] However, I have not found more specific information on this woman.

CONTRACTS AND FUNDING

In addition to the politics within the Catholic community, the OSFs had to compete with the federal schools and there was an apparent feeling of ill-will between the two. An 1893 article in *the Indian Advocate* stated that "The success of our school had been regarded with jealousy by the officials of the Government school and by a certain Methodist outfit" noting that "In spite of the ill-will of Government officials a first contract for the education of fifty Indian children was secured" in 1890 (this contract appears to be for religious education).[27] The competition between the two particularly influenced contract negotiations.

Like the other contract schools, the Sisters' school depended on government funds. The timeline of their work in Pawhuska corresponded with an era of government re-allotment of school funding, focusing on funding Protestant endeavors over Catholic ones. This meant that the federal school in Pawhuska would have had priority over St. Louis. The BCIM realized that many Catholic contract schools would have to close without government funds, so they fought against this reassignment of funds, emphasizing their history of work and past successes with the various Native communities.[28] Regarding the St. Louis School, Father Stephan outlined the situation in an 1899 letter, writing that if

> Government aid be withdrawn from the school, it will be impossible to keep the school in operation as a mission school, for there are no funds available for that purpose, and the result would be that the work of your community among the Osages would have to stop, and this Bureau would be forced to rent or sell the school to the government.[29]

The OSFs, therefore, had to do everything they could to keep the school going.

Between 1904 and 1910, there were continuous crises over contracts and funding. Contracts arrived late, leading to questions about the future of the school. The renewal date varied; for example, in 1905, Sister Gerard, the superior, asked Father Ketcham if the contract would be renewed. Ketcham responded that he would not find out until January and the contracts would probably not be signed until March. When faced with the possibility of a canceled contract, the Sisters networked with the local Osage leaders to get their contract renewed. However, it is unclear how effective this tactic was since the United States had disbanded the Osage's original governmental structure in 1900 and replaced it with one of their own that was under the control of the local agency, effectively limiting the authority and influence of the Osage political leaders.[30]

There were also concerns about the terms of the contract. At times, the Sisters found that the contract was not beneficial to them, such as the concern over the number of students in 1902, which led to attempts at negotiations and politicking. Worried about the lower enrollment, Sister Gerard wrote in 1902, "I spoke to the Governor and he thinks I did right not to sign the contract and also said he will do all he can to get me a contract for all we can take."[31] In 1909, the contract terms changed, allowing the Sisters to have students under 6 and over 20 and to receive medical services from the agency. In 1910, the Sisters faced losing their contract, causing them to advocate among the local Native community and agency leaders to maintain their place. Funding was also always an issue, with the OSFs regularly reporting that their government vouchers had not arrived. The school at Pawhuska was not alone in these issues; the BCIM reported to the OSFs in 1908 that they'd hired an attorney "to protect our interests."[32] Not only the school in Oklahoma was struggling, but all those overseen by the BCIM.

The insecurity about the contracts reflected the ongoing financial concerns. The Sisters were always struggling to find ways to feed the children, pay their bills, and more.[33] In 1899, this included requesting permission to have day students in addition to boarders. Such an idea would have brought in greater funds due to increased enrollment. However, Father Stephan pushed back against this idea, stating that it might lead to confusion over the purpose of the school since a boarding school for Indigenous persons had to follow set guidelines with an explicit emphasis on round-the-clock assimilation. Also, developing a second contract for the day school might lead to a delay in contracts or even the cancelation of contracts.[34]

The era of contract insecurity coincided with a larger trend in the boarding schools of defunding the contract schools. In response to these cuts, the BCIM argued that the local tribes should be allowed to choose how their funds were allotted. Father Ketcham even met with President Theodore Roosevelt in early 1904, arguing this case and gaining Roosevelt's support. Roosevelt held a meeting in favor of such a measure, as long as federal law did not already restrict said funds. Such a rule caused immense outrage among Protestants who believed that Catholics were abusing their authority and the tribal communities among whom they worked. The Indian Rights Association, led by its Baptist members, petitioned against the renewal of Catholic contracts and the choice of the tribes but was largely rebuffed. However, fights in Congress continued, with the BCIM continuing to argue that its schools were legitimate.[35]

Had the St.Louis School and other Catholic schools been fully defunded and closed, the students would have been transferred to the local federal schools. The federal schools would have seen an increase in funding, reflecting the new enrollment.

The OSFs were by no means the only group to deal with funding and other bureaucratic concerns. For example, when working with the Osage in Kansas in the 1840s, the Lorettines (chapter 2) struggled with oversight and finances. In 1847, the Jesuits reported that "the Osage Sub-Agency had been transferred to the Southern Superintendence, and that no money had been received for that purpose," questioning who would fund the mission in Kansas.[36] The missionaries wondered who would pay for their work and if their contract would be transferred to another group.[37] This type of contract concern was rather standard. However, the Lorettines faced a trickier situation with a later school in New Mexico.

The Lorettines faced worse funding issues when working in New Mexico at the Bernalillo School (1885–1935). According to a letter from Father Stephan that was recorded in the Sisters Annals, the Sisters stated that they had lost funding upon "alleg[ations] that the children carried on the contract school roll are not Indians." Father Stephan alleged that the accusations came from a person "whom I have never heard as a Government official" and who submitted an "unsupported report." He requested that the Lorettines receive their back-funds with due hast, as "the closing of this school will deprive seventy or more children of the means of an education. . . . and will certainly cripple for many years educational work in that Territory [Oklahoma]."[38]

It is possible that this incident was an attempt to challenge the authority of the Sisters. In an undated, handwritten source from the Bernalillo school, a chronicler, possibly a rough draft of the memoirs of one of the educators at the school, Sister Margaret Mary Keenan, recorded that the Sisters worked with the Pueblo. The Pueblo, according to the source, did not want to participate within the assimilationist attempts of the Catholic missionaries, and so "the council had decided not to let the girls attend any school." The source suggested that the Pueblo were terrified that having girls go to missions and federal schools would cause the girls to "get married & forsake the Pueblo which would cause the Pueblo soon to be broken up." The source noted that male education was fine, as it was believed that educated boys "would remain" with the community, while girls would not.[39] The handwritten source does not date the incident of the council decision, though context clues suggest it was in the 1890s. Could the report, suggesting that the students at the school were not Native, have come from the Pueblo as an attempt to keep the female students out of the school? Was the funding crisis a result of a moment of Native resistance? It is possible.

Whatever the cause, the BCIM took direct action regarding the funding crisis at the Lorettines' Bernalillo school, filing a case that sought reimbursement for the school from 1892 and 1893. In May 1894, Charles Lusk, who stood at the attorney representing the Lorettines, wrote that the Sisters would receive some of the money the government had withdrawn. Lusk noted that the process had been difficult, and "the Indian Office declined to reopen the case, and forced me to go before the Accounting Officers of the Treasury, where I won it."[40] Moreover, Lusk was able to expedite the process of reimbursement for some of the funds, so that the Sisters could receive some of the funds they had requested, although the process proved to be a long and frustrating one, similar to what the OSFs experienced in Oklahoma.[41]

Aside from questions of finance and contracts, the OSFs had other administrative hiccups as they competed with the federal school, even inadvertently. One headache came in 1910 over when the school year would start. Before 1910, the private and federal boarding schools had operated on approximately the same schedule. However, in 1910, the government changed the schedule so that the federal schools started in October while the Catholic schools continued to have the start of their term in September. The Sisters appreciated that timeline for the beginning of the school year, which coincided with "about the close of the Osage quarterly payment."[42] The timing of the payment was key for "If we opened later, the parents would return home with their children and it would be a difficult matter to have them return again by Oct."[43] The sources suggest that there remained confusion over the start of the school year. However, in

November, the Sisters reported that they had not been informed about the federal school opening on September 15 which coincided with the Catholic plans. This led to confusion as the Sisters tried to ensure that all enrolled students arrived on time.[44] If the students were not there, federal officials could suggest that the Sisters had reneged on their contract and limited funds or not renew it.

STEALING STUDENTS

Key to running a successful school was student enrollment and attendance. The Sisters' contracts specified various details, such as the ages of the students or how many students they were required to have enrolled to continue receiving funding. The number of contractually specified students often varied from the number attending.[45] The terms of the contracts reflected the number of enrolled students at the school during the academic year.

The issue of enrollment and attendance was a bit tricky, not just for the Sisters but also for federal schools. A study on the Chilocco School in Oklahoma noted that schools continuously admitted students to bolster their attendance numbers, which shifted due to disease, death, and desertion. For example, if a school stated it had 500 students at the beginning and end of the year, there was a good chance that not all these students had made it through the whole year. Schools were desperate to keep the number of students high, knowing any decline would lead to a decline in funding.[46]

Questions over enrollment and attendance came to the forefront in 1902 when the Sisters complained that government officials were taking students from their school and moving them to the federal school. The school struggled to keep its enrollment numbers up when Sister Gerard wrote to Father Stephan, "Agent has taken 11 children that were enrolled here and placed them in the Government School. I do not wish to complain but we have 68 now and I am anxious to keep them."[47] The priest expressed concern and further inquired into the matter. However, things worsened, with Sister Gerard writing later in December 1902 that a girl returned home with family but did not return to school at the expected time, so they sent a "Marshall" after the girl. Rather than returning the student to St. Louis, the police delivered the girl to the federal school.[48]

One of the key points to the conflict was the students' previous enrollment status. According to Sister Gerard, several had been at the federal school the previous year before transferring to St. Louis. Moreover, the agent stated that the Sisters did not have legal permission, although the Sisters did state they did.[49] Sister Gerard argued that she did have permission, stating that several adults had granted these students permission to go to the Sisters' school. She caveated to her claim in January 1903 by noting,

Now whether these are their legal guardians or not, I cannot positively say. However, I suppose that they were and that they had the same privileges as parents and therefore made no distinction. I will find out as soon as possible if they are their legal guardians and inform you.[50]

She was stymied by the agent's claim that he was the one in charge of making decisions regarding these students' education, exclaiming,

If Agent Mitscher is the legal guardian of those children, why did he let them remain at the St. Louis School from September 15 until October 14. He knew that they were in this School from the very time that they were enrolled.[51]

It is unclear why the students transferred to the OSFs' school. While the Osage had a long history of requesting a Catholic education, it is also possible that the Sisters' work at the federal school influenced this decision. The Sisters' correspondence does not indicate that they had met these students in catechism classes or other religious instructions, though such a situation is plausible. Could their relationship with these students have led to their guardians sending their children to a new school? Given a lack of sources, we cannot conclusively know, only postulate.

The Sisters turned to everyone they could to get the students back, including the BCIM and the now-Mother Katharine Drexel, SBS. At first, Mother Drexel initially voiced her promise of support, but by August 1903, she told Sister Gerard that she could no longer help.[52] The BCIM tried too to support the Sisters, but had other concerns as it fought with the government over budget cuts and nullified contracts (discussed further below).

The question of guardianship was interesting. An 1891 law allowed government agents to take children, by force if necessary, and place them in assimilationist schools, a shift from previous laws. This policy would change in 1917, when parents and guardians were required to give permission. However, the question was also that of off-reservation schools, such as the Carlisle Indian Industrial School. As of 1893, the federal government already required the student's parent's or guardian's permission to send a child to an off-reservation school.[53]

The larger fight over the Catholic schools' contracts made the situation more confusing. As Congress and other interested groups debated whether the local tribes could allot money specifically to the Catholic missions, some brought student attendance into the fray. Senator John T. Morgan argued in 1905 that it should not be the parents who decide where to send their children, but rather that of the parent's guardian, that is, the U.S. government. In doing so, Morgan hoped to focus on sending students to federal schools and defunding the Catholic missions.[54]

While Morgan's comments came a few years after the crisis in Pawhuska, it is not a leap to think that the government agent may have used this same logic when dealing with the Sisters. The debate over who had the power to grant permission to the students, emphasizing guardianship, foreshadows this later argument on the defunding of the Catholic missions. The OSFs were not the only ones to deal with fights over where the children should attend. In 1895, the director wrote to Father Harrity in Philadelphia, stating that the Bureau, not him, was biased against Catholic students. He gave an example:

> On one occasion, I requested an additional contract for 10 pupils who were being educated at one of our contract schools in excess of the quota. This request was refused on the plea of a lack of funds. A month or so later, the Secretary granted a request for 50 pupils to be placed in a Protestant contract school in Arizona.[55]

The director of the Catholic Bureau of Indian Missions insisted that he was restrained by the institutional anti-Catholicism that plagued the Bureau of Indian Affairs.

Concerns continued over which school children would attend. In 1908, BCIM secretary Charles Lusk wrote to Sister Gerard:

> I think it would be better that authority be obtained from the Commissioner of Indian Affairs for the enrollment in your school of the five children who were attending the Government school last year, but as you did not give the names of these children, I cannot ask for the necessary authority. You should, therefore, request the Commissioner to give the desired authority . . . stating that these children were transferred to your school with his consent, and recommending that your request be granted.[56]

Unfortunately, it is unclear what happened. However, the school remained opened.

CONCLUSION

In 1915, the Sisters of Loretto, who had worked with the Osage in Kansas from the 1840s through the 1860s, took over St. Louis School. The Loretto's archives described one reaction as "[rejoicing] that her Indians are once more under the care of Loretto."[57] The SBSs took over the school in 1942, renaming it St. Louis Academy. The school closed in 1949.[58] Nothing suggests that Lorettines or SBSs faced the troubles that the OSFs had. After all, attacks against Catholic contract schools increased after 1915 as the government sought to find more cost-effective ways to assimilate Indigenous persons.[59]

The tensions between the Sisters of St. Francis and the government over contracts demonstrates the multi-faceted struggles Catholic Sisters faced in asserting their authority over the contract schools. The success of the school relied on the number of the students enrolled, both in terms of receiving funding but also in terms of fulfilling mission. They were not alone in their struggles, but provide a case study. Yet, these debates were more than just about contracts; they were about who was in charge of the students. The Sisters fought to keep people they believed under their authority and control. To lose students would have meant failure in their mission. After all, how can you convert, if there is no one to convert?

NOTES

1. Sister Gerard, Letter to William Ketcham, November 4, 1902, Pawhuska Correspondence, 1888–1904, AOSF.

2. Sister Gerard, Letter to William Ketcham, December 15, 1902, Pawhuska Correspondence, 1888–1904.

3. Throughout this chapter, I use the term "Indian Territory." While this term is extremely troublesome and inaccurate (tribal nations were supposed to have land in this area, but it was continuously re-allotted to white settlers), it reflects the language of the period. When possible, I focus on specific locations or use "Oklahoma," which is the modern location of the OSFs' missions.

4. Throughout this chapter, I use the term "Indian Territory." While this term is extremely troublesome and inaccurate (tribal nations were supposed to have land in this area, but it was continuously re-allotted to white settlers), it reflects the language of the period. When possible, I focus on specific locations or use "Oklahoma," which is the modern location of the OSFs' missions; Joseph Murphy, *Tenacious Monks: The Oklahoma Benedictines, 1875-1975: Indian Missionaries, Catholic Founders, Educators, Agriculturists* (Shawnee, OK: Benedictine Color Press, 1974), 1–3.

5. "Among the Osage," *The Chickasha Daily Express* (Chickasha, "Indian Territory" [Okla.]), November 28, 1904; "Official Government Notice," *Tulsa Daily World* (Tulsa, "Indian Territory" [Okla.]), December 21, 1905; "Osage Allotments," *The Daily Ardmoreite* (Ardmore, Okla.), June 21, 1907; "Osage Indians Get 660 Acres Each," *The Vinita Daily Chieftain* (Vinita, "Indian Territory" [Okla.]), March 3, 1909.

Also see Blue Clark, *Indian Tribes of Oklahoma: A Guide* (Norman, OK: University of Oklahoma Press, 2009), 232–246; Janet Berry Hess, *Osage, and Settler: Reconstructing Shared History through an Oklahoma Family Archive* (Jefferson, NC: McFarland & Co., Publishers, 2015), 11–38.

6. "Among the Osage," *The Chickasha Daily Express* (Chickasha, "Indian Territory" [Okla.]), November 28, 1904.

7. Clark, *Indian Tribes of Oklahoma*, 232–246; Hess, *Osage, and Settler*, 11–38.

8. "The Osage Indians…," *Daily Public Ledger* (Maysville, Ky.), April 7, 1898; "Rich and Degenerate," *El Paso Daily Herald* (El Paso, Tex.), March 31, 1898.

Also see "From the "Indian Territory"," *The Russellville Democrat* (Russellville, Ark.), August 8, 1889; "Legislation for Indians Lands of the Five Civilized Tribes to be Apportion-Lazy Osages," *The Indianapolis Journal* (Indianapolis [Ind.]), December 15, 1897; "The Osage Indians are the Richest People in the World," *Audubon County Republican* (Audubon Co., Iowa), August 29, 1889; "Osage Indians By Far the Richest Nation in the World. Each Member of the Tribe is a Dissolute Nabob," *Clinch Valley News* (Jeffersonville, Va.), October 18, 1889; "Some Wealthy Indians," *The Morning News* (Savannah, Ga.), September 17, 1894; "They are Aristocrats," *The Madison Daily Leader* (Madison, S.D.), November 18, 1898.

9. "Osages Indians Come to the Front for Benefit of Bankrupt Law," *The Daily Ardmoreite* (Ardmore, Okla.), January 23, 1900; "Osages in Debt," *The Daily Ardmoreite* (Ardmore, Okla.), September 5, 1899; "Osages in Debt," *Passaic City Record* (Passaic City, N.J.), September 23, 1899.

10. Clark, *Indian Tribes of Oklahoma*, 232–246; Hess, *Osage and Settler*, 11–38.

11. Father Schoenmaker, Letter to Sister Mary Coaninoi Mongrain, February 27, 1871, LCH, Kansas Osage Mission Rev John Shonoemaker, SJ box 3-3.

12. "Among the Osage," *The Chickasha Daily Express* (Chickasha, "Indian Territory" [Okla.]), November 28, 1904; Clark, *Indian Tribes of Oklahoma*, 232–246; Hess, *Osage and the Settler*, 11–38, 93–107; "Official Government Notice," *Tulsa Daily World* (Tulsa, "Indian Territory" [Okla.]), December 21, 1905; "Osage Allotments," *The Daily Ardmoreite* (Ardmore, Okla.), June 21, 1907; "Osage Indians Get 660 Acres Each," *The Vinita Daily Chieftain* (Vinita, "Indian Territory" [Okla.]), March 3, 1909.

Also see Clark, *Indian Tribes of Oklahoma*, 232–246; Hess, *Osage, and Settler*, 11–38.

13. Murphy, *Tenacious Monks*, 1–26.

14. William Ketcham, "Catholic Educational Efforts in Two Territories," *The Indian Advocate* (Sacred Heart, OK), January 1, 1903, 20.

15. "Among the Osages," *The Indian Advocate,* April 1, 1893, 21–23; "Catholic Institutions of Oklahoma Territory," *The Guthrie Daily Leader* (Guthrie, OK), May 9, 1905; "The Quapaws III Work of the Catholic Church Among the Quapaws in the "Indian Territory"," *The Indian Advocate*, August 1, 1904, 250–253.

Also see Stephan Byrne, *Catholic Colonization in the Southwest: Arkansas, Texas, Louisiana, "Indian Territory", and New Mexico* (Chicago, IL: Rand, McNally, and Company, 1882), 50–51; William Ketcham, "Catholic Educational Efforts in Two Territories," *The Indian Advocate,* January 1, 1903, 20–25; Blanche E. Little, "Catholic Schools for Indians in the Oklahoma and Indian Territories," *The Indian Advocate,* October 1, 1899, 101–104; Oklahoma List, "Catholic Truth & Healing," accessed June 26, 2023, https://ctah.archivistsacwr.org/list/cat/oklahoma/.

16. Father Schoenmaker, Letter to Sister M. Cosina, March 8, 1878, LCH, Kansas Osage Mission Rev John Shonoemaker, SJ box 3-3.

17. "Miss Reel Teels About Indian Schools," *The Guthrie Daily Leader,* July 19, 1901.

18. "Among the Osage," *The Indian Advocate* 5, no. 2 (April 1, 1893). Also see MPFL 14 Propagation of Faith 1886–1900, NDA.

19. James D. White, "Essay: The Life of Theophile Meerschaert," in *Diary of a Frontier Bishop: The Journals of Theophile Meerschaert,* ed. James D. White (Tulsa,

OK: The Sarto Press, 1994), 14; Bryan C. Rindfleisch and Martha G. Beliveau, "The History and Uncomfortable Legacy of St. Patrick's Mission Indian School, Anadarko, Oklahoma, 1892-1966," *U.S. Catholic Historian* 41, no. 3 (Summer 2023): 53–54.

20. It was not just the Benedictines who reported to the Propagation of Faith, but also the local bishop. Such sources can be found in the Propagation of the Faith records at Notre Dame University, specifically MPFL 14 Propagation of Faith 1886-1900, NDA.

21. "About the Indian Advocate," *Chronicling America,* accessed June 1, 2023, https://chroniclingamerica.loc.gov/lccn/45043535/.

22. When reading through the Sisters' archival sources, the St. Louis School had the most documentation. Moreover, it is the earliest school run by the Sisters.
     Byrne, *Catholic Colonization in the Southwest,* 50–51; Ketcham, "Catholic Educational Efforts in Two Territories," 20–25; Oklahoma List, "Catholic Truth & Healing."

23. Adele Francis Gorman, *Celebrating the Journey, Volume II: History of the Sisters of St. Francis of Philadelphia 1855-1970* (Philadelphia, PA: Sisters of St. Francis of Philadelphia 2005); A member of the Community, "Sisters of the Third Order of St. Francis, 1855-1928," *Records of the American Catholic Historical Society* 40, no. 4 (December 1929): 347–381; Sisters of the Third Order of St Francis, *Institute of the Sisters of the Third Order of St. Francis: Philadelphia Foundation 1855-1964* (Glen Riddle, PA: Motherhouse and Novitiate Convent of Our Lady of Angels, 1963).

24. The school was initially under the directorate of the Prefecture Apostolic and later Vicariate Apostolic of "Indian Territory," between 1887 and 1905, and then the Diocese of Oklahoma (1905–1930), and finally the Diocese of Oklahoma City and Tulsa (1930–1949). The OSFs were the first to run the school from its opening in 1887, followed by the Sisters of Loretto in 1915 and the SBSs in 1942.
     Chronicles, Introduction, Pawhuska Chronicles--May 1908-Oct 1909, AOSF; Oklahoma List, "Catholic Truth & Healing"; "St. Louis Industrial School for Osage Girls," *The Indian Sentinel,* Pawhuska Correspondence 1904–1911, OSF, 5–8.

25. St. Louis Industrial School for Osage Girls," *The Indian Sentinel,* 1910, Pawhuska Correspondence 1904–1911, 7.

26. "St. Louis Industrial School for Osage Girls," *The Indian Sentinel,* 1910, Pawhuska Correspondence 1904–1911, OSF, 7.

27. "Among the Osage."

28. Francis Prucha, *The Churches and the Indian Schools, 1888-1912* (Lincoln, NE: University of Nebraska Press, 1979), 26–135.

29. J. A. Stephan, Letter to Rev. Sister Aquinata, July 31, 1899, Pawhuska Correspondence, 1888–1904.

30. Sister Gerard, Letter to Ketcham, November 7, 1905, Pawhuska Correspondence, 1904–1911; Ketcham, Letter to Gerard, November 10, 1905; Pawhuska Correspondence, 1904–1911; Ketcham, Letter to Gerard, January 2, 1906, Pawhuska Correspondence, 1904–1911; Ketcham, Letter to Gerard, March 19, 1906, Pawhuska Correspondence, 1904–1911; Unsigned [probably Lusk or Ketcham], Letter to Sister Basilissa, July 12, 1910, Pawhuska Correspondence, 1904–1911. Sister Basilissa, Letter to Ketcham, July 15, 1910, Pawhuska Correspondence, 1904–1911; Charles Lusk, Letter

to Gerard, August 14, 1909, Pawhuska Correspondence, 1904–1911; William Ketcham, Letter to Sister Gerard, March 7, 1904, Pawhuska Correspondence, 1904–1911; Charles Lusk, Letter to Sister Gerard, August 17, 1908, Pawhuska Correspondence, 1904–1911.

31. Sister Gerard, Letter to William Ketcham, November 4, 1902, Pawhuska Correspondence, 1888–1904.

32. William Ketcham, Letter to Sister Gerard, March 7, 1904, Pawhuska Correspondence, 1904–1911; Charles Lusk, Letter to Gerard, August 14, 1909, Pawhuska Correspondence, 1904–1911; Sister Gerard, Letter to Ketcham, November 7, 1905, Pawhuska Correspondence, 1904–1911; Ketcham, Letter to Gerard, November 10, 1905; Pawhuska Correspondence, 1904–1911; Ketcham, Letter to Gerard, January 2, 1906, Pawhuska Correspondence, 1904–1911; Ketcham, Letter to Gerard, March 19, 1906, Pawhuska Correspondence, 1904–1911; Charles Lusk, Letter to Sister Gerard, August 17, 1908, Pawhuska Correspondence, 1904–1911; Charles Lusk, Letter to Gerard, August 14, 1909, Pawhuska Correspondence, 1904–1911; Unsigned [probably Lusk or Ketcham], Letter to Sister Basilissa, July 12, 1910, Pawhuska Correspondence, 1904–1911; Sister Basilissa, Letter to Ketcham, July 15, 1910, Pawhuska Correspondence, 1904–1911; Sister Gerard, Letter to Ketcham, April 1, 1904, Pawhuska Correspondence, 1888–1904; Sister Gerard, Letter to Charles Lusk, August 12, 1904, Pawhuska Correspondence, 1888–1904; Ketcham, Letter to Sister Gerard, April 26, 1904, Pawhuska Correspondence, 1888–1904. Sister Gerard, Letter to Ketcham, April 1, 1904, Pawhuska Correspondence, 1888–1904; Sister Gerard, Letter to Charles Lusk, August 12, 1904, Pawhuska Correspondence, 1888–1904; Ketcham, Letter to Sister Gerard, April 26, 1904, Pawhuska Correspondence, 1888–1904.

33. Sister Gerard, Letter to Ketcham, April 1, 1904, Pawhuska Correspondence, 1888–1904; Sister Gerard, Letter to Charles Lusk, August 12, 1904, Pawhuska Correspondence, 1888–1904; Ketcham, Letter to Sister Gerard, April 26, 1904, Pawhuska Correspondence, 1888–1904.

34. Sr. M. Aquinata, Letter to Rev J.A.Stephan, August 19, 1899, Pawhuska Correspondence, 1888–1904; J. A. Stephan, Letter to Rev. Sister Aquinata, August 29, 1899, Pawhuska Correspondence, 1888–1904.

35. Prucha, *Churches, and Indian Schools,* 84–116.

36. J. Van de Velde, S. J. Letter to W. Medill, July 27, 1847, LHC, Osage Mission, St Ann's, St Francis historical data & memoirs RG-SCH, VII Box II-8.

37. J. Van de Velde, S. J. Letter to W. Medill, July 27, 1847, LHC, Osage Mission, St Ann's, St Francis historical data & memoirs RG-SCH, VII Box II-8.

38. J. A. Stephan, Letter to Hon. Commissioner of Indian Affairs, 1891, reproduced in Bernalillo Annals, 1891, LHC, LHC06.l.A.01.012 Annals, 1875–1966 (All Schools) Bernalillo, Bx 1–12.

39. Possibly Sister Margaret Mary Keenan, Memoirs, Undated, LHC, LHC06.K.A.0101.4 History of Bernalillo Schools and Memoirs by Dr Margaret M Keenan Bernalillo BX 1–14.

40. Charles Lusk, Letter to Rev. Sister Margaret Mary, May 25, 1894, LHC06.D.03.002 Indian Industrial School Correspondence, 1890–1936, Bernalillo, Bc 3-2.

41. Charles Lusk, Letters to Rev. Sister Margaret Mary, May 29, 1894, June 26, 1895, June 27, 1895, October 28, 1894. All letters from LHC06.D.03.002 Indian Industrial School Correspondence, 1890-1936, Bernalillo, BC 3-2.

42. Sister Basilissa, Letter to Ketcham, July 15, 1910, Pawhuska Correspondence, 1904–1911.

43. Sister Basilissa, Letter to Ketcham, July 15, 1910, Pawhuska Correspondence, 1904–1911.

44. Charles Lusk, Letter to Basilissa, November 17, 1910, Pawhuska Correspondence, 1904–1911; Sister Basilissa, Letter to Ketcham, December 3, 1910, Pawhuska Correspondence, 1904–1911.

45. Sister Gerard, Letter to William Ketcham, November 4, 1902, Pawhuska Correspondence, 1888–1904.

46. K. Tsiania Lomawaima, *They Called it Prairie Light: The Story of the Chilocco Indian School* (Lincoln, NE: University of Nebraska Press, 1994), 12.

47. Sister Gerard, Letter to William Ketcham, November 4, 1902, Pawhuska Correspondence, 1888–1904.

48. Sister Gerard, Letter to William Ketcham, December 15, 1902, Pawhuska Correspondence, 1888–1904.

49. Sister Gerard, Letter to William Ketcham, November 15, 1902, Pawhuska Correspondence, 1888–1904.

50. Sister Gerard, Letter to William Ketcham, January 3, 1903, Pawhuska Correspondence, 1888–1904.

51. Sister Gerard, Letter to William Ketcham, January 3, 1903, Pawhuska Correspondence, 1888–1904.

52. Mother Katharine Drexel, Letter to My Dear Sister, November 5, 1902, Pawhuska Correspondence, 1888–1904; Sister Gerard, Letter to William Ketcham, August 17, 1903, Pawhuska Correspondence, 1888–1904.

53. Adams, *Education for Extinction,* 61–65; Lomawainma, *Prairie Light,* 36.

54. Pruscha, *Church and Indian Schools,* 112.

55. Letter from Director of Catholic Indian Affairs to Father Harrity, December 19, 1895, Marquette Archives.

56. Charles Lusk, Letter to Gerard, October 3, 1908, Pawhuska Correspondence, 1904–1911.

57. Sister Mary Edith Laughlin, "Some Recollections of Mother Bridget Hayden The Osages," 1 , LHC, Osage Mission, St Ann's, St Francis historical data & memoirs RG-SCH, VII Box II-8.

58. "St. Louis School for Osage Indian Girls," *CTAH,* accessed July 19, 2023, https://ctah.archivistsacwr.org/list/cat/oklahoma/.

59. Adams, *Education for Extinction,* 307–335.

Chapter 7

The Sisters of St. Joseph at the Fort Yuma School, 1886–1900

On April 13, 1893, *The Daily Astoria* (Astoria, Oregon) ran a short blurb entitled "Yuma Chief Objects." The paragraph stated that the chief of the Quechan (commonly referred to as the Yuma) nation, identified as Miguel or Chief Miguel, was frustrated with Sisters of St. Joseph of Carondelet (the CSJs)[1] who ran a Catholic school on the reservation: "The chief says he is opposed to the manner in which the Sisters have been conducting the school, and that he is not in favor of the children being taught in the Catholic religion."[2] That same day, *The Morning Call* (San Francisco, California) ran an almost identical story entitled "Chief Miguel's Plaint," with one interesting caveat. The California article suggested that "the Sisters have threatened to have the chief deposed unless he ceased complaining."[3]

Did the CSJs threaten to depose the chief? Were they able to do so? Did they have the power to do so? This chapter looks at the CJSs at the Fort Yuma Indian School at Fort Yuma, California. In it, I contend that through their role as educators and assimilators, they were able to influence Native politics. The Sisters only did so to protect themselves in the face of adversity; the success of their school was at stake. Selectively choosing their battles, they focused on consolidating their authority over not only their students, but also the local tribal nation.

THE QUECHAN

The Fort Yuma Quechan historically has been known as the Yuma, but they prefer Quechan, meaning "those who descended."[4] Prior to colonization, they were largely agrarian, farming and living along the Colorado River in Arizona and California. This nation was divided into various settlements that

111

came together for large ceremonies but then returned to their own spaces. Leaders were elected officials rather than hereditary, selected for their qualifications such as oral skills and dreams or visions. There was no centralized governing party, with a variety of local leaders and parties. The Quechan had varying relations with other Indigenous nations, either through war or diplomacy. Most of the Quechan's regional political power in the region came from controlling their local crossing of the Colorado River.[5]

The Quechan encountered Europeans later than their counterparts on the east coast. While initial contact was in the early 1600s, it was short-lived and has had little impact. It was only in the last two decades of the eighteenth century that the Spanish actively started to settle in Quechan territory. The Quechan rebelled against the Spanish in July 1781, temporarily ending Euro-settler control for approximately 70 years.[6]

It was during the California Gold Rush that Americans came into contact with the Quechan. As more and more white settlers rushed to California, the tribe controlled the flow of settlers by limiting access to the Yuma Crossing and charging would-be hopefuls to cross. In 1850, a California militia raided their territory, leading to the tribe losing control of the river crossing. The army built a fort by the crossing, occupying the area. The intermittent conflict between the Quechan and the local garrison marked the years between 1850 and 1853. Due to a series of natural disasters and military maneuvers by the U.S. Army, such as destroying crops to starve them into submission, the Quechan made a treaty with the United States.[7]

In 1865, the government created a reservation for various Colorado River tribal nations, but the Quechan refused to live there. They remained at Fort Yuma and the small nearby town. The area became an important point of transportation for goods and people. At times, they worked for the Anglo settlers. The Quechan did not militarily resist the new political system, but evidence suggests that they lived alongside the white emigrants but maintained their own traditions. Moreover, they maintained control of the river bottomland, much to the chagrin of local settler entrepreneurs.[8]

By 1883, the government decided that a garrison was no longer needed at Fort Yuma, believing the Quechan to be compliant with settler policies for many years. However, there were still tensions over the Quechan's control of the river bottom, leading the U.S. government to create a reservation for the Quechan on the eastern side of the Colorado River. The nation was upset with the location and requested that if they must go to a reservation, it should remain on the west side of the river in California. The government concurred. In 1884, the U.S. government established a reservation at Fort Yuma. The reservation was approximately 45,000 acres.[9]

Local Quechan governance changed with the creation of the reservation. Leaders of the community lost their autonomy, coming fully under the authority of representatives of the U.S. government. The government initially appointed a white agent from the Colorado River Reservation to oversee the tribe, but the agent's office was 90 miles away, leading to a request for a subagency to oversee the new reservation. Instead, the government placed the Quechan under the control of the Mission Agency in Colton, California. In 1886, the government created a boarding school at Fort Yuma and awarded the contract to the Catholic Church, which acted as a subagency, holding a level of ad hoc jurisdiction over the nation on the reservation.[10]

SISTERS OF ST. JOSEPH

Catholicism in the American Southwest dates back further than in other parts of the country. Catholic missionaries arrived in modern-day Mexico in the 1500s, traveling north into the areas now known as Arizona, California, and New Mexico. The Jesuits dominated such missionary work in the area, sending preachers and establishing mission schools. In the nineteenth century, Catholicism was soundly established in the territory formerly belonging to Mexico. Despite the long tradition of the Catholic southwest, Catholics had a mixed relationship with the local nations. The communities of Pueblo and Navajo converted early, creating syncretic traditions. Other nations, such as the Quechan, only met with itinerant missionaries and preachers.[11] By the late nineteenth-century, multiple religious communities started to set up their own missions.

The CSJs arrived in the southwest in March 1886. The congregation originated in France in 1650, expanding to the United States in 1836. Their original missions were in Missouri and Illinois. While focusing on the education of deaf students, the Sisters had long harbored a desire to work with the Indigenous populations. The Sisters from the St. Louis Motherhouse initially sent a handful of missionaries to Minnesota in the 1850s, though it was after the Civil War that the Sisters worked more with the tribal nations. Sisters from both the Carondelet community as well as other ones, such as the Philadelphia congregation (which is autonomous from the St. Louis one), sent missionaries to work both on reservations as well as the federal boarding schools, such as the Carlisle Indian Industrial School.[12] (See figure 7.1.)

The government founded the Yuma Boarding School in 1886, with the CSJs gaining the government contract. They ran the school until 1900. The school was well attended, with records suggesting that 182 students attended at its height. Like the other schools in this study, the school was dependent upon government funding, but had close ties with the local Catholic community as well as the BCIM. What seems different is that the Fort Yuma school was not founded by Catholics, as was the case in Pawhuska or Avoca, but

Figure 7.1   The Original Missionaries to Fort Yuma. *Source: Courtesy of the Sisters of St. Joseph of Carondelet Angeles Providence.*

rather by the federal government itself. Arguably, the school's origins influenced how events would turn out.[13]

The Sisters' records show a long journey to Fort Yuma. Driven by a sense of mission, they were ready to start, although they had to wait for government contracts to go through. Due to bureaucratic delays from the Department of Interior Affairs, they were not able to move onto the Fort and open their school until early May. During those months, the Sisters boarded with a local family and made quick visits to the Fort to meet with the local Indigenous population and find out their needs.[14]

There is no doubt that the CSJs at Fort Yuma were on an imperialist mission. As Sister Mary Ambrosia wrote to the Carondelet motherhouse in 1887, "the Indian children [grow] from savaged to civilized habits fast."[15] The Sisters attempted to clothe their students in settler society clothing, meeting resistance "for the heat of Yuma was no inducement to clothing."[16] In addition to requiring western clothing, they also worked to convert the Yuma. An undated document, entitled "Statistics of the Fort Yuma School," notes that between 1671 persons were baptized, not just children but also adults, between the years 1886 and 1900. Indeed, the document notes that "chief Pascual [*sic*]" was baptized in 1887, along with 25 others. The school also provided First Communions, Confirmations, and Marriages.[17]

EARLY RELATIONS WITH THE QUECHAN

In addition to teaching at the school, the Sisters took on leadership roles, both at the school and as influential leaders within Quechan society. Sister Ambrosia (also known as Mary O'Neil in some sources) was the first superintendent. In a letter to the Carondelet motherhouse, Sister M. Aniceta wrote, "You would take her for the leader of the Salvation army. She is a regular temperance preacher and a genuine Boston School marm [*sic*]."[18] In addition to her educational duties, she also acted as a government agent for the nation.[19] Robert L. Bee argues that as a representative of the U.S. government it was Sister Ambrosia who held authority over the Quechan, not Miguel or any of the other chiefs, for "she was supported in her position by her immediate superior . . . and by the vast bureaucratic structure at the higher echelons."[20] Such an analysis appears to hold true, as Sister Ambrosia acted as a government agent, dealing with everyday matters with the Quechan, only sending for government or ecclesiastical representatives in times of extreme distress.

Relations between the Quechan and CJSs began to change after the death of Pasqual in May 1887. Pasqual had supported the CSJs as well as the government of the settler society. The Sisters mourned his loss, writing, "we feel like we lost a friend in him."[21] After Pasqual's death, there were more recorded instances of overt resistance. While the annals and newspaper sources do not link these to Pasqual's death, given Pasqual's soft policing of students at the school, we might conclude that students felt they were able to get away with more. An 1890 newspaper article on the Sisters' mission reported that the students "resented the trousers, shirt, shoes and fine tooth comb, and revolted outright at soap and water." There were other types of rebellion, particularly destruction of private property. The article stated that "The Sister superintendent was compelled to promise not to cut their hair unless the boys consented, and agreed also not to inflict corporal punishment."[22] According to the article, the children ceased to vandalize the school and accompanying buildings, suggesting the Sisters ceased the practice.

While anything published in the settler newspapers should be subject to critique, reading between the lines suggest a level of everyday resistance. The students' destruction of windows, and other parts of the school, was their attempt to express their anger at being required to attend school. There may have also been specific persons or policies that the students did not like, although that is supposition. Moreover, there was resistance to overt assimilation practices, such as clothing and hygiene, which were common at like all the boarding and mission schools of the period.[23] By bargaining with the students and promising to cease cutting their hair, the Sisters were able to achieve greater change: the ending of overt resistance through vandalism. While the students may have had some agency, it was limited as the Sisters worked to assume control.

INITIAL RELATIONS

In the succeeding years, the government pressured the Quechan to assimilate to white culture and adapt to life on the Fort. Like other reservations, the government tried to convince individual members of the tribe to accept private property, following in the tradition of the 1887 Dawes Act, which divided the reservation lands into individual allotments—and selling off additional lands to white settlers. Local treaties required children to attend a local contract school and boarding schools run by religious groups. However, the system started to falter as the government seized all but 8,000 acres of Yuma land, leading to most reservation land passing into white hands by the 1910s.[24]

The politics of assimilation reflected the physical layout of the reservation. The reservation straddled both sides of the Colorado River, with some families living on the California side of the river and some on the Arizona side. This river divide served as a natural basis for the various factions within the community. These groups largely corresponded with those who accepted assimilation and federal authority and those who did not. When the SJSs arrived, the white-acknowledged chief, Pasqual, and his followers lived near the settlement known as Indian Hill on the Arizona side.[25]

Pasqual had become chief in part due to white intervention. Between 1851 and 1853, what became the Fort Yuma Quechan community was trying to defend its land from Anglo settlers in the region. With the resulting treaty, the garrison began to meddle in their internal politics. Major Samuel Heintzelman was in charge of the negotiations and, later, political machinations. Heintzelman deposed the two chiefs who had been at the center of the previous conflict, one of whom he described as the "chief priest" and one as the "war chief." He then ordered the Quechan to vote for a new chief. At first, the Quechan elected a man named Macedon. (It is unclear is Macedon was his given name or one used by American forces.) Macedon was sympathetic to the American army but died shortly after in battle.[26]

Soon after Macedon's death, Pasqual became chief, although it is unclear whether the local community voted for him or if he was appointed by Heintzelman. The community often criticized the new chief for being too accommodating to white society. A contemporary commentary, *Arizona as It Is; or, The Coming Country,* published in 1877, described the chief as "a firm friend of the whites, whose manners and customers who often commends to his people, and urges them to adopt."[27] However, he may also have been using the policies of accommodation in order to negotiate spaces for the community's autonomy, while also trying to maintain his own political power.[28]

The Quechan considered those living near Pasqual to be "coffee drinkers," suggesting they had adopted the Euro-American habit of drinking coffee versus traditional tea. Members of this group moved to temporary housing by the river during the planting and harvesting seasons. To the north and south were communities that actively resisted assimilation, although those in the Somerton settlement did adapt to homesteading. Members of these communities represented different factions within the community, fighting among each other and challenging the authority of Pasqual, whom whites acknowledged as the main leader.[29]

Upon the CSJs' arrival, some Quechan themselves may have been initially wary of the Sisters. According to the memoirs of Sister Mary Thomas Lavin, the early months were a time of transition: "It was some time before the Indians became accustomed to the new arrivals."[30] However, some of the leaders soon started to support the Sisters. For example, Chief Pasqual, who was in charge before Manuel, supported the Sisters' school. According to one source, "the old chief was the truant officer, checking the number from the back of the room, and eventually rounding up those attempting to evade an education."[31] Pasqual's support, particularly in requiring children to attend school, suggests a level of accommodation to the Sisters' imperialist goals.[32] The Sisters respected Pasqual, although his appointment and support of them was contentious among the Quechan.

Changing Quechan politics influenced the relationship between the nation and the Sisters. Following his death, there was a power struggle within the Quechan. Throughout Pasqual's tenure, some members of the nation disagreed with his policies toward the settler society, finding them too accommodating. However, from the white standpoint, his successor must have the same approach to relations with the United States. According to one history of the Quechan, there were rumors that Pasqual had personally named Miguel his successor. Moreover, there is also evidence that the CSJs had a say in the matter. Sister Ambrosia requested that the army pick Pasqual's successor as they had with the former chief. She recommended Miguel, who had promised to support the school. Prior to his election to power, Sister Ambrosia saw him as an ally:

Captain Miguel the sub-chief made a grant speech in favor of the Sisters told the strange Indians all the good the Sisters were doing for the children and advised them all to send their children to school as soon as possible.[33]

Accordingly, he was promoted.[34]

Settler society initially approved Chief Miguel. A spring 1893 newspaper described the Fort Yuma Quechan leader as

> about 35 years of age and perhaps one of the finest specimens of aboriginal manhood . . . [he] stands nearly six feet, with [wide] shoulders. . . . His head and face are unusually large and the features prominent. His big black eyes are aglitter with intelligence. Altogether he reminds one of the noble Indian of Fennimore Cooper.[35]

He had historically been part of the assimilationist faction of the Quechan; an 1891 newspaper described him as "a faithful friend of the whites."[36] The CSJs agreed. Soon after his appointment, Sister Ambrosia wrote that "Miguel is a great big chief and he makes a splendid one. He has perfect order."[37] Later, in 1892, the *Arizona Sentinel* reported that Miguel was "very proud over the fact that one of his sons is becoming very proficient at the shoemaker's trade, and another as a carpenter in the Indian school."[38] However, this situation would soon change.

TENSIONS

Tensions between Miguel and the CSJs emerged quickly. One of the main contributing factors was disease. Various letters from the Sisters written in 1887 suggested that a variety of deadly diseases had infected the community, killing the children. A few months after Miguel's election, Sr. Ambrosia wrote that

> Miguel had proved himself a very poor Chief. . . . They told me that Miguel wanted them to take their children home, he said if the children were left in school they would all die by and by. The children have returned but we find it very hard to get along with them.[39]

The CSJs appealed for help. A local priest came to their aid. According to Sister Ambrosia:

> Father Stephan came just in time to help us out of difficulty. He gave Captain Miguel a good scolding, and told him he must send his children to school, and if he was not willing to send them here, the great Father in Washington would send an order to take his children by force and place them in an Eastern school. This frightened them considerably. Miguel promised Father to send the children back and they are slowly coming. . . . After Father left here, C. Miguel came to see me, and said that he would get all the children he could for school. He said that he did not like that man from Washington, he did not talk right to him. He

said they were not going to give their children to that man, they would give them to the Sisters, for the Sisters knew the Indian and the Indians knew the Sisters.[40]

Father Stephan threatened to send the children east was an act of coercion, demanding compliance in the face of a deadly disease. While Miguel initially resisted the CSJs' school, he seemed to have considered them the lesser of two evils. When forced to "choose" between sending students to a government boarding school in another part of the country, such as Carlisle, or back to the Sisters, he chose the Sisters. Miguel's negative response to the Sisters was tempered by a desire for some level of autonomy from other representatives of the U.S. government. However, relations did not improve.

The CSJs were not the only ones to have moments of conflict break out during times of disease. For example, while the Sisters of St. Francis were stationed in Oklahoma, cultural clashes over disease occurred. In March 1885, *The Portland Daily Press* reported an outbreak of consumption that "threatens to decimate the tribe."[41] However, the one in 1896 resulted in "death dances . . . on account of the alarming spread of consumption, among the Osage, which threatened the extinction of the tribe."[42] Most likely, this was the epidemic during which the instance occurred, given the widespread report of the epidemic from around the country. The Sisters of St. Francis did not record any moments of conflict between themselves and the local Osage in response to the disease, but other settlers did.

The Quechan continued to battle diseases such as measles, typhoid, and the flu.[43] In response to these deaths, various newspapers across the United States reported in 1892 and 1893 that members of the nation had murdered a local medicine man after several community members had died. The incident made national headlines, and there were rumors that Miguel was involved in the attack, particularly since one article reported that he tried to give them a pardon.[44] In 1893, another deadly wave of disease hit the school. It personally affected Miguel this time. Just after his deposition, Sister Ambrosia wrote, "He has as much as he can attend right now. His children are all stricken down with fever. Their [*sic*] were seven deaths last week. They were young children and baptized."[45] Referring to the earlier murder of a local medicine man, she stated, "I am afraid they will think we are the witches as they are looking for one."[46]

In addition to the emotional toll the death of the children must have taken, there were also cultural misunderstandings between Miquel and the Sisters. The Quechan's traditional funerary rituals involved the cremation of the body. However, the Sisters wanted to give the dead a Christian burial. The Sisters bury several of those who died in a local cemetery, supposedly without the approval of the Quechan. Sister Thomas went so far as to state that "they would dig up a body even after an indefinite period."[47]

Miguel responded to the children's death by removing students from the school. An April 1893 article from the *Los Angeles Herald* reported:

> Miguel kept his own children at the school but used his influence to keep other children away until the attendance had dwindled to a small number. From remarks made by him, Miguel wished to have considerable to say about the conduct of the school, and his vanity was hurt because he was not consulted by the principal. He even went so far as to demand of the commissioner that Mother Ambrosia should be removed as the head of the school. The effect of all this was seen on the school discipline, so that the control of the children was almost lost by the teachers.[48]

Miguel's initial resistance was a form of truancy, making sure that the number of students attending the school dwindled. This would have been effective, as the Sisters' funding depended upon the number of students attending the school. Miguel appeared to use this circumstance to challenge the authority of the school, demanding a new principal. Miguel's tactics were largely successful, as the teachers lost "the control of the children"; after all, how well could they teach when students were not there and did not listen?

Building upon his original plan, Miguel actively petitioned for the Sisters' removal, going so far as to visit the governor of California. According to one article reported in *The Seattle Post-Intelligencer,* "Chief Miguel . . . is in Sacramento to prevail upon Gov. Markham to intercede in behalf of the Indians in the management of the government school at Yuma, which is run by Sisters whose Catholic instructions do not meet with the approval of the chief."[49] The article placed Miguel's complaint not only within the realm of self-rule ("do not meet with the approval of the chief") but, more importantly, placed the blame on the religious group.

Miguel's complaint appeared to have registered with some Protestants. According to newspaper reports, he linked his protest to the anti-Catholic sentiment of the period. While the American Southwest was heavily Catholic, there were several Protestant Missionary groups, such as the Methodists, who resented the influences of the Catholics. In response to Miguel's complaints, Sister Ambrosia commented that

> he is very much applauded by the people belonging to the Church of the New Era in Los Angeles. They told him that they would send him a token of respect for the late action he took against the Sisters' school at Fort Yuma.

It is unclear which denomination the "Church of the New Era" was; there were several Protestant sects in Los Angeles, including the Congregationalists, Baptists, and Church of Unity. There were also several itinerant evangelical preachers during the 1890s.[50] No matter the denomination, whether members of the Church of the New Era did send Miguel anything, monetary or not, is unknown.[51]

Despite his attempts, Miguel did not succeed in removing the CSJs. A letter from Sister Ambrosia, written in April 1893, described Miguel's attitude toward the Sisters: "We have lost the good will of the Miguel portion of the tribe . . . He [the Inspector] gave Miguel three days to bring the girls [the students] back. He said no he would not bring the girls back to the Sisters. He wanted men teachers" Miguel was not against assimilation; he was not against the school itself; he was specifically rebelling against the Sisters. The letter went on to write that "He told the Indians that if the Sisters did not go that he would kill them [the Sisters]."[52]

This emphasis on the culpability of the Sisters suggests that Miguel correctly saw the Sisters as part of the imperial authority. I would argue that Miguel was not responding to gendered ideas of control, that is, women having authority over him, but rather imperial control. His actions would have been the same if men had been running the school. As Robert Bee asserts, "The school was not just a school; it was the embodiment of the federal government's presence and control over the Quechan tribe. To fight the school was to fight the government's increasing authority."[53] Thus, Miguel seems to have perceived the Sisters, particularly Sister Ambrosia, as an imperial authority that threatened his community's autonomy and survival.

Adding to the controversy over the Sisters' tenure were other political concerns. Miguel and one of his advisors, Walter Scott, had been protesting the increasing number of white settlers, particularly surveyors, on the reservation. They, and other Quechan leaders, feared that the reservation would be divided up into allotments. Indeed, there appears to have been a petition penned and signed by white settlers to divide the reservation according to the terms of the Dawes Act. The two were able to get a court injunction on the survey work. However, Scott was arrested in 1893.[54]

It must be noted that Scott later blamed Sister Ambrosia for his arrest. In a signed statement from decades after the incident (1935), he stated that "Mother O'Neil . . . ordered three policemen [to arrest me]. . . . When I appeared before her, Mother O'Neil told me . . . that I was a trouble-maker. For that reason she told me I was arrested."[55] Indeed, it must be noted that the *Arizona Sentinel* reported that Scott was arrested for "opposing the Indians in sending their children to school."[56] Whether Mother Ambrosia played any part in his arrest is not a part of the CSJs' records; however, the evidence suggests that the Sisters were involved in some way.

It is unclear what happened when Miguel was deposed, probably in late winter or early spring 1893. Newspapers offered a variety of accounts. Several suggested that he was deposed due to the murder of the medicine man, whom he may have blamed for the children's deaths.[57] Another article in the

Arizona Sentinel accused Miguel and his followers of "sedition."[58] Robert
Bee has suggested that Miguel was arrested after trying to break Scott out of
jail, a theory that a newspaper article from *Arizona* also supports.[59]

According to an undated source in the CSJs' archives, tensions mounted
even further after the police decided that they needed to speak to Miguel.
Whether it was to talk to him in response to the death of the medicine man
or for other reasons is not documented. A local police officer approached
Mother Ambrosia and asked if she knew where Miguel was. She stated he
was coming to the convent; the police waited and arrested the chief when he
arrived. According to the document, Miguel said, "I'll get even with you for
this."[60]

Did the Sisters set Miguel up? Chief Miguel's accusations appear well
founded. An 1893 article in the *Los Angeles Herald* reported, "the teacher
of the government school and Dr. Heffernan, the surgeon, are trying to have
another chief chosen."[61] More importantly, a letter from Sister Ambrosia
stated that "He [Miguel] feels very bitter towards me, as he blames me for
his removal, but it was the only means we could take to save the school."[62]
In other words, the Sisters had played a part in Miguel's fall from political
power.

After Miguel's arrest and loss of power, the new chief was "Capt Jose,"
whom local Indian agent William Harris reported "seems favorably inclined
towards the school."[63] However, the Sisters feared retribution from Miguel;
Sister Ambrosia wrote, "Pity us, then pray" after reporting that Miguel's trial
had been postponed. [64] In late September/early October 1893, multiple news
sources reported that Miguel had attacked the school. A paper from Salem,
Oregon, stated on 30 September that "Miguel, the deposed [*sic*] chief, with
a band of his tribe, is reported to have attacked the reservation school. It is
not yet known how serious the attack was or whether anyone was killed."[65]
In October 1893, The Los Angeles *Herald* reported that "Miguel and four
other Indians attempted to carry off Mary O'Neill [Sister Ambrosia], the
school superintendent."[66] *The Herald,* took a more satirical approach with a
story entitled "His Royal Nibs in Prison," which also reported the attempted
kidnapping. The article noted that "the whole affair is a purely political row,"
and that Miguel had "allowed his wrath to get the better of his diplomacy."[67]
According to one history of the CSJs, there was also a murder plot against
Mother Ambrosia in October 1893. The Sisters hid on the night of the
planned assassination, listening to the Quechan outside. Nothing happened,
however. Local police soon arrested Miguel and his followers.[68]

There were probably internal politics at play during this time that may have
influenced the deposition of Miguel. One history of the CSJs missions with
the Yuma suggested that Miguel was deposed by members of the Quechan
community who, "recognizing his defect, had signified to the Indian inspector

their willingness to choose a new chief."[69] Likewise, the Los *Angeles Herald* reported in April 1893, in an article entitled "Chief Miguel, not a Martyr," that Miguel "was never elected chief by the Yumas but got himself recognized as such by the government through the recommendation of the clerk at the school." Although the article did add the caveat that "the teacher of the government school and Dr. Heffernan, the surgeon, are trying to have another chief chosen," it ultimately sided with Sister Ambrosia's assessment that the election of the new chief was merely a matter of internal Quechan politics; however, the reality was much more complex as internal and external politics all intertwined.[70]

There is also the possibility that white governmental agents forced Miguel out as part of an extended effort to gain control over more Yuma land. In December 1893, the Department of the Interior signed a deal with "the principal men and other male adults of the Yuma Indians in the State of California," granting "the appropriation of $60,000 for the construction of a levee along the bank of the Colorado River to protect the lands allotted and sold, said sum to be reimbursed to the United States from the sale of the lands."[71] The agreement stated that the government would cover all costs associated with the project. While Miguel was on the Arizona side of the river, the timing of the agreement suggests that the community leaders were aware of this proposal. As one of the leaders, could Miguel have been opposed to this plan, either in part or in total? If so, could his deposition have been due to politics over the water levee and not with the Sisters at all? Or did all these events come together and lead to Miguel's fall? The evidence suggests they did.

After his arrest, local police officers whipped Miguel and his supporters and put them in jail. Sister Ambrosia described his incarceration as transforming his character:

> Miguel and his band walked home very humbly and I think they fully realize their defeat. Miguel did not want to be present [at meetings] but Mr. Estudillo [the reservation agent] sent a policeman after him. He was very much frightened now knowing what was in store for him.[72]

Even if temporarily subdued, Miguel and his supporters did not give up. He would continue to resist until an old man.

CONCLUSION

The role of the SJSs in internal Quechan politics ultimately led to the closure of the school. After the fire at the school, the Sisters left Fort Yuma less than a year later in 1900. Part of the reason was the fire, but there were also financial concerns, similar to those discussed in other chapters of this book. The Sisters continued to maintain reservation and residential schools throughout California and the southwest.[73]

In some ways, the SJSs' role at the Fort Yuma school is unique. From my reading of other sources, I have not found other instances of Catholic Sisters becoming so involved with Indigenous politics, going so far as to depose a leader. It is quite the opposite situation with the Sisters of St. Francis in Oklahoma. There we see a reliance upon tribal leaders during times of funding crises, as the OSFs hoped that the leaders would intervene on their behalf.

However, the underlying struggle that led to this situation was similar; like all the other case studies within this book, the CSJs were attempting to demonstrate their authority over the local community, particularly who had the right to determine whether the Quechan children attended the Catholic school or not. From the first school run by Catholic Sisters in Kansas through later iterations in the American west, Catholic Sisters struggled to determine their place as educators and assimilators at these schools. It was at Fort Yuma that the struggle took on another element, as the Sisters overthrew a local political leader, doing whatever they thought was best for their school to succeed.

NOTES

1. Chapter 4 also briefly examined the SJSs from the St. Louis Motherhouse. However, there I use the abbreviation CSJs. The original community of Sisters of St. Joseph were French missionaries, who looked to their leadership in the mother country during their first several decades of existence in the United States. Under the leadership of the St. Louis house, several communities of Sisters planned to become a separate community from their French counterpart in 1860. This led to the splintering of the community in the United States. Those who remiained under the leadership of St. Louis became the CSJs in 1877. However, in 1852, this consolidation had not occurred, which is why I use SSJs in a previous chapter. For more on the SSJs and CSJs see Elisabeth C. Davis, "The Disappearance of Mother Agnes Spencer: The Centralization Controversy and the Antebellum Catholic Church," *American Catholic Studies* 130, no. 2 (2019): 31–52; Elisabeth Davis, "We Know Not God's Designs in Permitting a Separation: Women Religious, the Consolidation Controversies, and the Nineteenth Century American Catholic Church" *Journal of Religious History* (December 2023):566–585; Mary M. McGlone, *Anything of Which a Woman is Capable: A History of the Sisters of St. Joseph in the United States, Vol. 1* (St. Louis: Bookbay, 2017); McGlone, *Called Forth by the Dear Neighbor: A History of the Sisters of St. Louis in the United States, Vol. 2* (St. Louis: Federation of the Sisters of St. Louis, 2020).

2. "Yuma Chief Objects," *The Daily Astoria,* April 13, 1893.

3. "Chief Miguel's Plaint," *The Morning Call,* April 13, 1893.

4. Based on readings from the Quechan's own sources, the name Quechan is one this nation prefers to show their heritage. It is part of reclaiming their heritage

and identity. "Fort Yuma-Quechan Tribe Community Profile," *The University of Arizona,* accessed January 4, 2023, https://naair.arizona.edu/fort-yuma-quechan-tribe; "Quechan Tribe," *Inter Trial Council of Arizona,* accessed January 4, 2023, https://itcaonline.com/member-tribes/quechan-tribe/.

5. Robert L. Bee, *Crosscurrents along the Colorado: The Impact of Government Policy on the Quechan Indians* (Tuscan: University of Arizona Press, 1981), 17–19; Duane Champagne, *American Indian Societies: Strategies and Conditions of Political and Cultural Survival* (Cambridge, MA: Cultural Survival Inc., 1989), 98–101; Bernard L. Fontana, "Yuma (Quechan) Indians," in *The New Encyclopedia of the American West,* ed. Howard R. Lamar (New Haven, CT: Yale University Press, 1998), online, *Credo Reference;* Amy Miller, *Stories from Quechan Oral Literature* (Cambridge: Open Book Publishers, 2016), 1–3; Teresa McNeil, "The Sisters of St. Joseph Under Fire: Pioneer Convent School on the Colorado River," *The Journal of Arizona History* 29, no. 1 (1988): 35–50.

6. Bee, *Crosscurrents,* 17–19; Fontana, "Yuma (Quechan) Indians."

7. Bee, *Crosscurrents,* 17–19; Fontana, "Yuma (Quechan) Indians."

8. Bee, *Crosscurrents,* 17–19.

9. Bee, *Crosscurrents,* 17–20; Fontana, "Yuma Quechan Indians."

10. Bee, *Crosscurrents,* 17–20.

11. Ross Enochs, "Native Americans on the Path to the Catholic Church: Cultural Crisis and Missionary Adaptation," *U.S. Catholic Historian* 27, no. 1 (2009): 71–88; Erika Perez, "Family, Spiritual Kinship, and Social Hierarchy in Early California," *Early American Studies* 14, no. 4 (2016): 661–687; Timothy Matovina, "Remapping American Catholicism," *U.S. Catholic Historian* 28, no. 4 (2010): 31–72; Robert H. Jackson, *Jesuits in Spanish America before the Suppression: Organization and Demographic and Quantitative Perspectives* (New York: Brill, 2021), 1–108.

12. Mary McGlone, *Called Forth by the Dear Neighbor: A History of the Sisters of St. Joseph in the United States Volume 2- from 1860-2010* (St. Louis, MO: Federation of the Sisters of St. Joseph, 2020); Elisabeth C. Davis, "Our Colored and Indian Charges Furnish So Much Amusement for Us": Catholicism, Assimilation, and the Racial Hierarchy in Carlisle, Pennsylvania, 1883-1918," *Pennsylvania History: A Journal of Mid-Atlantic Studies* 91, no. 1 (2024): 47–64.

13. McGlone, *Called Forth by the Dear Neighbor;* McNeil, "Pioneer Convent School," 35–50; Mary Lucina Savage, *The Century's Harvest Gathered by the Sisters of St. Joseph of Carondelet in the United States, 1836-1936* (St. Louis, MO: Sisters of St. Joseph, 1936).

Also see Sister Ambrosia, Letter to Rev. Mother M. Julia, November 17, 1893, Los Angeles Collection, CSJCA; Sr. M. Julia, Letter to Rev Mother, Palm Sunday 1886, March 22, 1886, March 28, 1886; April 5, 1886, April 10, 1886, April 15, 1886, April 19, 1886, April 26, 1886, May 3, 1886, CSJCA.

14. McGlone, *Called Forth by the Dear Neighbor;* McNeil, "Pioneer Convent School," 35–50; Savage, *The Century's Harvest.*

Also see Sister Ambrosia, Letter to Rev. Mother M. Julia, November 17, 1893, Los Angeles Collection, CSJCA; Sr. M. Julia, Letter to Rev Mother, Palm Sunday

1886, March 22, 1886, March 28, 1886; April 5, 1886, April 10, 1886, April 15, 1886, April 19, 1886, April 29, 1886, May 3, 1886, CSJCA.

15. Sister M. Ambrosia, Letter to Mother Agatha, January 4, 1887, Los Angeles Collection, CSJCA.

16. Sister Mary Thomas Lavin, "Fort Yuma Arizona," San Diego Collection, CSJCA.

17. "Statistics of the Fort Yuma School," undated, San Diego Collection, CSJCA.

18. Sr. M. Aniceta, Letter to Rev. Mother, March 7, 1890, CSJCA.

19. Bee, *Crosscurrents,* 20.

20. Bee, *Crosscurrents,* 27.

21. Sister Ambroisa, Letter to Rev. M. Agatha, May 9, 1887, CSJCA.

22. "Civilizing the Yumas. Noble Work of Catholic Missionaries Among the Indians," *Staunton Vindicator* (Staunton, Virginia), September 12, 1890.

23. For example, Adams, *Education for Extinction;* John R. Gram, "Acting Out Assimilation: Playing Indian and Becoming American in the Federal Indian Boarding Schools," *American Indian Quarterly* 40, no. 3 (2016): 25–273; White, "White Power and the Performance of Assimilation," 106–123.

24. Bee, *Crosscurrents,* 17–20.

25. Bee, *Crosscurrents,* 22–24; Fontana, "Yuma (Quechan) Indians"; Charles R. Quinn, *The Story of St. Thomas Indian Mission, and the Forgotten Colorado River Missions at the Historic Yuma Crossing* (Downey, CA: E. Quinn, 1968), 2–28.

26. Bee, *Crosscurrents,* 17–18.

27. Hiram C. Hodge, *Arizona as It Is; or, The Coming Country* (New York: Hurd and Houghton, 1877), 157.

28. Bee, *Crosscurrents,* 17–18; J. N. Mack, "Inside and Out: The Sisters of St. Joseph, Chief Pasqual, and the Education of Native Children in Yuma," *The Catholic Historical Review* 109, no. 1 (2023): 77–106.

29. Bee, *Crosscurrents,* 22–24; Fontana, "Yuma (Quechan) Indians"; Quinn, *The Story of St. Thomas Indian Mission,* 2–28.

30. Sister Mary Thomas Lavin, "Fort Yuma Arizona," San Diego Collection, CSJCA.

31. Sister Mary Thomas Lavin, "Fort Yuma Arizona," San Diego Collection, CSJCA.

32. Mack, "Inside and Out," 77–106.

33. Sister Salesia, Letter to Rev. Mother Agatha, September 6, 1886, CSJCA, 208.7.

34. Lee, *Crosscurrents,* 25–27.

35. "Big Chief Miguel," *The Morning Call,* San Francisco, April 9, 1893.

36. "Indians Arrested," *The Morning Call,* San Francisco, March 9, 1891.

37. Sister M. Ambrosia, Letter to Mother Assistant, July 15, 1887, CSJCA.

38. "Local Items," *The Arizona Sentinel,* Yuma, AZ, September 3, 1892.

39. Sister Ambrosia, Letter to Mother Assistant, October 30, 1887, CSJCA.

40. Sister Ambroisa, Letter to Rev. M. Agatha, November 20, 1887, CSJCA.

41. "Consumption Among the Indians," *The Portland Daily Press* (Portland ME), March 11, 1885.

42. "Death Dances Discontinued," *The Providence News* (Providence RI), February 22, 1896.

Also see "Death Dances Stopped," *The Houston Daily Post* (Houston, Tex.), February 23, 1896; "Is Indeed the 'Dance of Death'," *St. Paul Daily Globe* (Saint Paul, Minn.), February 23, 1896; "News in Brief," *Hutchinson Gazette* (Hutchinson, Kan.), February 27, 1896; "No More Death Dances," *Daily Kennebec Journal* (Augusta, Me.), February 24, 1896.

43. Sister M. Ambrosia, Letter to M. Agatha, November 13, 1886, CSJCA; Sister Ambrosia, Letter to Mother Assistant, April 6, 1887, CSJCA; Sister Ambrosia, Letter to Rev. Mother Agatha, April 23, 1887, CSJCA; Sister Ambrosia, Letter to Rev. Mother Agatha, January 14, 1889, CSJCA; Sister Ambrosia, Letter to Mother M. Julia, February 2, 1890, CSJCA; Sister Alphonsa, Letter to Dearest Mother, June 18, 1886, CSJCA.

44. "Strangled Their Doctor," *The Cheyenne Daily Leader* (Cheyenne, WY), January 15, 1892; "Miguel, Chief of the Yuma Indians . . ." *The Arizona Sentinel*, March 19, 1892.

45. Sister M. Ambrosia, Letter to Mother M. Julia, April 25, 1893, CSJCA.

46. Sister M. Ambrosia, Letter to Mother M. Julia, April 25, 1893, CSJCA.

47. Sister Thomas, "Fort Yuma," CSJCA.

48. "Chief Miguel Not a Martyr," *Los Angeles Herald,* April 30, 1893.

49. "Chief Miguel...." *The Seattle Post-Intelligencer* (Seattle, WA), April 14, 1893.

50. Michael E. Engh, "A Multiplicity and Diversity of Faiths,": Religion's Impact on Los Angeles and the Urban West, 1890-1940," *The Western Historical Quarterly* 28, no. 4 (1997): 463–492.

51. Quote from Sister M. Ambrosia to Mother M. Julia, April 25, 1893, CSJCA. Also, see "Chief Miguel....," *The Seattle Post-Intelligencer* (Seattle, WA), April 14, 1893; "Chief Miguel's Plaint," *The Morning Call* (San Francisco, CA), April 13, 1893; "Yuma Chief Objects," *The Daily Morning Astorian* (Astoria, OR), April 13, 1893.

52. Sister Ambrosia, Letter to Rev. Mother M. Julia, April 5, 1893, CSJCA.

53. Bee, *Crosscurrents,* 32–43.

54. "Hon. Francisco, Estudillo...." *The Arizona Sentinel,* September 23, 1893.

55. Walter Scott, Signed Statement, November 7, 1935, quoted in Bee, *Crosscurrents,* 31–32.

56. "Hon. Francisco, Estudillo...."

57. "Fought with their Fists," *The Indianapolis Journal* (Indianapolis, Indiana), September 30, 1893; "Indians in a Fist Fight," *The Evening World* (New York, NY), September 30, 1893; "Rebellion Among Indians," *The Columbus Journal* (Columbus, Nebraska), October 4, 1893.

58. "Trouble in Camp," *The Arizona Sentinel,* September 30, 1893.

59. Bee, *Crossroads,* 31–32; "Trouble in Camp," *The Arizona Sentinel,* September 30, 1893.

60. Unknown, "A Narrow Escape," undated, CSJCA.

61. "Chief Miguel Not a Martyr," *Los Angeles Herald* (Los Angeles), April 30, 1893.

62. Sister M. Ambrosia to Mother M. Julia, April 25, 1893, CSJCA.

63. WTH [possibly William Harris], Letter to Sister Aniceta, November 25, 1894, CSJCA.

64. Sister Ambrosia, Letter to Rev. Mother M. Julia, November 22, 1893, CSHJCA.

65. "Indian Outbreak," *Capital Journal* (Salem, OR), September 30, 1893.

66. "His Royal Nibs in Prison," *The Herald* (Los Angeles, CA), October 2, 1893.

67. "His Royal Nibs in Prison," *The Herald,* October 2, 1893.

68. Sister Thomas Marie McMahon, "The Sisters of St. Joseph of Carondelet Arizona's Pioneer Religious Congregation" (MA Thesis, St. Louis University, St. Louis, MO, 1952), 144.

69. McMahon, "Arizona's Pioneer Religious Congregation," 143.

70. "Chief Miguel Not a Martyr," *Los Angeles Herald,* April 30, 1893.

71. Hoke Smith, "Letter from the Secretary of the Interior," March 19, 1894, CSJCA.

72. Sister Ambrosia, Letter to Rev. Mother M. Julia, November 20, 1894, CSJCA.

73. McGlone, *Called Forth by the Dear Neighbor;* McNeil, "Pioneer Convent School," 35–50.

Conclusion

In early 1915, William Ketcham, the head of the Bureau of Catholic Indian Missions, made an impassioned speech before Congress, begging for funding. Ketcham described Catholic work at the boarding schools in the early decades of the twentieth century as coming about at the "initiative" of the federal government and as having been profitable. He argued that attacks on funding the Catholic schools were an attack on tribal sovereignty over their own funds. Moreover, he suggested that such political machinations were unpatriotic, describing his Protestant opponents as "Un-American in character, [as they] apparently would rejoice to see Catholic Indians deprived for the consolations of the religion of their choice."[1] Ketcham relied upon concepts of First Amendment promises of religious freedom to suggest that Indigenous persons choose who should run their schools. Ketcham's argument was not fully unique, being a reiteration of Catholic arguments for Indigenous autonomy in choosing a Catholic education.

Exhausted by years of negotiating, Ketcham was tired and frustrated. At the end of his speech, Ketcham seemed to lose his control, exclaiming:

> Must our entire work again be revolutionized? How can you expect us to carry on successful work if the status of our Indian school is to be changed during every session of congress? As an American citizen I will say with chagrin and regret, if our work must be destroyed by ever-changing policies, if we must be driven out of Indian educational work, it would be more frank on the park of congress to enact a law to that effect in unmistakable terms, so that the public might be properly enlightened and the Catholic church might know just what course to pursue.[2]

The fights of the late 1800s had only intensified in the early 1900s as Congress continued to defund the Catholic schools. Catholics were willing to

129

continue with the experiment but needed to know where they stood. Where they stood was on rocky ground.

Despite these funding woes, Catholic Sisters continued to run the Native American mission schools, a position they hold to this day. Some of the religious communities discussed in this book continued to work with Indigenous communities until the late twentieth century. The Sisters of Loretto worked with the Osage in Oklahoma until 1942. The Sisters of St. Francis of Philadelphia worked at the St. Stephan's Indian School in Wyoming until 1985 (though as of the writing of this book, the school is still operational). Sisters of St. Joseph of Carondelet's last assignment with an Indigenous school ended in 1980, when the St. Joseph Industrial School in Keshena, Wisconsin closed in 1980. Other communities continue to work at reservation and boarding schools, such as the Missionary Benedictine Sisters at the St. Augustine Indian Mission School in Nebraska. (For a more complete timeline of schools run by Catholic Sisters, see the appendix).[3]

FINAL THOUGHTS

Catholic Sisters crafted their stories so as to emphasize their own authority and agency over the situations and people with whom they engaged. This book has tracked the varied experiences these women in the nineteenth-through twentieth centuries had while working on reservations and boarding schools, joining them together through the theme of authority. Despite the common assumption that Catholic Sisters are separate from the larger trends in American society, nothing ever exists in a bubble. These women were influenced by and participated in larger trends around them, from education reform in the 1840s to the performances of the World's Fairs in the 1890s. The Sisters of Loretto in Kansas were the first group to run a boarding school, creating practices and policies that would become standard. The Sisters of the Holy Child Jesus had their students perform both as examples of "authentic" Indigenous persons and as "civilized" ones. The Sisters of St. Francis in Oklahoma found themselves in competition with the local federal schools, while the Sisters of St. Joseph at Fort Yuma became enmeshed in tribal politics.

Today, Catholic women religious are coming to terms with the history of the Native American boarding schools. Various congregations were members of the Catholic Truth and Healing Project, as well as other initiatives seeking open transparency around the 74 schools they ran prior to 1978. These commissions have also largely focused on making archival sources available to survivors and their descendants, as well as researchers.[4] However, some of these attempts are limited. For example, the Sisters of St. Francis of Philadelphia's website states that "ministries included . . . nine Native American missions" without further elaborating; however, the OSFs have been active members of the Catholic Truth and Healing Commission.[5]

Despite these attempts at reconciliation, the question remains: What was lost? This book has been limited in scope, focusing only on the narratives the Sisters created. A missing aspect is the students' experiences, which have not been recorded. Denise Lajimodiere's powerful history, *Stringing Rosaries,* demonstrates the heart wrenching impact of the Sisters' push for authority in the twentieth century.[6] However, with most of the survivors of these early schools long gone, we cannot know the toll and trauma that the Sisters' actions had on their students.

Even if student voices were to turn up saying they supported the Sisters' actions and authority, the history of Catholic Sisters in a boarding school is ultimately one of imperialism, with a focus on cultural conquest and determination. Though not using guns and other forms of militarized violence, Catholic Sisters undermined Indigenous autonomy, imposing their own authority and beliefs over those of others.

NOTES

1. Ketcham, "Plea for the Catholic Indian Schools."
2. Ketcham, "Plea for the Catholic Indian Schools."
3. All material taken from "List," Catholic Truth and Healing, accessed February 18, 2024, https://ctah.archivistsacwr.org/list/.
4. Dan Stockman, "Newly Published List Shows Catholic Sisters Ran 74 US Native American Boarding Schools," National Catholic Reporter, May 9, 2023, https://www.ncronline.org/news/newly-published-list-shows-catholic-entities-ran-87-us-Native-american-boarding-schools#:~:text=The%20Catholic%20Truth%20%26%20Healing%20website,were%20affiliated%20with%20the%20schools.; Dan Stockman, "Inside the Effort to Identify Catholic-Run Boarding Schools for Indigenous Children," Global Sisters Report, March 30, 2023, https://www.globalsistersreport.org/news/inside-effort-identify-catholic-run-boarding-schools-indigenous-children; Nancy Marie Spears, "New Archive Sheds Light on Indian Boarding Schools Run by the Catholic Church," The Imprint, June 8 2023, https://imprintnews.org/top-stories/new-archive-sheds-light-on-indian-boarding-schools-run-by-the-catholic-church/242011.
5. "Our History," The Sisters of St. Francis of Philadelphia, accessed October 11, 2023, https://osfphila.org/about/our-history/.
6. Denise K. Lajimodiere, *Stringing Rosaries: The History, the Unforgivable, and the Healing of the Northern Plains American Indian Boarding School Survivors* (Fargo, ND: North Dakota State University Press, 2019).

Appendix

Schools for Native Students Run By Catholic Sisters

What follows is a chart listing all the schools at which Catholic Sisters worked between 1847 and mid-2024. I have organized it by community rather than school. All material comes from the Catholic Truth and Healing Database. This chart is meant to spur interest in future research, but also to delineate the scope of the involvement of Catholic Sisters at the Native American Boarding Schools.

In crafting this chart, I have had to make multiple choices that may over-generalize communities. For example, when categorizing the Benedictine Sisters or members of the Sisters of St. Joseph (non-Carondelet community), I've simplified to just note the order or congregation, rather than the individualized community. I've done this to help make the chart more accessible. (See table A.1.)

Table A.1 Table of Catholic Schools for Native Students Run by Catholic Sisters, 1847–present

Community	School	Dates Involved	Native Community
Benedictine Sisters (I am overgeneralizing and am not identifying individual communities)	Immaculate Conception Indian School	1887–1963	Santee, Sisseton-Wahpeton Dakota
	Immaculate Conception Indian School	1963–1971	Santee, Sisseton-Wahpeton Dakota
	Sacred Heart Academy	1897–1901	Cherokee, Creeks, Miami, Osage, Peoria, Quapaws
	Sacred Heart School (Fort Berthold Reservation)	1910–1916, 1916–1938	Arikara, Hidatsa, Mandan
	St. Benedict Indian School	1882–1906	Blackfeet, Unkpapa, Yanktonai-Dakota
	St. Joseph Indian School	1934–1975	Brulé Lakota; Cheyenne River Sioux; Crow Creek Reservation; Pine Ridge Reservation; Sans Arc Lakota; Santee Dakota; Sisseton-Wahpeton Dakota; Standing Rock Reservation
	St. Mary's Indian Industrial School	1882–1900	Grand Ronde
	St. Scholastica Indian Boarding School	1881–1923	Sioux
Congregation of the Sisters of St. Agnes	St. Joseph's Orphanage and School	1906–1956	Odaawa, Ojibwe
Dominican Sisters (now members of the Dominican Sisters of Peace)	St. Joseph Indian School	1972–1973	Brulé Lakota; Cheyenne River Sioux; Crow Creek Reservation; Pine Ridge Reservation; Sans Arc Lakota; Santee Dakota; Sisseton-Wahpeton Dakota; Standing Rock Reservation

(Continued)

Table A.1 (Continued)

Community	School	Dates Involved	Native Community
Dominican Sisters of Sparkill	St. Paul's Mission School	1973–2020	Assiniboine; Chippewa-Cree; Cree; Crow; Dakota; Gros Ventres; Nakona; Ojibwe; Sioux
Franciscan Sisters of Christian Charity	St. John's School (Laveen, AZ)	1939–1995	Apache, Maricopa, Pima, Tohono O'odham
Franciscan Sisters of Perpetual Adoration	St. Mary's Indian School	1883–1969	Lac Court-Oreille and Lac du Flambeau Reservations; Ojibwa and LaPoint Agency, Red Cliff
Franciscan Sisters of the Sacred Heart	St. Joseph's Normal School for Indian Boys	1888–1890	Dakota, Ojibwe
Missionary Benedictine Sisters	St. Augustine Indian Mission School	1957–2023 (ongoing as the publication of this book)	Omaha, Ho-Hunk
Notre Dame Sisters	Our Lady of Loudres (Porcupine, South Dakota)	1937–2002, 2010–2017	Lakota
Oblate Sisters of the Blessed Sacrament	St. Paul's Indian Boarding School	1935–1975	Yankton Sioux
School Sisters of Notre Dame (Central Pacific Province)	Holy Childhood of Jesus School	1886–1988	Ojibwa, Ottawa
Sisters of Charity of Leavenworth	St. Stephan's Indian School	1888–1890	Eastern Shoshoni, Northern Arapaho
School Sisters of St. Francis	St. Labre Mission School	1933–1995	Cheyenne, Crow
	St. Paul's Mission School	1936–1985	Assiniboine; Chippewa-Cree; Cree; Crow; Dakota; Gros Ventres; Nakona; Ojibwe; Sioux
Sisters of the Blessed Sacrament	St. Augustine Indian Mission School	1909–1945	Omaha, Ho-Chun
	St. Louis School for Osage Indian Girls	1942–1949	Cherokee, Osage, Potawatomi, Quapaw

(Continued)

Table A.1 (Continued)

Community	School	Dates Involved	Native Community
	St. Michael Indian School	1902–the writing of this book	Acoma; Apache; Hopi; Jemez; Laguna; Navajo; Taos, as well as mission tribes of California and tribes from Southern Arizona
	St. Paul's Indian Boarding School	1935–1975	Yankton Sioux
Sisters of Charity of Montreal	Little Flower School	1928–1971	Sisseton-Wahpeton Dakota
	Our Lady of Sorrows	1875–1883	Sisseton-Wahpeton Dakota
	St. Michael's Indian School	1922–1972	Sisseton-Wahpeton Dakota
Sisters of the Divine Savior	Tekakwitha Indian Mission Orphanage	1938–1973	Sisseton Wahpeton Oyate
Sisters of the Good Shepherd	House of the Good Shepherd	1885–1891	Dakota
Sisters of the Holy Child Jesus	Academy of the Holy Child	1883–1890	Hunkpapa Sioux Ojibwa
Sisters of the Holy Humility of Mary	Our Lady of Loudres, Porcupine, South Dakota	1931–1937	Lakota
Sisters of the Holy Names of Mary and Jesus	St. Mary's Indian Industrial School	1874–1880	Grand Ronde
Sisters of Loretto	Bernalillo Boarding School for Indian Girls	1885–1935	Genizaro Mestizo Tiwa
	Osage Manual Labor School	1847–1870	Miami, Osage, Peoria, Piankosha, Quapaw, Wea
	St. Louis School for Osage Indian Girls	1915–1942	Cherokee, Osage, Potawatomi, Quapaw
Sisters of Mercy	St. Anne's School	1883–1886	Umatilla Reservation
Sisters of Mercy of the Americas	Indian Girls' Industrial School	1886–1934	Mohawk

(Continued)

Table A.1 (Continued)

Community	School	Dates Involved	Native Community
	Mission of Our Lady of the Sacred Heart Indian Industrial School	1887–1889	Ojibwe, Sioux
	St. Agnes Academy for Girls	1898–1949	Chickasaw, Choctaw
	St. John's School (Laveen, AZ)	1899–1900	Apache, Maricopa, Pima, Tohono O'odham
	St. Mary's Academy	1884–1946	Potawatomi, Shawnee
	St. Mary's Industrial Boarding School	1884–1907	Turtle Mountain Ojibwe
Sisters of Mount Carmel	Sacred Heart Academy	1899–1904	Cherokee, Creeks, Miami, Osage, Peoria, Quapaws
Sisters of Notre Dame of the United States	St. Augustine Indian Mission School	1946–1954	Omaha, Ho-Chunk
Sisters of the Order of St. Benedict	St. Mary's Indian Industrial School	1881–1882	Grand Ronde
Sisters of Providence (formerly Daughters of Charity, Servants of the Poor)	St. Ignatius Indian School	1865–1919	Confederated Salish and Kootenai Tribes
	Mary Immaculate School	1878–1974	Coeur d'Alene
	Our Lady of Seven Dolors	1868–1901	Clallam, Tulalip
	Sacred Heart School (Ward, Washington)	1873–1921	Colville Reservation
	St. Joseph Academy	1888–1896	Yakama
Sisters, Servants of the Immaculate Heart of Mary	St. Stephan's Indian School	1974–1989	Eastern Shoshoni, Northern Arapaho

138   *Appendix*

Table A.1   (Continued)

Community	School	Dates Involved	Native Community
Sisters of St. Ann	Copper Valley School	1956–1971	Ahtna
	Holy Cross Mission School	1888–1956, 1965–1969	Ingalik, Ten'a, Yupik Eskimo
	Pius X Mission	1932–1959	Denaina, Eskimo, Tlingit
	St. Mary's Mission School	1894–1898, 1974–1982	Eskimo, Ingalik, Yupik
Sisters of St. Benedict (various communities; Includes Sisters of the Order of St. Benedict)	St. Benedict Indian School	1878–1882	Blackfeet, Unkpapa, Yanktonai-Dakota
	St. Benedict's Industrial School	1884–1896	Ojibwe
	St. Benedict's Industrial School for Indian Girls	1878–1969	Ojibwe
	St. Mary's Mission School (Red Lake, Minnesota)	1888–2009	Red Lake Chippewa
	St. Scholastica Indian Boarding School	1878–1881	Sioux
Sisters of St. Dominic of the Immaculate Heart of Mary Province	St. Mary's Indian Mission School	1936–1967	Chehalis; Colville; Entiat; Flathead; Lakota; Methow; Nespelin; Nez Perce; Noakask; Ojibwe; Okanogan; Paloos; Sanpoil; Senijextee; Wenatchi; Yakama
Sisters of St. Francis of Mary Immaculate	St. Mary's Industrial Institute	1880–1938	Metis, Ojibwe
Sisters of St. Francis of Penance and Christian Charity (North American Province)	Holy Rosary Mission	1888–1939	Oglala Lakota

(Continued)

Table A.1 (Continued)

Community	School	Dates Involved	Native Community
Sisters of St. Francis	St. Xavier Mission School	1935–1998	Cree, Crow
Sisters of St. Francis of Penance and Christian Charity (Sacred Heart Community)	Holy Rosary Mission	1939–1991	Oglala Lakota
Sisters of St. Francis of Philadelphia	St. Andrew's School	1890–1971	Umatilla Reservation
	St. John's School (Hominy Creek, Oklahoma)	1888–1907	Osage
	St. Joseph Academy	1899–1968	Chickasaw
	St. Joseph Indian School	1928–1933	Brulé Lakota; Cheyenne River Sioux; Crow Creek Reservation; Pine Ridge Reservation; Sans Arc Lakota; Santee Dakota; Sisseton-Wahpeton Dakota; Standing Rock Reservation
	St. Louis School for Osage Indian Girls	1887–1915	Cherokee, Osage, Potawatomi, Quapaw
	St. Patrick Indian Mission	1892–1965	Apache, Caddo, Comache, Kiowa
	St. Stephan's Indian School	1892–1985	Eastern Shoshoni, Norther Arapaho
Sisters of St. Joseph (Independent Congregations)	Nazareth Institute	1896–1899	
	St Agnes Academy	1897–1898	Choctaw
	St. Joseph Mission School	1902–1904	Lapwai, Nez Pearce
	St. Mary of the Quapaw	1894–1987	Miami, Osage, Ottawa, Peoria, Quapaw
	St. Stephan's Indian School	1974–1976	Eastern Shoshoni, Norther Arapaho

(Continued)

Table A.1 (Continued)

Community	School	Dates Involved	Native Community
Sisters of St. Joseph of Carondelet	Academy of the Holy Child	1890–1902	Hunkpapa Sioux Ojibwa
	Convent of Our Lady of the Lake	1885–1896	Sisseton Reservation
	Fort Yuma Indian School	1886–1900	Quechan
	Nazareth Institute	1900–1928	Cherokee, Choctaw, Creek, Muskogee
	St. Anthony's Industrial School	1887–1908	Campo, Kumiai, Luseno
	St. Boniface Indian Industrial School	1891–1956	Cahuilla; Gabrielino-Tongva; JuanenoKumeyaay; Luiseno; Serrano
	St. John's School (Laveen, AZ)	1901–1938	Apache, Maricopa, Pima, Tohono O'odham
	St. Joseph Industrial School	1881–1980	Menominee, Oneida, Stockbridge
	St. Joseph Mission School	1904–1968	Lapwai, Nez Perce
	St. Joseph Orphanage and School	1866–1906	Odaawa, Ojibwe
Sisters of St. Rose of Lima	St. Agnes Academy	1902–1945	Choctaw
Ursuline Sisters of the Roman Union (Western Province)	Holy Family Mission School	1890–1940	Blackfeet, Cree, Ojibwe, Piegan
	Our Lady of Loudres (Pilgrim Springs, Alaska)	1919–1941	Eskimo Innuit
	St. Mary's Mission School	1905–1987	Eskimo, Ingalik, Yupik
	St. Paul's Mission School	1936–1985	Assiniboine; Chippewa-Cree; Cree; Crow; Dakota; Gros Ventres; Nakona; Ojibwe; Sioux

(Continued)

Table A.1 (Continued)

Community	School	Dates Involved	Native Community
	St. Peter Mission School	1884–1918	Assiniboine; Blackfeet; Cheyenne; Choteaux; Cree; Flathead; Gros Ventres; Iroquois; Ojibwe; Piegan; Snake
	St. Xavier Mission School	1887–1921	Cree, Crow
	Villa Ursula	1924–1972	Blackfoot; Cheyenne; Coeur d'Alene; Colville; Cree; Flathead; Gros Ventre; Iroquois; Kalispel; Kootenai; Nez Perce; Ojibwe; Piegan; Salish; Snake; Spokane; Umatilla; Upper Pend d'Oreilles

Source: Created by the author.

Bibliography

Adams, David Wallace. *Education for Extinction: American Indians and the Boarding School Experience, 1875-1928.* Lawrence, KS: University Press of Kansas, 1995.

Adlred, Lisa. "Plastic Shamans the Astroturf Sun Dances: New Age Commercialization of Native American Spirituality," *American Indian Quarterly* 24, no. 3 (Summer 2000): 329–352.

Alexander, Jeffrey. "Cultural Pragmatics: Social Performance between Ritual and Strategy." *Sociological Review* 22, no. 4 (December 2004): 527–573.

Anonymous. *Gleanings of fifty years: the Sisters of the Holy Names of Jesus and Mary in the northwest, 1859-1909.* Portland, OR: Glass & Prudhomme Company, 1909.

Appel, Livia and Theodore C. Blegen. "Official Encouragement of Immigration to Minnesota during the Territorial Period." *Minnesota History Bulletin* 5, no. 3 (August 1923): 167–203.

Austen, Ian and Dan Bilefsky. "Hundreds More Unmarked Graves Found at Former Residential School in Canada." *New York Times,* June 24, 2021. https://www.nytimes.com/2021/06/24/world/canada/indigenous-children-graves-saskatchewan-canada.html.

Avella, Steven M. "Catholicism on the Pacific: Building a Regional Scaffolding." *U.S. Catholic Historian* 31, no. 2 (Spring 2013): 1–24.

Barkwell, Lawrence, ed. *Women of the Metis Nation:* Winnipeg, NB: The Metis Heritage & Resource Center, 2009.

Barman, Jean and Bruce M. Watson. "Fort Colville's Fur Trade Families and the Dynamics of Race in the Pacific Northwest." *The Pacific Northwest Quarterly* 90, no. 3 (Summer 1999): 140–153.

BBC News. "Canada: 751 Unmarked Graves found at Residential School." June 25, 2021. https://www.rnz.co.nz/news/world/445484/canada-751-unmarked-graves-found-at-residential-school-in-saskatchewan.

Bederman, Gail. *Manliness and Civilization: A Cultural History of Gender and Race in the United States, 1880–1917.* Chicago, IL: The University of Chicago Press, 1995.

Bee, Robert L. *Crosscurrents along the Colorado: The Impact of Government Policy on the Quechan Indians.* Tucson, AZ: University of Arizona Press, 1981.

Beecher, Catherine E. *A Treatise on Domestic Economy for the Use of Young Ladies at Home and at School.* New York: Harper & Brothers, 1845.

Berkhofer, Robert F. *Salvation and the Savage: An Analysis of Protestan Missions and American Indian Response, 1787-1862.* Lexington, KY: University of Kentucky Press, 1965.

Berkshire, The Edge. "Is 'Squaw' Really an Offensive Name and to Whom?" February 1, 2022. https://theberkshireedge.com/is-squaw-really-offensive-and-to-whom/.

Billington, Ray Allen. *The Protestant Crusade 1800-1860: A Study of the Origins of American Nativism.* New York: Quadrangle Book, 1964.

Blackhawk, Ned. *The Rediscovery of America: Native Peoples and the Unmaking of U.S. History.* New Haven, CT: Yale University Press, 2023.

Blair, Karen J. "The State of Research on Pacific Northwest Women." *Frontiers: A Journal of Women Studies* 22, no. 3 (2001): 48–56.

Blanchet, A. M. A. *Selected Letters of A.M.A. Blanchet: Bishop of Walla Walla & Nesqualy.* Edited by Roberta Stringham Brown. and Patricia O'Connell Killen. Translated by Roberta Stringham Brown. Seattle, WA: University of Washington Press, 2013.

Blanchet, Francis Norbit. *Letters of the Most Rev. F. N. Blanchet, D.D.* Portland, OR: Herman & Atkinson, Catholic Sentinel Job Print, 1871.

Bold, Christine. *"Vaudeville Indians" on Global Circuits, 1880s to 1930s.* New Haven, CT: Yale University Press, 2022.

Bomberry, Michelle. "Negotiating Two Worlds: Learning through the Stories of Haudenosaunee Youth and Adults." *Canadian Journal of Education* 36, no. 2 (2013): 248–283.

Bonde, Deborah Dawson. "Missionary Ways in the Wilderness: Eliza Hart Spalding, Maternal Associations, and the Nez Perce Indians." *American Presbyterians* 69, no. 4 (1991): 271–282.

Booth, Tabatha Toney. "Cheaper than Bullets: American Indian Boarding Schools and Assimilation Policy, 1890-1930." In *Images, Imaginations, and Beyond: Proceedings of the Eighth Native American Symposium, South-Eastern Oklahoma State University.* Edited by Mark B. Spencer, 46–56. (Durant: Southeastern Oklahoma State University, 2009.

Boyd, Robert. "The Pacific Northwest Measles Epidemic of 1847-1848." *Oregon Historical Quarterly* 95, no. 1 (1994): 6–47.

Bradley, Marie Merriman. "Political Beginnings in Oregon. The Period of Provisional Government, 1839-1849." *The Quarterly of the Oregon Historical Society* 9, no. 1 (March 1908): 42–72.

Brands, H.W. *Bound to Empire: The United States and the Philippines.* New York: Oxford University Press, 1992.

Braude, Ann. *Radical Spirits: Spiritualism and Women's Rights in Nineteenth-Century America.* Indianapolis, IN: Indiana University Press, 2001.

Bresie, Amanda. "Katharine Drexel's Benevolent Empire: The Bureau of Catholic Indian Missions and the Education of Native Americans, 1885-1935." *U.S. Catholic Historian* 32, no. 3 (Summer 2014): 1–24.

Briggs, Laura. *Taking Children: A History of American Terror* Oakland, CA: University of California Press, 2020.

Brownell, Susan, editor. *The Anthropology Days of the 1904 St. Louis Olympic Games.* Lincoln, NE: University of Nebraska Press, 2008.

Bunson, Margaret. *Faith in the Wilderness: The Story of the Catholic Indian Missions.* Huntington, IN: Our Sunday Visitor, 2000.

Burich, Keith R. *The Thomas Indian School and the "Irredeemable" Children of New York.* Syracuse, NY: Syracuse University Press, 2016.

Burns, Louis F. *Osage Missions Baptisms, Marriages, and Internments 1820-1886.* Fallbrook, CA: Ciga Press, 1986.

Bussel, Robert and Daniel J. Tichenor. "Trouble in Paradise: A Historical Perspective on Immigration in Oregon." *Oregon Historical Quarterly* 118, no. 4 (Winter 2017): 460–487.

Butler, Anne M. *Across God's Frontiers: Catholic Sisters in the American West 1850-1920.* Chapel Hill, NC: University of North Carolina Press, 2012.

Byrne, Stephan, O. S. D. *Catholic Colonization in the Southwest: Arkansas, Texas, Louisiana, Indian Territory and New Mexico.* Chicago, IL: Rand, McNally and Company, 1882.

Cahill, Cathleen D. *Federal Fathers & Mothers: A Social History of the United States Indian Service,1869-1933.* Chapel Hill, NC: University of North Carolina Press, 2011.

Caldwell, Michael. *A Mustard Seed Down in a Vast Field: Modest Demers, Early Catholic Missionary and Bishop, Establishing Catholicism in the Pacific Northwest.* Crescent City, CA: Michael Caldwell, 2020.

Calloway, Colin. *The Chiefs Now in This City: Indians and the Urban Frontier in Early America.* New York: Oxford University Press, 2021.

Cambridge Dictionary. "Authority." Cambridge University Press & Assessment, 2023. http://dictionary.cambridge.org/us/dictionary/english/authority.

Cameron, Linda A. "Common Threads: The Minnesota Immigrant Experience." *Minnesota History* 62, no. 3 (Fall 2010): 96–106.

Campbell, Joan. *Loretto: An Early American Congregation in the Antebellum South.* St. Louis, MO: Bluebird Publishing, 2015.

Campbell, Malcom. "Immigrants on the Land: Irish Rural Settlement in Minnesota and New South Wales, 1830-1890." *New Hibernia Review* 2, no. 1 (Spring 1998): 43–61.

Campbell, Malcolm. *Ireland's Farest Shores: Mobility, Migration, and Settlement in the Pacific World.* Madison, WI: University of Wisconsin Press, 2022.

Carroll, James T. *Seeds of Faith: Catholic Indian Boarding Schools.* New York: Garland, 2000.

Carroll, James T. "Self-Direction, Activity, and Syncretism: Catholic Indian Boarding Schools on the Northern Great Plains in Contact." *U.S. Catholic Historian* 16, no. 2 (1998): 78–89.

———. "The Smell of the White Man is Killing Us: Education and Assimilation Among Indigenous Peoples." *U.S. Catholic Historian* 27, no. 1 (Winter 2009): 21–49.

Castile, George Pierre. "The Commodification of Indian Identity." *American Anthropologist* 98, no. 4 (1996): 743–749.

Catholic Colonization Bureau. *Catholic Colonization in Minnesota. Colony of Avoca, Murray County, Southwestern Minnesota.* St. Paul, MN: The Pioneer Press, 1880.

Catholic Truth and Healing Commission. "Catholic-Operated Boarding Schools in the United States pre-1978." Accessed August 29, 2023, https://ctah.archivistsacwr .org/.

Churchill, Ward. *Kill the Indian, Save the Man: The Genocidal Impact of American Indian Residential Schools.* New York: City Lights Books, 2004.

Cipolla, Craig N. "Native American Historical Archaeology and the Trope of Authenticity." *Historical Archaeology* 47, no. 3 (2013): 12–22.

Clark, Blue. *Indian Tribes of Oklahoma: A Guide.* Norman, OK: University of Oklahoma Press, 2009.

Clarke, Kevin. "A Burial Site for Indigenous Children was Found in Canada. Could it Happen in the United States." *America: The Jesuit Review,* June 14, 2021. https:// www.americamagazine.org/faith/2021/06/14/kamloops-burial-sites-indigenous -children-native-american-boarding-schools.

Clemmons, Linda. "'Our Children Are in Danger of Becoming Little Indians': Protestant Missionary Children and Dakotas, 1835-1862." *Michigan Historical Review* 25, no. 2 (1999): 69–90.

Clemmons, Linda. "'We Find It a Difficult Work': Educating Dakota Children in Missionary Homes, 1835-1862." *American Indian Quarterly* 24, no. 4 (2000): 570–600.

Clevenger, Sydney. "Oregon Places: St. Vincent's and the Sisters of Providence: Oregon's First Permanent Hospital." *Oregon Historical Quarterly* 102, no. 2 (Summer 2001): 210–221.

Clymer, Kenton. *Protestant Missionaries in the Philippines, 1898-1916: An Inquiry into the American Colonial Mentality.* Chicago, IL: University of Illinois Press, 1986.

Coburn, Carol and Martha Smith, *Spirited Lives: How Nuns Shaped Catholic Culture and American Life, 1836-1920.* Chapel Hill, NC: University of North Carolina Press, 1999.

Colgan, Denise and Doris Gottemoeller. *Union and Charity: The Story of the Sisters of Mercy of the Americas.* Silver Spring, MD: Institute of the Sisters of Mercy of the Americas, 2017.

Connelly, Mary Beth Fraser. *The Chicago Sisters of Mercy and the Revolution of a Religious Community.* New York: Fordham University Press, 2014.

Conroy-Krutz, Emily. *Christian Imperialism: Converting the World in the Early American Republic.* Ithaca, NY: Cornell University Press, 2015.

Cowan, Mairi. "Education, Francisation, and Shifting Colonial Priorities at the Ursuline Convent in Seventeenth-Century Québec." *Canadian Historical Review* 99, no. 1 (2018): 1–29.

Cyprian, Mary. "'The Catholic Sentinel', Pioneer Catholic Newspaper of Oregon." *Records of the American Catholic Historical Society of Philadelphia* 7, no. 3/4 (September, December 1960): 85–92.

Davis, Elisabeth. ""Any Violation of This Arrangement": Catholic Negotiations at the Carlisle Indian Industrial School, 1883-1918)." *Pennsylvania History: A Journal of Mid-Atlantic Studies* 90 (Summer 2023): 419–441.

———. "The Disappearance of Mother Agnes Spencer: The Centralization Controversy and the Antebellum Catholic Church." *American Catholic Studies* 130, no. 2 (2019): 31–52.

———. "For Actions He Took Against the Sisters' School": Imperial Politics, Quechan Resistance, and the Sisters of St. Joseph at the Fort Yuma Mission." *Journal of Arizona History* 65, no. 1 (Spring 2024): 3–30.

———. ""Our Colored and Indian Charges Furnish So Much Amusement for Us": Catholicism, Assimilation, and the Racial Hierarchy in Carlisle, Pennsylvania, 1883-1918." *Pennsylvania History: A Journal of Mid-Atlantic Studies* 91, no. 1 (2024): 47–64.

———. "'To Keep the Catholics Intact': The Catholic Experience at the Carlisle Indian Industrial School, 1883-1918." *U.S. Catholic Historian* 40 (Fall 2022): 1–20.

———. "We Know Not God's Designs in Permitting a Separation: Women Religious, the Consolidation Controversies, and the Nineteenth Century American Catholic Church." *Journal of Religious History* 47 (December 2023): 566–585.

Davis, Ethan. "An Administrative Trail of Tears: Indian Removal." *The American Journal of Legal History* 50, no. 1 (2008): 49–100.

Davis, Julie. "American Indian Boarding School Experiences: Recent Studies from Native Perspectives." *OAH Magazine of History* 15, no. 2 (2001): 20–22.

Davis, W. L. "Peter John De Smet: The Journey of 1840." *The Pacific Northwest Quarterly* 35, no. 1 (January 1944): 29–43.

Dean, Joan Fitzpatrick, *All Dressed Up: Modern Irish Historical Pageantry*. Syracuse, NY: Syracuse University Press, 2014.

Dejong, David H. "'Unless They Are Kept Alive': Federal Indian Schools and Student Health, 1878-1918." *American Indian Quarterly* 31, no. 2 (2007): 256–282.

Delios, Ilia. "The Catholic Social Gospelers: Women Religious in the Nineteenth Century." *U.S. Catholic Historian* 13, no. 3 (Summer 1995): 1–22.

Demos John. *The Heathen School: A Story of Hope and Betrayal in the Age of the Early Republic*. New York: Alfred A. Knopf, 2014.

Dennis, Matthew. "Natives and Pioneers: Death and the Settling and Unsettling of Oregon." *Oregon Historical Quarterly* 115, no. 3 (Fall 2014): 282–297.

De Smet, P. J. "Father De Smet's Narrative Describing Upper Washington Territory, 1859." *The American Catholic Historical Researches* 12, no. 3 (July 1895): 102–106.

———. *Life, Letters and Travels of Father Pierre-Jean De Smet, S.J., 1801-1878*. New York: Francis P. Harper, 1905.

———. *Western Missions and Missionaries: A Series of Letters*. New York: James B. Kirker, 1863.

Devens, Carol. "'If We Get the Girls, We Get the Race': Missionary Education of Native American Girls." *Journal of World History* 3, no. 2 (1992): 219–237.

Dolan, Jay P. *The Catholic American Experience: A History from Colonial Times to the Present*. New York: Image Books, 1985.

———. *Catholic Revivalism: The American Experience 1830-1900*. Notre Dame, IN: University of Notre Dame Press, 1978.

———. *In Search of an American Catholicism: A History of Religion and Culture in Tension*. New York: Oxford University Press, 2002.

Dolan, Sarah A., M. Marie Meier, and Charles A. Dill. "The Changing Image of Catholic Women." *Journal of Religion and Health* (Summer 1993): 91–106.

Dorsey, Bruce. *Reforming Men and Women: Gender in the Antebellum City*. Ithaca, NY: Cornell University Press, 2002.

Dunbar-Ortiz, Roxanne. *An Indigenous Peoples' History of the United States*. Boston, MA: Beacon Press, 2014.

———. *Not "a Nation of Immigrants": Settler Colonialism White Supremacy and a History of Erasure and Exclusion*. New York: Beacon Press, 2021.

Dunn, Mary. "'The Cruelest of All Mothers': Marie de l'Incarnation, Motherhood, and Christian Discipleship." *Journal of Feminist Studies in Religion* 28, no. 1 (2012): 43–62.

———. "Mysticism, Motherhood, and Pathological Narcissism? A Kohutian Analysis of Marie de l'Incarnation." *Journal of Religion and Health* 52, no. 2 (2013): 642–656.

Edwards, Rebecca. *New Spirits: Americans in the Gilded Age, 1865–1905*. New York: Oxford University Press, 2005.

Edwards, Richard, Jacob K. Friefeld, and Rebecca S. Wingo. *Homesteading the Plains: Toward A New History*. Lincoln, NE: University of Nebraska Press, 2017.

Eittreim, Elisabeth M. *Teaching Empire: Native Americans, Filipinos, and US Imperial Education, 1879-1918*. Lawrence, KS: University of Kansas Press, 2019.

Ellis, Clyde. "Boarding School Life at the Kiowa-Comanche Agency, 1893-1920." *The Historian* 58, no. 4 (1996): 777–793.

Emmons, David M. *Beyond the American Pale: The Irish in the West, 1845-1910*. Norman, OK: University of Oklahoma Press, 2010.

Endres, David J. *A Bicentennial History of the Archdiocese of Cincinnati: The Catholic Church in Southwest Ohio 1821-2021*. Milford, OH: Little Miami Publishing Co., 2021.

Engh, Michael E. "A Multiplicity and Diversity of Faiths": Religion's Impact on Los Angeles and the Urban West, 1890-1940." *The Western Historical Quarterly* 28, no. 4 (1997): 463–492.

Enochs, Ross. "Native Americans on the Path to the Catholic Church: Cultural Crisis and Missionary Adaptation." *U.S. Catholic Historian* 27, no. 1 (2009): 71–88.

Estrine, Judith and Edward Rohs. *Raised by the Church: Growing up in New York City's Catholic Orphanages*. New York: Fordham University Press, 2011.

Ewans, Mary. *The Role of the Nun in Nineteenth-Century America*. Thiensville, WI: Caritas Communications, 2014.

Ewing, Charles. *Circular of the Catholic Commissioner for Indian Missions to the Catholics of the United States*. Baltimore, MD: John Murphy & Co., 1874.

Fear-Segal, Jacqueline and Susan D. Rose, eds. *Carlisle Indian Industrial School: Indigenous Histories, Memories, and Reclamations*. Lincoln, NE: University of Nebraska Press, 2016.

Ficken, Robert E. "After the Treaties: Administering Pacific Northwest Indian Reservations." *Oregon Historical Quarterly* 106, no. 3 (Fall 2005): 442–461.

Fifteenth Congress, Session II, Chapter 85, March 3, 1819.

Fischer-Tiné, Harold et al., eds. *Spreading Protestant Modernity: Global Perspectives on the Social Work of the YMCA and the YWCA, 1889-1970.* Honolulu, HI: University of Hawai'i Press, 2021.

Fitzgerald, Sr. Mary Paul. *Beacon on the Plains.* Leavenworth, KS: The Saint Mary College, 1939.

Fixio, Donald L. *Bureau of Indian Affairs.* Santa Barbara, CA: Greenwood, 2012.

Flaxman, Radegune. *A Woman Styled Bold: The Life of Cornelia Connelly, 1809-1879.* London: Darton, Longman, and Todd, 1991.

Foley, Thomas W. "Father Francis M. Craft and the Indian Sisters." *U.S. Catholic Historian* 16, no. 2 (Spring 1998): 41–55.

Foner, Eric. *The Second Founding: how the Civil War and Reconstruction made the Constitution.* New York: W. W. Norton & CO., 2020.

Fossey, Richard and Stephanie Morris. "St. Katharine Drexel and St. Patrick's Mission to the Indians of the Southern Plains: A Study in Saintly Administration." *Catholic Southwest* 18 (2007): 61–82.

Fredericks, Linda, Dan Jesse, Robert Brave Heart Sr., and Melissa Strickland. "The Lakota Language Project at Red Cloud Indian School: Turning the Tide of Native Language Loss." *Journal of American Indian Education* 57, no. 3 (2018): 51–71.

Ganss, Henry George. *History of St. Patrick's Church.* Carlisle, PA: DJ Gallagher & Company, 1895.

Gaul, Anita Talsma. "'Living in Perfect Harmony': A Multiethnic Catholic Parish on the Minnesota Prairie, 1881-1910." *Journal of American Ethnic History* 30, no. 1 (Fall 2010): 37–71.

Gerber, David A. and Alan M. Kraut. "Becoming White: Irish Immigrants in the Nineteenth Century." In *American Immigration and Ethnicity: A Reader.* Edited by David Gerber and Alan M. Kraut, 161–182. New York: Palgrave Macmillian, 2005..

Gerlach, Dominic E. "St. Joseph's Indian Normal School, 1888-1896." *Indian Magazine of History* 69, no. 1 (1973): 1–42.

Gilman, Rhoda R. "The History and Peopling of Minnesota: Its Culture." *Daedalus* 129, no. 3 (Summer 2000): 1–29.

Gittinger, Roy. "The Separation of Nebraska and Kansas from the Indian Territory." *The Mississippi Valley Historical Review* 3, no. 4 (1917): 442–461.

Gladue Rights Research Database. "The Anishinaabe (Ojibwe, Saulteaux)." Accessed February 12, 2024. https://gladue.usask.ca/anishinaabeg.

Glancy, Diane. *Fort Marion Prisoners and the Trauma of Native Education.* Lincoln, NE: University of Nebraska Press, 2014.

Glassberg, David. *American Historical Pageantry: The Uses of Tradition in the Early Twentieth Century.* Chapel Hill, NC: University of North Carolina Press, 1990.

Gorman, Adele Francis. *Celebrating the Journey. Volume II History of the Sisters of St. Francis of Philadelphia 1855-1970.* Philadelphia, PA: Sisters of St. Francis of Philadelphia 2005.

Graber, Jennifer. "'If a War It Be Called': The Peace Policy with American Indians." *Religion and American Culture* 24, no. 1 (2014): 36–69.

———. "Mighty Upheaval on the Minnesota Frontier: Violence, War, and Death in Dakota and Missionary Christianity." *Church History* 80, no. 1 (March 2011): 76–108.

Grabill, Joseph L. *Protestant Diplomacy and the Near East: Missionary Influence on American Policy, 1810-1927*. Minneapolis, MN: University of Minnesota Press, 1971.

Gram, John R. "Acting Out Assimilation: Playing Indian and Becoming American in the Federal Indian Boarding Schools." *American Indian Quarterly* 40, no. 3 (2016): 251–273.

Graves, William Whites, editor. *Life and Letters of Fathers Ponziglione, Schoenmakers, and other Early Jesuits at   Osage Mission: Sketch of St. Francis' Church. Life of Mother Bridget*. St. Paul, KS: W.W. Graves, 1916.

Green, Steven K. *The Bible, the School, and the Constitution: The Clash that Shaped Modern Church-State Doctrine*. New York: Oxford University Press, 2012.

Grim, Ronald E. "Mapping Kansas and Nebraska: The Role of the General Land Office." *Great Plains Quarterly* 5, no. 3 (1985): 177–197.

Grinde, Donald A. "Taking the Indian out of the Indian: U.S. Policies of Ethnocide Through Education." *Wicazo Sa Review* 19, no. 2 (2004): 25–32.

Guilday, Peter. *A History of the Councils of Baltimore (1791-1884)*. New York: The MacMillan Company, 1932.

Haig-Brown, Celia, Garry Gottfriedson, Randy Fred, and the Kirs Survivors. *Tsqelmucwíc: The Kamloops Indian Residential School- Resistance and Reckoning*. Vancouver: Arsenal Pulp Press, 2022.

Harley, R. Bruce. "The Founding of St. Boniface Indian School, 1888-1890." *Southern California Quarterly* 81, no. 4 (Winter 1999): 449–466.

Harmon, Alexandra, Colleen O'Neill, and Paul C. Rosier. "Interwoven Economic Histories: American Indians in a Capitalist America." *The Journal of American History* 98, no. 3 (2011): 698–722.

Hassett, M. M. "An Historical Sketch of the Diocese of Harrisburg." *Records of the American Catholic Historical Society of Philadelphia* 29, no. 3 (September 1918): 183–218.

Healy, Kathleen. *Sisters of Mercy: Spirituality in America 1843-1900*. New York: Paulist Press, 1992.

Hegman, Susan. "Native American 'Texts' and the Problem of Authenticity." *American Quarterly* 41, no. 2 (June 1989): 265–283.

Herron, Mary Eulalia. "Work of the Sisters of Mercy in the United States, Diocese of New York, 1846-1921." *Records of the American Catholic Historical Society of Philadelphia* 33, no. 3 (1922): 216–237.

Hess, Janet Berry. *Osage and Settler: Reconstructing Shared History though an Oklahoma Family Archive*. Jefferson, NC: McFarland & Co., Publishers, 2015.

Hobsbawm, Eric. *The Age of Empire: 1875-1914*. New York: Vintage Books, 1987.

Hodge, Hiram C. *Arizona as It Is; or, The Coming Country*. New York: Hurd and Houghton, 1877.

Hogan, Margaret A. "Sister Servants: Catholic Women Religious in Antebellum Kentucky." PhD Dissertation, University of Wisconsin–Madison, Madison, WI, 2008.

Holscher, Kathleen. *Religious Lessons: Catholic Sisters and the Captured School Crisis in New Mexico.* New York: Oxford University Press, 2012.

Hopkins, H. G. *American Empire: A Global History.* Princeton, NJ: Princeton University Press, 2018.

Howe, Daniel Walker. *What Hath God Wrought: The Transformation of America, 1815-1848.* New York: Oxford University Press, 2007.

Hunt, Brittany. "Sinister Schooling: Modern-Day Implications of Hampton Model Industrial Schools and American Indian Boarding Schools." *Zanj: The Journal of Critical Global South Studies* 3, no. 1 (2019): 70–83.

Hunter, Judith Amanda. *Before Pluralism: The Political Culture of Nativism in Antebellum Philadelphia.* New Haven, CT: Yale University, Press, 1991.

Hurley, Helen Angela. *On Good Ground: The Story of the Sisters of St. Joseph in St. Paul.* Minneapolis, MN: University of Minnesota Press, 1951.

Isenberg Nancy. *Sex and Citizenship in Antebellum America.* Chapel Hill, NC: University of North Carolina Press, 1998.

Jackson, Robert H. "Jesuits in Spanish America before the Suppression: Organization and Demographic and Quantitative Perspectives." In *Jesuits in Spanish America before the Suppression: Organization and Demographic and Quantitative Perspectives,* 1–108. Brill, 2021. http://www.jstor.org/stable/10.1163/j.ctv1sr6hzt.3.

Jackson, Willis Glenn. "Missions Among the Kickapoo and Osage in Kansas, 1820-1860." MA Thesis, Kansas State University, Manhattan, KS, 1965.

Jacobson, Matthew Frye. *Barbarian Virtues: The United States Encounters Foreign People at Home and Abroad, 1876–1917.* New York: Hill and Wang, 2001.

Johnson, Kimberley S. *Governing the American State: Congress and the New Federalism, 1877–1929.* Princeton, NJ: Princeton University Press, 2006.

Kaplan, Amy. *The Anarchy of Empire in the Making of U.S. Culture.* Cambridge, MA: Harvard University Press, 2002.

———. "Manifest Domesticity." *American Literature* 70, no. 3 (1998): 581–606.

Karson, Jennifer, ed. *Wiyazayxt/ Wiyaakaa'awn/ As Days Go By: Our History, Our Land, Our People-The Cayuse, Umatilla, and Walla Walla.* Seattle, WA: University of Washington Press, 2006.

Keliiaa, Caitlin. "Unsettling Domesticity: Native Women and 20th-Century US Indian Policy in the San Francisco Bay Area." PhD Dissertation, University of California, Berkeley, Berkeley, CA, 2019.

Keeler, Kasey. *American Indians and the American Dream: Policies, Place, and Property in Minnesota.* Minneapolis, MN: University of Minnesota Press, 2023.

Kelly, Mary. *Private Women, Public Stage: Literary Domesticity in Nineteenth-Century America.* Chapel Hill, NC: University of North Carolina Press, 2017.

Kelly, Sister Mary De Sales. "A Study of the Osage Mission Schools Based on United States Archival Material 1847-1870." MA Thesis, Catholic University of America, Washington, DC, 1955.

Kerber, Linda. "Separate Spheres, Female Worlds, Women's Place: The Rhetoric of Women's History." *The Journal of American History* 75, no. 1 (1988): 9–39.

Kessler-Harris, Alice. *Out to Work: A History of Wage-Earning Women in the United States.* New York: Oxford University Press, 1982.

Killen, Patricia O'Connell. "The Geography of a Minority Religion: Catholicism in the Pacific Northwest." *U.S. Catholic Historian* 18, no. 3 (Summer 2000): 51–71.

Killoren, John J. *"Come, Blackrobe" De Smet and the Indian Tragedy.* Norman, OK: University of Oklahoma Press, 1994.

Kilpinen, Jon T. "The Supreme Court's Role in Choctaw and Chickasaw Dispossession." *Geographical Review* 94, no. 4 (2004): 484–501.

Kim, Jessica M. *Imperial Metropolis: Los Angeles, Mexico, and the borderlands of American empire, 1865-1941.* Chapel Hill, NC: University of North Carolina Press, 2019.

Kinsella, Thomas. *A Centenary of Catholicity in Kansas, 1822-1922 ; The History of our Cradle Land (Miami and Linn Counties) ; Catholic Indian missions and missionaries of Kansas ; The Pioneers on the Prairies : Notes on St. Mary's Mission, Sugar Creek, Linn County; Holy Trinity Church, Paola, Miami County; Holy Rosary Church, Wea; Immaculate Conception, B.V.M., Louisburg; St. Philip's Church, Osawatomie; Church of the Assumption, Edgerton, Johnson County; to Which is Added a Short Sketch of the Ursuline Academy at Paola; The Diary of Father Hoecken, and Old Indian Records.* Kansas City, MO: Casey Printing, 1921.

Kreis, Karl Markus, editor. *Lakotas, Black Robes, and Holy Women: German Reports from The Indian Missions In South Dakota, 1886-1900.* Lincoln: University of Nebraska Press, 2007.

Krupat, Arnold. *Boarding School Voices: Carlisle Indian School Students Speak.* Lincoln, NE: University of Nebraska Press, 2021.

Lajimodiere, Denise K. *Stringing Rosaries: The History, the Unforgivable, and the Healing of Northern Plains American Indian Boarding School Survivors.* Fargo, ND: North Dakota State University Press, 2019.

Lambert, Valerie and Michael Lambert. "Teach Our Children Well: On Addressing Negative Stereotypes in Schools." *American Indian Quarterly* 38, no. 4 (2014): 524–540.

Lazerson, Marvin. "Understanding American Catholic Educational History." *History of Education Quarterly* 17, no. 3 (1977): 297–317.

Lentis, Marinella. *Colonized through Art: American Indian Schools and Art Education, 1889-1915.* Lincoln, NE: University of Nebraska Press, 2017.

Lewandowski, Tadeusz. *Ojibwe, Activist, Priest: The Life of Father Philip Bergin Gordon, Tibishkogijik.* Madison, WI: University of Wisconsin Press, 2019.

Lipperini, Patricia T. "Privileged to Educate: Katharine Drexel and Catholic Social Teaching- An Embodied Pedagogy." *Religious Education* 108, no. 4 (2013): 392–402.

Loretto Community. "Only One Heart: Loretto and Indigenous Peoples." *Loretto Community,* October 4, 2020. http://lorettocommunity.org/author/lorettocommunity/.

Lomawaima, K. Tsianina. "Domesticity in the Federal Indian Schools: The Power of Authority over Mind and Body." *American Ethnologist* 20, no. 2 (1993): 227–240.

———. *They Called it Prairie Light: The Story of the Chilocco Indian School.* Lincoln, NE: University of Nebraska Press, 1994.

Love, Eric T. L. *Race over Empire: Racism and U.S. Imperialism, 1865–1900.* Chapel Hill, NC: University of North Carolina Press, 2004.

Mack, J. N. "Inside and Out: The Sisters of St. Joseph, Chief Pasqual, and the Education of Native Children in Yuma." *The Catholic Historical Review 109,* no. 1 (2023): 77–106.

Mack, John. "Osage Mission: The Story of Catholic Missionary Work in Southeast Kansas." *The Catholic Historical Review* 96, no. 2 (April 2010): 262–281.

Macleod, William. *American Indian Frontier.* New York: Alfred A. Knopf, 1928.

Mahoney, Irene. *Lady Blackrobes: Missionaries in the Heart Of Indian Country.* Golden, CO: Fulcrum Publishing: 2006.

Mannard, Joseph G. ""Our Dear Houses Are Here, There and Every Where" The Convent Revolution in Antebellum America." *American Catholic Studies* 128, no. 2 (2017): 1–27.

Markowitz, Harvey. *Converting the Rosebud: Catholic Mission and the Lakotas, 1886-1916.* Norman, OK: University of Oklahoma Press, 2018.

Martin, Joel W. "Crisscrossing Projects of Sovereignty and Conversion: Cherokee Christians and the New England Missionaries during the 1820s." In *Native Americans, Christianity, and the Reshaping of the American Religious Landscape.* Edited by Joel W. Martin and Mark A. Nicholas, 67–89. Chapel Hill, NC: University of North Carolina Press, 2010.

———. *The Land Looks After Us: A History of Native American Religion.* New York: Oxford University Press, 1999.

Martinez, Doreen E. "Wrong Directions and New Maps of Voice, Representation, and Engagement: Theorizing Cultural Tourism, Indigenous Commodities, and the Intelligence of Participation." *American Indian Quarterly* 36, no. 4 (2012): 545–573.

Marty, Martin E. *Righteous Empire: The Protestant Experience in America.* New York: Harper & Row, 1977.

Massa, Mark S. *Anti-Catholicism in America: The Last Acceptable Prejudice.* New York: The Crossroad Publishing Company, 2003.

Masterson, James R. "The Records of the Washington Superintendency of Indian Affairs, 1853-1874." *The Pacific Northwest Quarterly* 37, no. 1 (January 1946): 31–57.

Mathews, John Joseph. *The Osages: Children of the Middle Waters.* Norman, OK: University of Oklahoma Press, 1961.

Matovina, Timothy. "Remapping American Catholicism." *U.S. Catholic Historian* 28, no. 4 (2010): 31–72.

Mattick, Barbara E. *Teaching in Black and White: The Sisters of St. Joseph in the American South.* Washington, DC: Catholic University Press, 2022.

McAnally, J. Kent. "The Haskell (Institute) Indian Band in 1904: The World's Fair and Beyond." *Journal of Band Research* 31, no. 2 (1996): 1.

McBeth, Sally J. "Indian Boarding Schools and Ethnic Identity: An Example from the Southern Plains Tribes of Oklahoma." *Plains Anthropologist* 28, no. 100 (1983): 119–128.

McCaffrey, Lawrence. "Ireland and Irish America: Connections and Disconnections." *U.S. Catholic Historian* 22, no. 3 (Summer 2004): 1–18.

McCrossen, Catherine, Mary Leopoldine, and Maria Theresa. *The Bell and the River*. Palo Alto, CA: Pacific Books, 1957.

McGlone, Mary M. *Anything of Which a Woman is Capable: A History of the Sisters of St. Joseph in the United States, Vol. 1*. St. Louis, MO: Bookbay, 2017.

———. *Called Forth by the Dear Neighbor: A History of the Sisters of St. Joseph in the United States Volume 2- from 1860-2010*. St. Louis, MO: Federation of the Sisters of St. Joseph, 2020.

McGougall, Roseane and Emily Siegal. "The Life of the Society of the Holy Child Jesus in the United States, 1862 to Present: An Ecclesial Perspective." *American Catholic Studies* 132, no. 4 (Winter 2021): 95–117.

McGuiness, Margaret. *Called to Serve: A History of Nuns in America*. New York: New York University Press, 2013.

———. *Katharine Drexel and the Sisters who Shared Her Vision*. New York: Paulist Press, 2023.

McKevitt, Gerald. "Northwest Indian Evangelization by European Jesuits, 1841-1909." *The Catholic Historical Review* 91, no. 4 (October 2005): 688–713.

McMahon, Thomas Marie. "The Sisters of St. Joseph of Carondelet Arizona's Pioneer Religious Congregation." MA Thesis, St. Louis University, St. Louis, MO, 1952.

McNally, Michael David. *Ojibwe Singers: Hymns, Grief, and a Native Culture in motion*. Oxford: Oxford University Press, 2000.

McNeil, Teresa. "The Sisters of St. Joseph Under Fire: Pioneer Convent School on the Colorado River." *The Journal of Arizona History* 29, no. 1 (1988): 35–50.

Meerschaert, Theophile. *Diary of a Frontier Bishop: The Journals of Theophile Meerschaert*. Edited by James D. White. Tulsa, OK: The Sarto Press, 1994.

A Member of the Community. "Sisters of the Third Order of St. Francis, 1855-1928." *Records of the American Catholic Society of Philadelphia* 40, no. 4 (December 1929): 347–381.

Minogue, Anna C. *Loretto: Annals of the Century*. New York: The America Press, 1912.

Moffatt, Catherine A. *The Hope of Harvest: The Life of Mother Veronica of the Crucifix Second Superior General of the Sisters of the Holy Names of Jesus and Mary 1820-1903*. Portland, OR: Kilham Stationery and Printing Company, 1944.

———. *So Short a Day: The Life of Mother Marie-Rose Foundress of the Congregation of the Sisters of the Holy Names of Jesus and Mary 1811-1849*. New York: McMullen Books, Inc, 1954.

Moran, Katherine D. *The Imperial Church: Catholic Founding Fathers and United States Empire*. Ithaca, NY: Cornell University Press, 2020.

Moses, L. G. "Indians on the Midway: Wild West Shows and the Indian Bureau at World's Fairs, 1893-1904." *South Dakota State Historical Society* 21 (1991): 206–229.

———. *Wild West Shows and Images of American Indians 1883-1933*. Albuquerque, NM: University of New Mexico Press, 1999.

M. T. B. "CORPORAL PUNISHMENT AS A MEANS OF SCHOOL DISCI-PLINE." *The Connecticut Common School Journal and Annals of Education* 3 (11), no. 5 (1856): 138–142.

Murphy, Joseph F. *Tenacious Monks: The Oklahoma Benedictines, 1875-1975.* Shawnee, OK: Benedictine Color Press, 1974.

Native Languages of the Americas. "Setting the Record Straight about Native Languages: Squaw." Accessed August 27, 2023. http://www.Native-languages.org/iaq5.htm.

Native Northeast Portal. "Editorial Note: The Use of the Word Squaw." Accessed August 27, 2023. http://Nativenortheastportal.com/editorial-note-use-word-squaw.

Neanias. "MODES OF CORPORAL PUNISHMENT IN SCHOOLS." *The Connecticut Common School Journal and Annals of Education* 3 (11), no. 5 (1856): 142–143.

Newson, Michael. "Pan-Protestantism and Proselytizing: Minority Religions in a Protestant Empire." *Widener Law Review* 15 (2009): 1–91.

O'Daniel, Hannah. "Southern Veils: The Sisters of Loretto in Early National Kentucky." PhD Dissertation, University of Louisville, Louisville, KY, 2017.

Office of Indian Affairs. *Some Things that Girls Should Know How to do and Hence Should Learn How to do When in School.* Washington, DC: Government Printing Office.

O'Hara, Edwin. "Catholic Pioneers of Oregon Country." *The Catholic Historical Review* 3, no. 2 (July 1917): 187–201.

———. *Pioneer Catholic History of Oregon.* Portland, OR: Press of Glass & Prudhomme Company, 1911.

Oliphant, J. Orin. "Some Neglected Aspects of the History of the Pacific Northwest." *The Pacific Northwest Quarterly* 61, no. 1 (January 1970): 1–9.

Original Broadway Cast. "Who Lives? Who Dies? Who Tells Your Story." Track 46 on *Hamilton: Original Broadway Cast Recording*, 2015, Amazon Digital Music.

Outka, Elizabeth. *Consuming Traditions: Modernity, Modernism, and the Commodified Authentic.* New York: Oxford University Press, 2009.

Owens, M. Liliana. "The Early Work of the Lorettines in Southeastern Kansas." *The Kansas Historical Quarterly* 15, no. 3 (August 1947): 263–276.

———."The Pioneer Days of the Lorettines in Missouri, 1823-1841." *Records of the American Catholic Historical Society of Philadelphia* 70, no. ¾ (December 1959): 67–87.

Oxford English Dictionary. "Authority." Oxford University Press. Accessed October 3, 2023. https://www.oed.com/search/dictionary/?scope=Entries&q=authority&tl=true.

Oxx, Katie. *The Nativist Movement in America: Religious Conflict in the 19th Century.* New York: Routledge, 2013.

Parham, Vera. "'These Indians Are Apparently Well to Do': The Myth of Capitalism and Native American Labor." *International Review of Social History* 57, no. 3 (2012): 447–470.

Parker, Benjamin E., ed. *A Companion to American Religious History.* New York: Wiley-Blackwell, 2021.

Patterson, Michelle Wick. "'Real' Indian Songs: The Society of American Indians and the Use of Native American Culture as a Means of Reform." *American Indian Quarterly* 26, no. 1 (2002): 44–66.

Perez, Erika. "Family, Spiritual Kinship, and Social Hierarchy in Early California." *Early American Studies* 14, no. 4 (2016): 661–687.

Piatote, Beth H. *Domestic Subjects: Gender, Citizenship, and Law in Native American Literature.* New Haven, CT: Yale University Press, 2013.

Pond, Ronald J. and Daniel W. Hester. "Through Change and Transition: Treaty Commitments Made and Broken." In *Wiyaxayxt/Wiyaakaa'awn/As Days go By: Our History, Our Land, Our People- The Cayuse, Umatilla, and Walla Walla.* Edited by Jennifer Karson, 93–142. Seattle, WA: University of Washington Press: 2006.

Prucha, Francis Paul. *American Indian Policy in Crisis: Christian Reformers and the Indian, 1865-1900.* Norman, OK: University of Oklahoma Press, 1976.

———. *The Churches and the Indian Schools, 1888-1912.* Lincoln, NE: University of Nebraska Press, 1979.

———. "Two Roads to Conversion: Protestant and Catholic Missionaries in the Pacific Northwest." *The Pacific Northwest Quarterly* 79, no. 4 (October 1988): 130–137.

Rahill, Peter J. *The Catholic Indian Missions and Grant's Peace Policy, 1870-1884.* Washington, DC: Catholic University of America Press, 1953.

Raibmon, Paige. *Authentic Indians: Episodes of Encounter from the Late-Nineteenth-Century Northwest Coast.* Durham, NC: Duke University Press, 2005.

Ramirez, Renya. "Healing, Violence, and Native American Women." *Social Justice* 31, no. 4 (98) (2004): 103–116.

Reeves-Ellington, Barbara et al., *Competing Kingdoms: Women, Mission, Nation, and the American Protestant Empire, 1812-1960.* Durham, NC: Duke University Press, 2010.

Regensburg, Margaret. "The Religious Sisters of the Good Shepard and the Professionalization of Social Word." PhD Dissertation, Stony Brook University, Stony Brook, NY, 2007.

Reyhner, Jon. "American Indian Boarding Schools: What Went Wrong? What Is Going Right?" *Journal of American Indian Education* 57, no. 1 (2018): 58–78.

Reyhner, Jon and Jeanne Eder. *American Indian Education: A History. Second Edition.* Norman, OK: University of Oklahoma Press, 2017.

Richardson, Ellen. "Catholic Women as Institutional Innovators: The Sisters of Charity and the Rise of the Modern Urban Hospital in Buffalo, N.Y., 1848-1900." PhD Dissertation, State University of New York at Buffalo, Buffalo, NY, 1996.

Riggs, Christopher K. "American Indian Citizenship, Past and Present." In *Rising from the Ashes: Survival, Sovereignty, and Native Americans.* Edited by William Willard, Allan G. Marshall, and J. Diane Pearson, 169–211. Lincoln, NE: University of Nebraska Press, 2020.

Rindfleisch, Bryan C. and Martha G. Beliveau, "The History and Uncomfortable Legacy of St. Patrick's Mission Indian School, Anadarko, Oklahoma, 1892-1966." *U.S. Catholic Historian* 41, no. 3 (Summer 2023): 49–71.

Rinehart, Melissa. "To Hell with Wigs! Native American Representation and Resistance at the World's Columbian Exposition." *American Indian Quarterly* 36, no. 4 (2012): 403–442.

Robertson, Dwanna L. "Invisibility in the Color-Blind Era: Examining Legitimized Racism against Indigenous Peoples." *American Indian Quarterly* 39, no. 2 (2015): 113–153.

Rockwell, Sr. M. Georgiana. *St. Katharine's Hall: Carlisle, Pennsylvania- The Unfolding Apostolate of the Sisters of the Blessed Sacrament-1906-1918.* Bensalem, PA: Sisters of the Blessed Sacrament, 1980.

Rose, Susan D. and Jacqueline Fear-Segal. *Carlisle Indian Industrial School: Indigenous Histories Memories and Reclamations.* Lincoln, NE: University of Nebraska Press, 2016.

Rosenberg, Emily S. *Spreading the American Dream: American Economic and Cultural Expansion, 1890–1945.* New York: Hill and Wang, 1982.

Roy, Loriene. "Ojibwe." In *Gale Encyclopedia of Multicultural America.* Edited by Gale, 3rd ed., Detroit, MI: Gale, 2014. Credo Reference.

Ryan, M. S. "Loretto and Its History." In *Loretto Centennial Discourses 1812-1912.* St. Louis, MO: B. Herder, 1913.

Savage, Mary Lucina. *The Century's Harvest Gathered by the Sisters of St. Joseph of Carondelet in the United States, 1836-1936.* St. Louis, MO: Sisters of St. Joseph, 1936.

Schoenberg, Wilfred. "Catholics in the Pacific Northwest." *U.S. Catholic Historian* 12, no. 4 (Fall 1994): 65–84.

———. *A History of the Catholic Church in the Pacific Northwest, 1743-1983.* Washington, DC: The Pastoral Press, 1987.

Scott, Gertrude M. "Village Performance at the Chicago World's Columbian Exposition 1893." PhD Dissertation, New York University, New York, 1991.

Shannon, James P. "Catholic Boarding Schools on the Western Frontier." *Minnesota History* 35 (September 1956): 133–139.

Shelley, Thomas J. "American Catholic Identities: A Documentary History." *U.S. Catholic Historian* 24, no. 2 (Spring 2006); 27–40.

The Sisters of St. Francis of Philadelphia. "Our History." Accessed October 11, 2023. https://osfphila.org/about/our-history/.

Sisters of the Third Order of St Francis. Glen Riddle, PA: Motherhouse and Novitiate Convent of Our Lady of Angels, 1963.

Slikva, Kevin. "Art, Craft, and Assimilation: Curriculum for Native Students during the Boarding School Era." *Studies in Art Education* 52, no. 3 (2011): 225–242.

Smith, Alice E. "The Sweetman Irish Colony." *Minnesota History* 9, no. 4 (December 1928): 331–346.

Smithers, Gregory D. "The 'Pursuits of the Civilized Man': Race and the Meaning of Civilization in the United States and Australia, 1790s-1850s." *Journal of World History* 20, no. 2 (2009): 245–272.

Smith-Rosenberg, Carroll. "The Hysterical Woman: Sex roles and Role Conflict in 19th-Century America." *Social Research* 39 (1972): 652–678.

Spalding, Thomas W. "Frontier Catholicism." *The Catholic Historical Review* 77, no. 3 (July 1991): 470–484.

Spears, Nancy Marie. "New Archive Sheds Light on Indian Boarding Schools Run by the Catholic Church." *The Imprint,* June 8, 2023. https://imprintnews.org/top -stories/new-archive-sheds-light-on-indian-boarding-schools-run-by-the-catholic -church/242011.

Stanciu, Cristina. "Americanization on Native Terms: The Society of American Indians, Citizenship Debates, and Tropes of "Racial Difference"." *Native American and Indigenous Studies* 6, no. 1 (2019): 111–148.

———. *The Makings and Unmakings of Americans: Indian and Immigrants in American Literature and Culture, 1879-1924.* New Haven, CT: Yale University Press, 2023.

Stephan, J. A. *The Bureau of Catholic Indian Missions, 1874-1895.* Washington, DC: The Church News Publishing Company, 1895.

Stewart, George C. *Marvels of Charity: History of American Sisters and Nuns.* Huntington, IN: Our Sunday Visitor, Inc., 1994.

Stockman, Dan. "Inside the Effort to Identify Catholic-Run Boarding Schools for Indigenous Children." *Global Sisters Report,* March 30, 2023. https://www .globalsistersreport.org/news/inside-effort-identify-catholic-run-boarding-schools -indigenous-children.

———. "New Published List Shows Catholic Sisters Ran 74 US Native Boarding Schools." *National Catholic Reporter,* May 9, 2023. https://www.ncron line.org/news/newly-published-list-shows-catholic-entities-ran-87-us-native -american-boarding-schools#:~:text=The%20Catholic%20Truth%20%26 %20Healing%20website,were%20affiliated%20with%20the%20schools.

Stuart, John. "Beyond Sovereignty?: Protestant Missions, Empire and Transnationalism, 1890–1950." In *Beyond Sovereignty: Britian, Empire and Transnationalism.* Edited by Kevin Grant, Phillipa Levine, and Frank Trentmann, 103–125. London: Palgrave Macmillan, 2007.

Suval, John. ""The Nomadic Race to Which I Belong": Squatter Democracy and the Claiming of Oregon." *Oregon Historical Quarterly* 118, no. 3 (Fall 2017): 306–337.

Talahongva, Patty. "No More 'Die Bread': How Boarding Schools Impacted Native Diet and the Resurgence of Indigenous Food Sovereignty." *Journal of American Indian Education* 57, no. 1 (2018): 145–153.

Taylor, Mary Christine. *A History of Catholicism in the North Country: Diocese of Ogdenburg Centennial 1872-1972.* Camden, NY: A.M. Farnsworth, 1972.

Tentler, Leslie Woodcock. *American Catholics: A History.* New Haven, CT: Yale University Press, 2020.

Thiel, Mark G. "Catholic Ladders and Native American Evangelization." In *Native American Catholic Studies Reader: History and Theology.* Edited by David Endres, 27–58. Washington, DC: Catholic University of American Press, 2022.

Tollefson, Kenneth D., Marin L. Abbott, and Eugene Wiggins, "Tribal Estates: A Comparative and Case Study." *Ethnology* 35, no. 4 (Autumn 1996): 322.

Trachtenberg, Alan. *The Incorporation of America: Culture and Society in the Gilded Age.* New York: Hill and Wang, 2007.

Trafzer, Clifford E., ed. *Boarding School Blues: Revisiting American Indian Educational Experiences.* Lincoln, NE: University of Nebraska Press, 2006.

Trennert, Robert. "Educating Indian Girls at Nonreservation Boarding Schools, 1878-1920." *Western Historical Quarterly* 13, no. 3 (July 1982): 271–290.

———. "Selling Indian Education at World's Fairs and Expositions, 1893-1904." *American Indian Quarterly* 11 (1987): 203–220.

Treuer, Anton. *Ojibwe in Minnesota.* St. Paul, MN: Minnesota Historical Society, 2010.

Unknown. "The Sisters of Mercy in New York." *The Catholic World, A Monthly Magazine of General Literature and Science* 50 297 (December 1889): 382.

U.S. Constitution. First Amendment.

U.S. Department of the Interior. "Secretary Haaland Announces Federal Indian Boarding School Initiative." June 22, 2021. https://www.doi.gov/pressreleases/secretary-haaland-announces-federal-indian-boarding-school-initiative.

Various. *Loretto Centennial Discourses 1812-1912.* St. Louis, MO: B. Herder, 1913.

Vizenor, Gerald. "Minnesota Chipewa: Woodland Treaties to Tribal Bingo." *American Indian Quarterly* 13, no. 1 (Winter 1989): 30–57.

Vogeler, Ingolf. "The Roman Catholic Culture Region of Central Minnesota." *Pioneer America* 8, no. 2 (July 1976): 71–83.

Vuckovic, Miriam. *Voices from Haskell: Indian Students between Two Worlds, 1884-1928.* Lawrence, KS: University of Kansas Press, 2008.

Waggett, George M. O. M. I. "The Oblates of Mary Immaculate in the Pacific Northwest, 1847-1878." *Records of the American Catholic Historical Society of Philadelphia* 64, no. 2 (June 1953): 72–93.

———. "The Oblates of Mary in the Pacific Northwest, 1847-1878." *Records of the American Catholic Historical Society of Philadelphia* 63, no. 3 (September 1952): 177–187.

———. "The Oblates of Mary in the Pacific Northwest, 1847-1878." *Records of the American Catholic Historical Society of Philadelphia* 64, no. 3 (September 1953): 166–182.

———. "The Oblates of Mary in the Pacific Northwest, 1847-1878." *Records of the American Catholic Historical Society of Philadelphia* 64, no. 4 (December 1953): 199–212.

Walden Sarah. *Tasteful Domesticity: Women's Rhetoric & the American Cookbook 1790-1940.* Pittsburgh, PA: University of Pittsburgh Press, 2018.

Warren, William W. *History of the Ojibway People.* St. Paul, MN: Minnesota Society Press, 1984.

Weber, Carolyn A. "Caught between Catholic and Government Traditions: Americanization and Assimilation at St. Joseph's Indian Normal School." *American Educational History* 40, no. 1–2 (2013): 75+.

Weed Willis, Park Weed. "Early Recollections and Impressions of Umatilla County, Oregon." *The Pacific Northwest Quarterly* 28, no. 3 (July 1937): 301–311.

Welter, Barbara. "The Cult of True Womanhood: 1820-1860." *American Quarterly* 18, no. 2 (1966): 151–174.

White, James D., ed. *Diary of a Frontier Bishop: The Journals of Theophile Meer-schaert.* Tulsa, OK: The Sarto Press, 1994.

White, Richard. *Railroaded: The Transcontinentals and the Making of Modern America.* New York: W.W. Norton & Company, 2011.

————. *The Republic for Which It Stands: The United States during Reconstruction and the Gilded Age, 1865-1896.* New York: Oxford University Press, 2017.

Widdler, Keith R. "Magdelaine LaFrambroise: The First Lady of Mackinac Island." *Mackinac History: A Continuing Series of Illustrated Vignettes* 4, no. 1 (2007): 2–11.

Willging, Eugene P. and Herta Hatzfeld. "Catholic Series of the Nineteenth Century in Oregon." *Records of the American Catholic Historical Society of Philadelphia* 72, no. ½ (March, June 1961): 46–61.

Williams, Samantha M. *Assimilation, Resilience, and Survival: A History of the Stewart Indian School, 1890-2020.* Lincoln, NE: University of Nebraska Press, 2022.

Wingerd, Mary L. *North Country: The Making of Minnesota.* Minneapolis, MN: University of Minnesota Press, 2010.

Woidat, Caroline M. "Captivity, Freedom, and the New World Convent: The Spiritual Autobiography of Marie de l'Incarnation Guyart." *Legacy* 25, no. 1 (2008): 1–22.

Wolffe, John. "Protestant–Catholic Divisions in Europe and the United States: An Historical and Comparative Perspective," *Politics, Religion & Ideology* 12, no. 3 (2011): 241–256.

Yacovazzi, Cassandra L. "Down with the Convent!: Anti-Catholicism and Opposition to Nuns in Antebellum America." In *A Companion to American Religious History.* Edited by Benjamine E. Park, 150–164. New York: Wiley Blackwell, 2021.

Zamir, Shamoon, Alexander B. Upshaw, and Edward S. Curtis. "Native Agency and the Making of 'The North American Indian': Alexander B. Upshaw and Edward S. Curtis." *American Indian Quarterly* 31, no. 4 (2007): 613–653.

Zink, Amanda J. *Fictions of Western American Domesticity: Indian, Mexican, and Anglo Women in Print Culture, 1850–1950.* Albuquerque, NM: University of New Mexico Press, 2018.

Index

About the Author

Dr. Elisabeth C. Davis earned her PhD in history at the University at Buffalo. She is currently an assistant professor of history at East Central University in Ada, Oklahoma.